# The Book of
# NEWDIGATE

*Portrait of a Wealden Village*

COMPILED BY JOHN CALLCUT &
THE NEWDIGATE SOCIETY

HALSGROVE

First published in Great Britain in 2002

Frontispiece photograph: *The junction of Henfold Lane with Village Street, 1921.*

British Library Cataloguing-in-Publication Data
A CIP record for this title is available from the British Library

ISBN 1 84114 147 X

HALSGROVE

Halsgrove House
Lower Moor Way
Tiverton, Devon EX16 6SS
Tel: 01884 243242
Fax: 01884 243325
email: sales@halsgrove.com
website: www.halsgrove.com

Printed and bound by
Bookcraft Ltd, Midsomer Norton

*Whilst every care has been taken to ensure the accuracy of the
information contained in this book, the author disclaims responsibility
for any mistakes which may have inadvertently been included.*

# NEWDIGATE - A WEALDEN VILLAGE

*The roads that lead to Newdigate are never very wide,*
*They wander past the lovely fields and arching trees beside;*
*They twist and turn in sun and shade past cottages and church,*
*And spinneys dark with ancient yew, with oak and silver birch.*

*From Reigate-way, through Betchworth, Leigh or Brockham by the Mole*
*(Where waterfall and willows meet to gladden every soul*
*Who rides the 'double-decker' bus with shopping-laden knee!)*
*We know when Shellwood's left behind we're nearly home for tea.*

*From Dorking, on the Horsham Road, we leave the trains behind,*
*And from Beare Green we climb the hill, and turn and darkly wind*
*The leafy lane by Broomells, pass the village club and sign*
*Into the heart of Newdigate, to your house and mine.*

*And roundabout the farmsteads lie, the cottages, the fields,*
*The dark old barns wherein are stored the grain the harvest yields,*
*The herd of gentle Guernsey cows within the shadowy byre;*
*The moated manor in the vale; the church with shingled spire.*

*What Wealden loveliness abides in all these simple things –*
*The cawing of the homing rooks, the white owl's whirring wings;*
*The bright eye of the dormouse; the song of mistle thrush –*
*Etched on the dark'ning pear tree, breaking the twilight hush.*

*We love the lanes of Newdigate – the homes, the woods, the streams;*
*And though we travel far and wide, they come again in dreams.*
*But more than all – to bless us, to gladden and renew -*
*Are the friendly folk in Newdigate, the kind hearts and true.*

**Vere Wallis, 1960**

*Village street, looking south, c.1900.*

'At Newdigate, Surrey' by Patrick Nasmyth (1787–1831).

# CONTENTS

*Maps by Jane Lilley

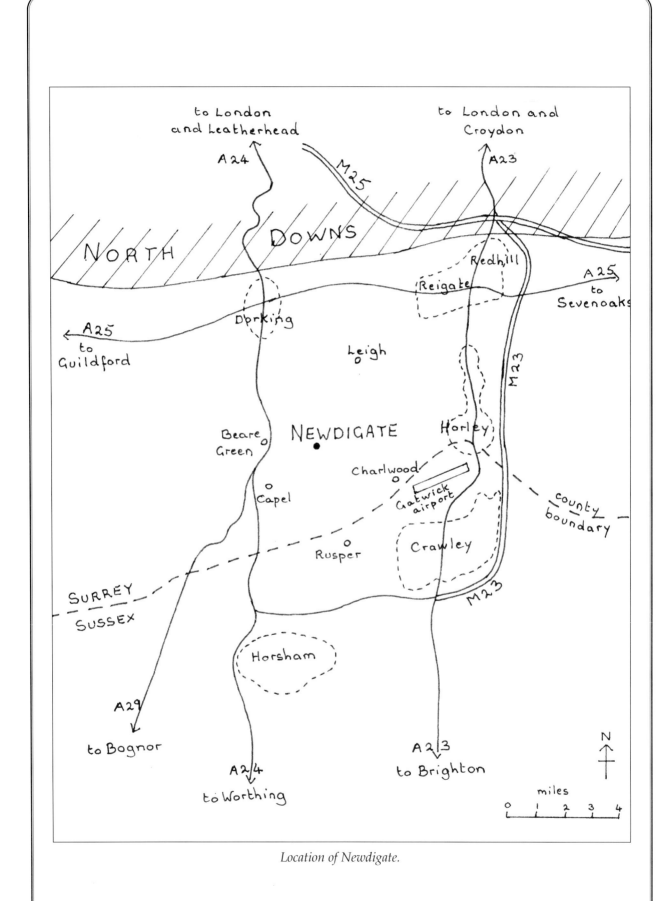

*Location of Newdigate.*

to London
and Leatherhead

to London and
Croydon

A24

M25

A23

NORTH        DOWNS

Redhill

Reigate

A25
to
Sevenoaks

A25
to
Guildford

Dorking

Leigh

M23

Beare
Green

NEWDIGATE

Horley

Charlwood

Gatwick
airport

county
boundary

Capel

Rusper

Crawley

M23

SURREY
SUSSEX

Horsham

A29

A23
to Brighton

N

to Bognor

A24
to Worthing

miles
0  1  2  3  4

# ACKNOWLEDGEMENTS

I have enjoyed compiling this book but little that I have written would have been possible without the research, expertise and knowledge of Joyce Banks and the late Charles Thompson for which I offer my thanks.

I would like also to acknowledge contributions and support from the following: Paul Bailey, Ann Baldwin, the late Alan Banks, Derek Brearley, George Brind, Neil Carter, Jean Charbonneau (née Brett), Nan Crutcher, Tony Crutcher, John Ede, Jim Elliott, Rhonna Farrin (née Davy), Charlie Frost, Christine Gallivan, the late George Green, Jeffrey Herbert, Harold Hopkins, Eric Longhurst, Marian Medhurst, the late Alice Melville (née Whiffen), Pearl Moore (née Jones), Robert Pols, Hugh Richards, Jean Shelley, Charles Smith, Wendy Stott, Bill Tanner, Carola Thompson, Bob Verner-Jeffreys, the late Vere Wallis, the late Alan Warman, the late Lawrence Wheeler, Dr William Wheeler, John Williams and all the committee members of the Newdigate Society, namely Susan Brind, Barbara Capel, Pam Keeble, Jane Lilley, Peter Monk, Diana Salisbury, Rosemary Thompson and Donald Thwaites.

Extracts from the Tithe Apportionment and Baptisms Register have been reproduced by permission of the Surrey History Service.

I would also like to acknowledge the numerous people, too many to mention by name, who have assisted me with photographs, anecdotes and facts about our village.

**John Callcut, 2002.**

*A rabbit shoot at Chaffolds Farm.*

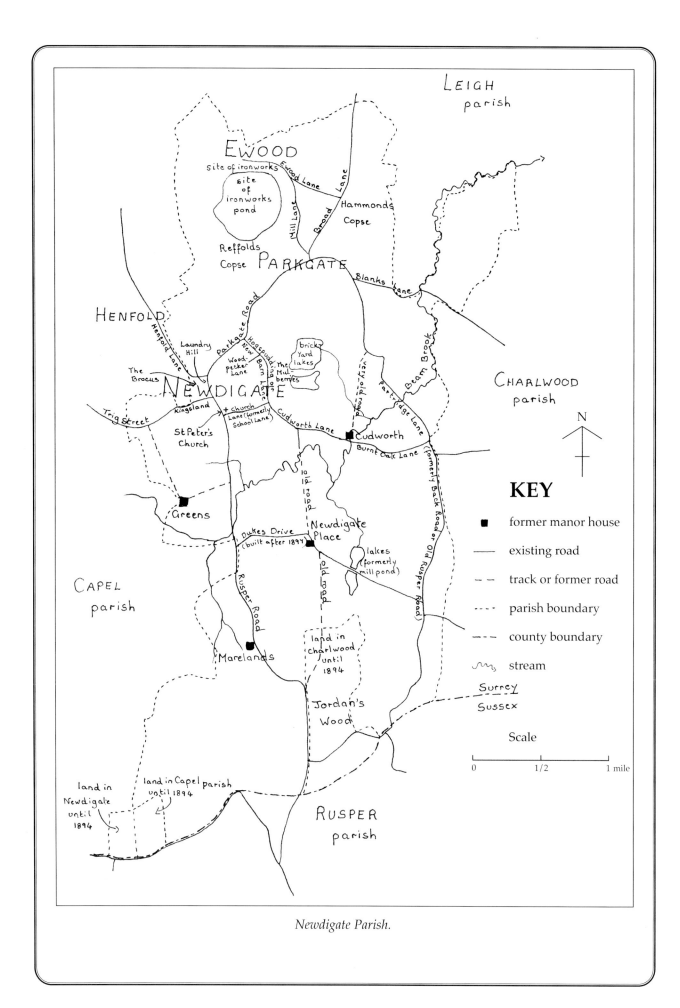

*Newdigate Parish.*

# Chapter 1

# THE VILLAGE ENVIRONMENT

## Introduction

Newdigate is in the Weald of Southern England, in the land of clay that lies between the chalk hills of the North and South Downs. It is in the middle of a triangle of three towns, Dorking, Reigate and Horsham, and lies between the A24 and A23 roads which are the main routes to the north and south.

It is a Surrey village adjoining West Sussex to the south. The parish is long and narrow, and according to the local inhabitants who last 'walked the bounds' in 1880, the total distance around the border was 26 miles (although in 1894 the boundaries were changed and the distance was estimated to be closer to 18 miles). Due to its position it has always been very isolated and even today some of the older residents still talk with a unique Surrey/Sussex border accent, which is on the verge of becoming extinct. It is not a Kentish or West-Country burr but it has a sharp, rustic resonance, recalling the days when generations of the same family lived, worked and died within the confines of the village.

The story of the village is traced from Saxon times, through the prosperous iron-making period to the difficult years of farming on Wealden clay. The coming of the railways to nearby Holmwood made the area accessible and brought dramatic changes, leading to the present day with its struggles to maintain and preserve the very fabric of the village.

The name 'Newdigate' is unique. There is no other place in the world that spells the name as in Surrey. There is a Newdegate Lake in southern Tasmania, and in Western Australia there is a Newdegate Island near Albany. On the south coast of Australia is a town called Newdegate, founded in 1922, whose children wear the same coloured school uniform as those in Newdigate. These names originated from Sir Francis Alexander Newdigate-Newdegate who was governor of Tasmania from 1917–20 and governor of Western Australia from 1920–24. He was a senior member of that ancient family who originally settled in Newdigate in the early 1100s and took their name from the village.

## The Natural Habitat
### *By Diana Salisbury*

From the top of Box Hill on the chalky North Downs, one can see – on a clear day – the English Channel twinkling in the sunlight through gaps in the South Downs. At one's feet is the Greensand Way, a sandstone ridge running parallel with the North Downs, and used in part by the pilgrims to Canterbury. The wide, largely undulating area between the North and South Downs is the Weald of Southern England.

In ancient times the area was thickly wooded and today there are still so many trees that, although you know it is there, Newdigate is impossible to see. From this vantage point on Box Hill only smoke coming from the brickworks at Beare Green and the aircraft taking off from Gatwick allow the observer to estimate where Newdigate lies.

Newdigate is a parish within the most wooded county in Britain. The predominant species is the pedunculate oak (the one with stems to the acorns), and there are plenty of hornbeam, hazel, holly, ash, birch, chestnut, sweet chestnut, field maple, sycamore and wild cherry. There is also some beech, although this usually prefers chalky ground.

There are several areas of 'ancient wood' in the parish, i.e. wood that was here prior to AD1600. These are identified by certain plants and trees growing within them, including the small-leafed lime and wild service tree. Hammonds Copse, which belongs to the Woodland Trust, has many wild service trees, but there are others dotted around and some are quite old. Bluebells and dog's mercury are other indicators of ancient woods.

Shaws, the remaining strips of woodland between fields which are found in several parts of the parish, are also often remnants of old woodland and many contain hornbeam which has been coppiced in the past or laid into hedges. One of the main woodland management forms was coppicing and this is once again being carried out in Hammonds Copse. The hazel is cut to ground level every 12 to 15 years and the new straight stems are used in hedge laying or as bean poles, broom handles, etc., while the brush is transformed into pea sticks or besom brooms. Coppicing also encourages wild flowers and forms habitats of differing ages for the wildlife.

The main large woodland areas in the parish are Jordan's Wood, Reffolds Copse and Hammonds Copse, but there are many smaller areas and several newly planted woodlands, as at Rolls Farmhouse and Green Lane Farm.

The wildlife of the parish is typical of Wealden woodland. Roe deer are very numerous, as well as foxes, rabbits and grey squirrels. Badgers, although a protected species, are always under threat so the locations of their setts are kept secret; there are believed to be one or two in the parish. Badgers prefer drier conditions than the clay provides, so there are more setts on the North Downs. Other mammals include stoats, weasels, woodmice, fieldmice, moles and the occasional dormouse. Hares have become a rare sight. A number of mink have been seen attacking ducks.

Amphibians are in good numbers due to the brickyard lakes and the many lakes dug in recent times as farmers have broadened their interests to include leisure and related activities. Toads, frogs and common newts are plentiful but the great crested newt is top of the list as a protected species that is found in the brickyard lakes. There are also a number of alien amphibians which escaped from the former field station at Beam Brook. The most numerous of these is the marsh frog with its very raucous mating call from May to July.

Reptiles are also common, particularly grass snakes, which like water and swim well. Slow-worms are also present.

There are five different types of damselfly and dragonfly that thrive in the brickyard lakes and around the many other lakes and garden pools. Butterflies are not as numerous as in the past but even so the brimstone, red admiral, tortoiseshell, peacock, grizzled skipper and the rare brown hairstreak have all been spotted in the area. Glow-worms, though less common than they were, are still found at several sites in the parish.

The flora is typical of Wealden clay. Bluebells are spectacular in spring, followed by primroses, cow parsley, wood anemones, milkmaid (or cuckoo flower), celandines and dog violets. Later in the year sheepsbit scabious is plentiful in the fields and woods together with foxgloves, agrimony, bugle, meadowsweet, herb bennet, herb robert, rosebay and willowherb, etc. Orchids found locally include the early purple and common spotted. The woodlands also support a wide variety of ferns.

Bird life is well represented in the parish. Garden birds include the robin, blackbird, starling, sparrow, song thrush, dunnock, goldfinch, chaffinch, pied wagtail, greenfinch, green woodpecker, great spotted woodpecker, jackdaw, blue tit, great tit, ringed dove, woodpigeon and wren. Slightly less common but in fair numbers are nuthatches, tree creepers, coal tits, longtailed tits and bullfinches. Away from gardens you may be lucky enough to see a kingfisher and in summer there are the cuckoos, housemartins (which particularly seem to like the new Becket Wood estate) and a few swallows. There were many swifts around the church until the roof was repaired, which meant

*The lake at Newdigate's brickworks in 1986.*

they could no longer get under the eaves, but hopefully the population is gradually increasing. Lapwings or peewits can also be seen in the fields together with pheasants and partridges. All the woodland migrants – including the chiffchaff, willow warbler, garden warbler and blackcap – are found here. Nightingales are heard in the scrub areas of Ewood where the Schermuly factory used to be, and used to be heard at the brickworks before the Mulberries housing development was built. Owls are represented by tawnys, little owls and a few barn owls. Herons visit the lakes and garden ponds, and large numbers of rooks, crows, jays, magpies, kestrels and sparrowhawks find habitats within the parish.

From 1919–49 the occupants of Normans Cottage (now Holly Tree Cottage) on Rusper Road recorded the birds seen within two miles of there. Apart from the above-mentioned birds they recorded spotting the linnet, yellowhammer, green plover, goldcrest, whitethroat, spotted flycatcher, redwing, fieldfare, nightjar, tree pipit, grasshopper warbler, brambling, lesser whitethroat, black redstart, hawfinch, grey wagtail, red-backed shrike, sandpiper and, rarest of all, two nutcrackers at Beare Green in 1949.

# Geology

*Carola Thompson submitted a dissertation on the effect of clay on a Wealden community for her geography degree. The following are edited extracts:*

*The clay deposits were laid down over 100 million years ago in a large lake which extended from just north of London, across the present English Channel and into northern France as far as Paris. The clay can reach 60 metres thick; the top 5 to 7 metres are usually well weathered and yellow in colour, whilst below, the unweathered clays are blue. Some other rocks appear in parts of the parish and they are shown in the map on the following page.*

*Before man entered the area the natural vegetation was deciduous forest. Frequent rain on the uncleared land, unable to penetrate the clay and preserved from evaporation by the dense woodland, would have formed marshland in every hollow. Early man could not clear the forest with his stone axes nor remove the tree stumps without great difficulty. Any paths made through the forest would have turned into slippery mud when trodden by man or animals, and only in frost or drought would they be passable, hardening and cracking into a rugged hoof-pitted surface. There was no waterway large enough to permit passage through the forest near Newdigate, since the parish lies just below the watershed between the River Mole flowing north to the Thames and the Rivers Adur and Arun flowing south to the coast...*

*Newdigate is low-lying and natural drainage is poor. Roads and fields are liable to flood and pools of water linger long after rain has stopped. Patches of mist hang in hollows and in dips in the road, captured by the tall roadside hedges...*

*Normans Cottage (now Holly Tree Cottage) in 1910.*

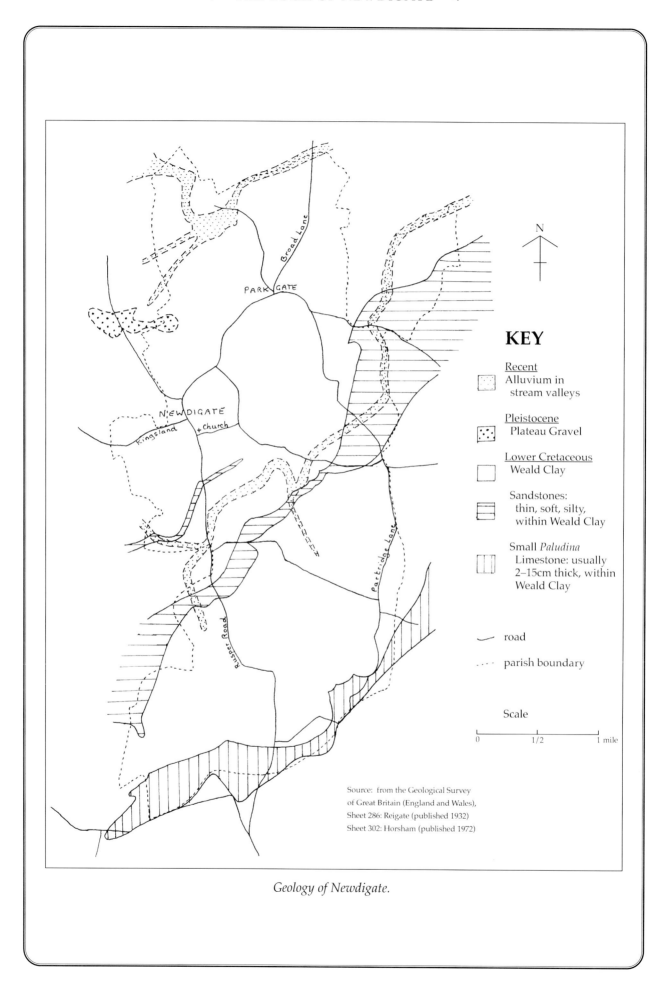

**KEY**

<u>Recent</u>
Alluvium in
stream valleys

<u>Pleistocene</u>
Plateau Gravel

<u>Lower Cretaceous</u>
Weald Clay

Sandstones:
thin, soft, silty,
within Weald Clay

Small *Paludina*
Limestone: usually
2–15cm thick, within
Weald Clay

— road

···· parish boundary

Scale

0       1/2       1 mile

Source: from the Geological Survey
of Great Britain (England and Wales),
Sheet 286: Reigate (published 1932)
Sheet 302: Horsham (published 1972)

*Geology of Newdigate.*

## Chapter 2

# EARLY TIMES

In the early centuries AD the Romans passed close by Newdigate along Stane Street in nearby Ockley. The area was thickly wooded and this was the strategic route from London to Chichester enabling travellers to pass through the oak forests.

The Romans withdrew in about AD410 and the area was later settled by the Anglo-Saxons, who set up small villages with houses of wattle and daub and roofs of rushes, which they shared with their animals. The Saxons were cattle drovers and swineherds and would winter in their villages and then drive their cattle to distant pastures amongst the woodlands. The pedunculate oak (*Quercus robur*) has flourished here since the Ice Ages and, until the forests were cleared, acorns must have been an important autumn food for fattening the pigs before the winter.

Nearby Beare Green has a Saxon element to its name (*beru*, meaning a swine pasture) while Cudworth, in the parish, is derived from the Anglo-Saxon 'Cudda's Ford'.

## Domesday

Newdigate does not appear in the Domesday Book as it was an outlying area of the manors of Reigate and Dorking, both of which were held by the de Warenne family. However, under a description of Merton, a royal manor in the hundred of Brixton, the following paragraph appears:

*A man named Orcas holds two hides, which always lay in the manor and were in another hundred. He held them at the time of King Edward the Confessor (1042–66). It was then assessed for two hides and now for nothing.* [A hide was the land that could be ploughed by a single plough in one year – about 60 acres].

Although there is no conclusive evidence, there is nevertheless a strong possibility that this refers to land in Newdigate; it is known that the prior of Merton, whose priory had been endowed with the manor of Merton, held in 1291 a dwelling-house and 60 acres of land in Newdigate. The land was described as 'ancient demesne', which means that it was described in the Domesday Book as having been royal land under Edward, and may be the land in the village still known as Kingsland.

## The Warennes

Shortly after William the Conqueror's death William de Warenne, one of the King's Norman followers, was created Earl of Surrey and endowed with the manors of Reigate, Dorking, Shere Vachery and Fetcham. He had fought at Hastings and married Gundrada who may have been the Conqueror's step-daughter. Joyce Banks has researched the Warenne family and tells us in the book *Newdigate – Its History and Houses*, published in 1993:

*The Warennes, Earls of Surrey, figure largely in the history of Reigate and Dorking, but only marginal references to them appear in Newdigate records. Isabel, only child of the 3rd Earl who was killed on a Crusade, married firstly William de Blois, eldest surviving son of King Stephen, who was invested as the 4th Earl of Surrey in 1148 by right of his wife. By the Treaty of Wallingford he also succeeded to all that his father had held before he became King, which included the honours of Pevensey, Rye, Lancaster and Norwich castles. At the same time he acquired further estates in Sussex and Surrey in addition to the old Warenne lands to which he had succeeded on marriage. He accompanied King Henry II to France and died at the siege of Toulouse. A second marriage of Isabel to William, brother of the King, was proposed, but was violently opposed by Archbishop Becket on the grounds of consanguinity. Instead, Isabel married his step-brother, Hamelin Plantagenet, the illegitimate son of Geoffrey of Anjou, who in his turn became 5th Earl of Surrey. Thus the*

 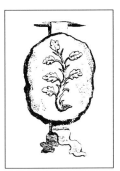

*The Seal of Isabella, Countess of Warenne, and the Seal of Hamelin, Earl of Warenne.*

Right: *Kingsland in 2002. The fields are larger but the landscape will not have changed much since Newdigate's forebears toiled in the unforgiving clay.*

Above: *William de Warenne who supported William the Conqueror –* from John Watson's Memoirs of the Earls of Warren and Surrey, *1782.*

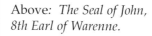

Above: *The Seal of John, 8th Earl of Warenne.*

Left: *Traditionally thought of as being the tomb of William de Newdigate who died in 1377. The tomb is under the great tower, in St Peter's Church.*

Right: *The pen-and-ink sketch is an optimistic reconstruction taken from the indentations in the stone.*

Below far left: *The Seal of William de Newdigate which is a cross composed of four acorns; very apt for an area abundant with oaks.*

Left centre: *The Seal of John Newdigate, 1424.*

Left: *The Seal of Thomas Newdigate, 1496.*

*family were extremely wealthy; the notarial sign on the reverse of the mandate for the church indicates that the family probably had their own chancery, an indication of their power. Hamelin's life thereafter seems to be marked with disputes with Becket and with the Abbot of Cluny; a dispute over Newdigate church, although minor, was part of the pattern.*

*Passing over the 6th and 7th Earls of Warenne, who lived eventful and roisterous lives full of intrigue, we come to the 8th Earl (John), who complained about trespass in his park of Ewood. A field to the west of Ewood is marked Old St John's on the Ordnance Survey map – this is a corruption of Old Sir John's and is correctly marked on the Tithe Map. It may well be the 16 acres added to Ewood by the 8th Earl in 1337.*

The advowson of the church remained in the family of the Warennes until the early-fourteenth century when they also owned Ewood.

John attempted to divorce his wife Joan of Bar and settle his estates on his illegitimate children by Maude de Nerford. In 1317 the Earl of Lancaster attempted to put a stop to this and in retaliation Warenne seized Lancaster's wife at Canford in Dorset and conducted her to Reigate Castle. This created a sensation and resulted in a private war between the two earls. Warenne died in 1347 without lawful issue and his estates passed to his sister, Alice, who had married Edmund Fitzalan, Earl of Arundel and Duke of Norfolk. Thus much land in Newdigate passed to successive Dukes of Norfolk.

Ewood (Yew Wood) was described from early times as a 'park', i.e. an enclosure of the forest for the purpose of deer hunting. The patent rolls of 1312 mention it and earthen banks for retaining the deer can still be seen amongst the woods.

# The Origins of 'Newdigate'

The place name Newdigate derives from 'on-Ewood-gate', i.e. on the road to Ewood. 'Gate' in Middle English meant 'road' and Newdigate began as a road through the forest rather than as a fixed settlement – hence today there is no cluster of cottages around a village green. The hamlet of Parkgate to the north of Newdigate was named at the time when gate took the meaning of 'entrance', that is, the entrance to the park.

The parish was divided between two of the administrative areas called hundreds. The northern part, together with two areas on the Sussex border, were in Reigate Hundred, and the area now called Parkgate was described as 'The Hamlet'. The remainder, 'the parish part', was in Copthorne Hundred. The reason for this division was that Ewood was held with Reigate by the de Warennes, while from the early-thirteenth century the rest of the land was held with Ashtead, which belonged to Copthorne Hundred, by the de Mara family.

# The Manors

## Marelands

The de Mara family gave their name to Marelands. Over the years this has been spelt Mar(e)lande, Mayland, Marishland and Marshland; today, two nearby cottages are called Marshland while the house is named Marelands.

The property passed to the Crown in the time of Henry VIII and is thought to be one of the original endowments of Trinity College, Cambridge which was established in 1543. Although the manor declined in the following years, this was still an important area for the supply of timber. In 1581, John Cowper (of the neighbouring Temple Elfold) bought 688 oaks, marked for timber and growing on Horsielands, Beameland and Marelands, 469 oaks marked for tall trees and 322 beech trees. Other names are mentioned in these Tudor surveys which are familiar today, including Chawfields (Chaffolds), Rolphs (Pancrass Rolls, now The Elms) and Clarks Land (the site of George Horley Place). After 1546 the Trinity College lands included Horsieland, now called Simons, and Beameland to the south of it.

## Cudworth

Cudworth Manor is on a moated site and is possibly the oldest settlement in the area as the name derives from the Anglo-Saxon 'Cudda's Ford' – the ford crosses Beam Brook, which is Anglo-Saxon for 'tree brook'. 'Cudiford' appears in a transaction of 1229 but the earliest surviving parts of the existing house date from the 1550s, indicating that an earlier medieval house was demolished. Nearby King John's Barn contained medieval timbers which may have come from the old house.

In the early-fourteenth century the de la Poyle family were described as lords of the manor of Cudeford in the hundred of Coppedethorne. The manor of Poyle was extensive and the lands extended to the neighbouring parish of Leigh. In 1353/4 there was a dispute between the priory of Merton, which held Shellwood in Leigh, and Robert de Codeford as to who should repair the bridge at Brookelandsbridge (now Brook Farm); Robert was bound to repair the bridge as 'from time immemorial it had been used for horses, packhorses and men on foot.'

The land later passed to the Newdigate family and after they disposed of all their Newdigate lands in 1636 it passed to the Budgen family.

The manor included six farms, all of which bore old names – Goosings, Deanland, Batchelors (now Boothlands), Woodmans (linked with Rolls or Rolfes), Souters (now Oaklands Park Farm Cottage), Cockmans (now Ivy House) and Pitter's which is in present-day West Sussex (probably Peter's Farm).

In 1807 the manor of Cudworth was acquired by the Duke of Norfolk.

17

## Newdigate Place & the Newdigate Family

According to John Aubrey the Newdigate family settled in the area during the reign of Henry I (1100–35) and took their name from the village. Their home was at Newdigate Place, described as being one mile south of the church. It was at one time a large house with a courtyard but towards the end of the seventeenth century it was reduced in size and occupied by a series of yeoman farmers and later by the Duke of Norfolk's steward.

When the Herron family built a new Newdigate Place in 1897 the old house became known as Home Farm, and still retains that name.

In the fourteenth century the family was prosperous and important and during the reign of Edward III arms were granted to John Newdigate. The shield was 'three lions jambs erased argent', the crest a 'Fleur de Lys argent'; this latter emblem is now used as the school badge.

William de Newdigate was Sheriff of Surrey and Sussex in 1372 and was also one of three Justices of the Peace for Surrey. He died in 1377 and the ancient gravestone under the belfry in the church is believed to be that of William, which is fitting because the advowson of the church had passed to him in 1357 and it seems likely that the church tower was constructed at this time. His son, John, was a Knight in Parliament in 1386, and was one of a commission of seven appointed to keep the peace after the Peasants' Revolt of 1381.

In Tudor times, Newdigate Place was improved and updated and the wills of both Thomas (1576) and Agnes (1583) mention furniture in the old parlour, the new parlour and the chamber over the new parlour. The furnishings were of some substance – long tables, covered chairs, great beds with testers

and linen. 'Glasse' windows were also mentioned.

The Newdigate family had also established itself at Harefield, Middlesex and in 1585 John Newdigate exchanged the Harefield property for Arbury in Warwickshire where a house had been built on the site of an Augustinian priory. The last head of the family remaining in Newdigate was Thomas (d.1612), who left his lands and tenements to his nephew West Newdigate, who sold it to John Budgen in 1636. The manor of Newdigate remained in the Budgen family until it was sold to the Duke of Norfolk in 1807.

Sir Roger Newdigate (1719–1806) instigated the Newdigate Prize in 1806. This was a prize open to Oxford undergraduates, originally for English verse, with a maximum of 50 lines, connected with the history of ancient sculpture, painting or architecture. The restrictions were removed in 1826 and the verse can now be of any length and subject.

### Greens

In 1576 this area was called the manor of Greens when it was held by Thomas Boorde and Edward Willett but the house is much older.

Greens Farmhouse is one of the finest hall houses in Surrey, probably built in the twelfth century. It straddles the Capel and Newdigate boundary and is quite remote, being approached by long lanes from Rusper Road and Trig Street. John Grene held land in Newdigate in 1449 and there were still members of the family here in 1497 so this is possibly from whence the name is derived.

Considering the remoteness of the farm, it is an unexpectedly magnificent building. Is it too fanciful to suggest that it was built as a grand royal hunting lodge for the king and his followers?

*Extract from a baptism register which includes a daughter of Thomas Newdigat. The family regularly initialled entries, which was unusual at that time.*
Reproduced by kind permission of the Surrey History Service.

Newdigat          Christininges A[nn]o Dom[in]i 1560

Samuell wright the son of Richard wright was christined the 5 Daie of October./

Fines Newdigat daughter of Thomas Newdigat christined the 4 daie of Novemb[er]

Anno Do[min]i 1562

Nicholas Misbroke son of Will[ia]m Misbroke christined the 10 Daie of November

Joane wright y[e] daughter of Nicholas wright christined y[e] 20th Daie of March

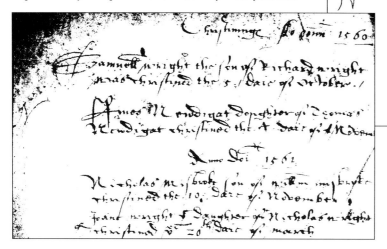

# Chapter 3

# MIDDLE AGES & BEYOND

## *The Militia in Newdigate*

From early times local defence forces, generally called militia, were organised and maintained for mobilisation in the event of a threat to the country. These units were organised on a local basis, and if a call came the militia were required immediately to give up their normal occupations and become soldiers. Some Elizabethan muster rolls still exist and a few relate to Newdigate. Thus in 1569 the following list was made:

### *Nudgate*

| | | |
|---|---|---|
| *Edmond Chawndler* | *a* *p* *s* | |
| *Hugh Bowrer* | *p* *m* | |
| *John Kemp* | *a* *p* *m* | |
| *John Laborne* | *a* *p* *s* | |
| *Thomas Jackman* | *a* *p* *s* | |
| *Richard Tailour* | *p* *s* | |
| *Larrance Laborne* | *p* *m* | |

### *Leighe et pars Nudgate*
[meaning 'Leigh and part of Newdigate'
i.e. Parkgate?]

| | | |
|---|---|---|
| *John Ellis* | *p* *s* | |
| *Henrie Bonicke* | *p* *s* | |
| *William Constable* | *s* | |

[It is thought that 'a' stood for arquebus (a portable long-barrelled gun) 'p' for pike, 's' for sword, and 'm' possibly for a sheet of mail.]

In the *Book of All Such Armour and Weapons*, also dated 1569, the following are shown under Newdigate:

| | |
|---|---|
| *Thomas Newdigate gent.* | *Corsle(te)* |
| *Chandeler* | *Coats of Plate 1* |
| | *Corseletes 1* |

Another list records those rated to keep horses and geldings for service. There is only one entry for Newdigate, under 'lighthorseman': 'Walter Newdigate gent. – a grey fleabitten gelding.' 'Fleabitten', when referring to a horse, means having reddish-brown tufts of hair on a lighter background. A lighthorseman had to have:

> *... a sufficient geldinge with a strong sadle and lether harnis furnyshed, the man to be furnyshed with a coate of plate or brigandyne or the curate of a corslett, sleves with chaines of mayle, a northern stafe, a case of pistolls, sword and dagger, a cassock of red clothe with twoe gardes of white clothe one jnch broad.*

In a list dated 26 March 1627, 100 foot-soldiers were levied in Surrey to serve in the Low Countries, including one man from Newdigate – John Nicholls. It is not known whether he survived and returned to the parish.

Following the establishment of the standing army in the 1660s, militia units declined in effectiveness, and an Act of 1757 instituted a form of conscription. Lists of all males of eligible age in the parish were made, and some were then chosen by ballot to serve compulsorily as militiamen.

During the Napoleonic Wars most of the militia were on permanent duty and whilst away from home the wives and families were paid an allowance which was noted in the parish records. One such Newdigate entry, dated 26 March 1812, shows that Benjamin Henton, aged 30, of the Second Regiment of Militia, with his wife Sarah and two young children, was paid 7s.6d. per week. Sarah was the daughter of James Penfold, a cooper who lived at Brooklag.

## *Crime*

Life was very hard during this period and sometimes the people of Newdigate resorted to crime.

At the Croydon Assizes on 10 March 1580 Christopher Scriven of Newdigate, a labourer, together with two men from other parishes, was indicted for petty larceny, having stolen six geese valued at 11d. from William Finche of Leigh. He had previously stolen a purse from a house in Brockham Green.

In 1583 at the same court, a butcher named Robert Oswyn and a yeoman, Henry Goodman, were indicted for grand larceny for stealing a bay gelding worth 50s. and a grey mare valued at £5 from Walter Newdigate. Larceny was described as 'grand' when the value of the stolen goods was a shilling or more, and the penalty on conviction was hanging. Oswyn was found guilty and sentenced to be hanged, but Goodman remained at large.

In 1594 Mary Willsonne of Newdigate, a spinster, broke into the close of Richard Weller of Headley and stole two sheep worth 8d. Although her case was heard she was not in court, being still at large.

Robert Sypas of Newdigate (or Ockley) was indicted for grand larceny and burglary. At Ockley he stole £3 in money, a doublet, a cloak, a smock, several pieces of linen, a pair of hose and a purse, with a total value of over £3. Thomas Bax, a sawyer, and Richard Pricklove, a tailor of Ockley, were indicted as accessories. Earlier Sypas and Bax had burgled the house of Oliver Gardiner of Newdigate to steal three bushels of barley and three bushels of wheatmeal with a total value of 26s. Sypas cheated the hangman by dying in gaol, and Bax and Pricklove were acquitted.

Oliver Gardiner's house was again burgled two years later by a spinster, Faith Lee of Newdigate, who stole a loaf of bread valued at 2d. and a cheese valued at 4d. She was found guilty and received a whipping. In 1601 another spinster named Blanche Weller of Newdigate was indicted for petty larceny for stealing three napkins from Edward Willett of Newdigate. Her confession did not save her from a whipping – she was 13 years old.

In 1623, Thomas Graysborough (or Westbrook), a labourer, Sarah his wife and Helen Burnett, a spinster, all of Newdigate, were indicted for burgling the house of William Deane of Newdigate. They stole two cheeses, a crock of lard and a piece of beef worth in total 1s.2d.; they must have been desperately hungry to risk the ultimate penalty. Thomas Graysborough and Helen Burnett were found guilty and sentenced to be hanged but the spinster was remanded on a plea of pregnancy. She may have been hanged after the birth of her child.

In 1609, John Terry junr and Thomas Dunnynge, both husbandmen of Charlwood, John Terry senr of Newdigate, also a husbandman, and Grace Myttens, a widow of Charlwood, were indicted for the murder of Eleanor Fyste. They were accused of attacking her at Charlwood on 18 February that year while John Terry junr, aided and abetted by the others, was also accused of strangling her. Only John Terry junr was found guilty and was to be hanged.

Almost 100 years later, Thomas Patching, the son of a famous Quaker of the same name who had died in prison in Southwark for his beliefs in 1660, and described as of the manor of Greens with land in Newdigate and Capel, was found guilty of murdering a widow named Sarah Hurst. He was declared bankrupt in 1706 owing more than £6,000, a huge sum for those times. He became a fugitive and was never found.

This was a time of religious dissent, with an established community of Quakers along the Newdigate/Capel border and much Protestant antagonism towards the Roman Catholics. The law at the time required that everyone should attend the Church of England services at their own Parish Church every Sunday and those who did not attend were accused of recusancy. In 1581 a return showed that there were 105 recusants in Surrey who regularly paid fines. In 1605, Henry Darrell junr, a gentleman of Newdigate and a member of the family which had run the Ewood iron mill, was indicted. In 1624 a yeoman, John Kellam of Newdigate, was indicted for harbouring his servants, Catherine Eaton and John Lee, as recusants for 11 months.

The Quakers continued to have difficulty with the law. In 1662, after the restoration of the monarchy, several yeomen of Newdigate – Allen Wallis of Chaffolds, Henry Sturges, John Dymocke, and widow Wonham, together with Richard Bax of Capel, were all accused, with others, of assembling at Charlwood to perform an act of religious worship:

*... other than as it is set out by the law of the Realm to the great terror of the people and disturbance of the peace, in contempt of the King and his laws, an evil example... and against the peace.*

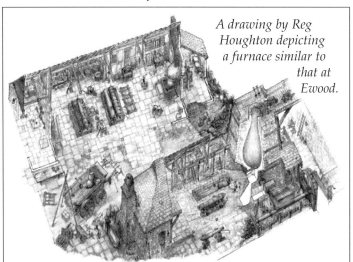

*A drawing by Reg Houghton depicting a furnace similar to that at Ewood.*

Reproduced by kind permission of the Wealden Iron Research Group.

## Forestry

It has already been seen that trees were an important resource for the area, and as early as 1289 Thomas de la Lynde assigned William Newdigate and others to sell 100 loads of timber in the woods of Lynde.

At the time of the Dissolution of the Monasteries in 1538 Henry VIII decided to build a palace called Nonsuch that would rival any in Europe. Merton Priory surrendered in that year and stone for the new palace was plundered from the priory while its land in Newdigate – Beamlands, Horsielands, Ockley,

Rolfs and Marelands – was given to Trinity College in Cambridge by Henry. Vast quantities of timber were also required for Nonsuch and it would appear that much of this was obtained from the lands formerly held by the priory.

Carpenters were sent out from Nonsuch to choose and mark trees that would be suitable. In Rusper and Newdigate in the June/July period the accounts show payment for felling, hewing and squaring 21½ loads of timber at 1s.2d. per load (a load of timber was 50 feet). At Ewood, only 1½ loads were taken, probably because the wood was already coppiced to provide fuel for the furnaces of the ironworks there.

Sawpits were constructed by two labourers who worked for 15 days at a rate of 5d. per day – the working day had been established by statute in 1495 as from 5a.m. until between 7p.m. and 8p.m.

A pale or fence was being constructed around the deer park at Nonsuch and large quantities of posts, shores and rails were required. The local carters delivered 59 loads from Newdigate at 2s.2d. per load.

The biggest timbers were the 'principal rafters' for the two towers of the palace. First a special wagon – the Great Wain – had to be built, strong and large enough to be capable of carrying these from the place of felling to the building site. A Robert Wryghte was paid 6s. to make this wagon. There was a man of that name living in Newdigate in 1552 (he was the defendant in a suit to establish the true ownership of a messuage, barn, orchard and 73 acres here), so possibly the Great Wain was constructed by a Newdigate man. It was involved in a formidable task as 14 of these great timbers were 80 feet long and one was longer at 89 feet. Two of these giant timbers came from Newdigate woodland; it is doubtful if there are any oaks in the area today that can boast such a height. The men at that time must have had great physical strength and been very resourceful to be able to cope with such a project with essentially simple tools.

# Iron Making
### By Jean Shelley and Joyce Banks

When one looks over the fields south of Ewood Farmhouse it is hard to believe that 500 years ago this was a lake of some 90 acres and the whole area was alive with activity. The remote valley of Ewood was once a smoky, noisy, dirty and busy place with heavy carts loaded with iron ore, charcoal, iron and slag coming and going all the time. For this was one of the most important iron-making areas in the country.

The central part of the Weald, from Horsham eastwards, lies on sandstone and is known as the High Weald. Newdigate and its neighbours are on the Low Weald, which is heavy clay.

From about 400BC until around AD1800 parts of the Weald formed a busy industrial landscape. Some of the strata, especially in the High Weald, contained iron ore from which iron could be smelted, but there is also a smaller amount of iron-bearing rock in the Low Weald. To smelt iron, charcoal is needed as wood itself will not produce enough heat, and much wood and labour are needed to produce charcoal. Fortunately trees grow readily on clay; they were managed as coppiced woodland, larger timber not being used for charcoal.

Until about 1500 the smelting of iron was on a small scale in chimney-like furnaces called bloomeries, made of thick clay and about 3 feet high and 2 feet in diameter. Each bloomery had a hole low down on one side for hand-operated bellows which were essential to maintain the required heat, 1100°C. A bloomery produced a solid 'bloom' of iron which could then be worked by a blacksmith. Smelting produced a waste product, slag, which is a dull grey-to-black colour with small holes caused by trapped gases, and is virtually indestructible. Pieces of slag can still be found on the ground around Ewood.

In 1496, in the Ashdown Forest, the French technique of using water power to operate the bellows via an overshot water-wheel was first used, changing the whole industry. Blast furnaces came into use and were much larger than the bloomeries, being about 20 feet square and 20 feet high. To operate the water-wheel, streams were dammed to make large ponds, the dams being known as bays; the streams and deep valleys of the High Weald ensured reliable water power. The new furnaces produced iron which could be cast directly into moulds to make fire backs, cannons and cannonballs. For domestic uses further processes were carried out at the forge to convert the cast iron into wrought iron; often furnaces and forges were on separate sites. The forges used water power to operate the bellows that heated two hearths and lifted the large hammer. Blast furnace slag may be black, greenish or grey, but is always very hard and shiny. Forge slag is similar to bloomery slag.

The industry was at its height in the 1500s and 1600s, driven by the wars of those times. It required a substantial workforce for which there was no employment when iron making ceased. Documents list 178 water-powered sites, most of which were in the High Weald.

*Mill Cottage.*

*The broken culvert which started to crumble after the dry summer of 1976 and the cold winter of 1981/82. The bay was intact in 1966.*

*The former iron-mill pond, now a field.*

At Ewood it is still possible to see the pond bay behind Mill Cottage; it is a very long bay in order to retain enough water as the valley behind is very wide and exceedingly shallow. The size of the pond recorded at different times varied from 20 to 100 acres. It was drained some time between 1813 and 1840.

There are two stone culverts through which water can flow, probably built when the pond was drained; by the early 1970s they were in poor condition. In front of the bay near Mill Cottage an area of widening and deepening is thought to have been the location of the wheel pit. Today the main stream flows to the west of Mill Cottage.

It is impossible to say whether there was a bloomery at Ewood although the site seems suitable. When Lord Abergavenny, the then owner, conveyed Ewood to George and Christopher Darrell in 1536, there was already 'uno molendino ferreo, vocato An Iron Myll'. It is not known when it was established, but there had been an earlier transaction of land here during the reign of Henry VIII, and Lord Abergavenny was already involved in other iron-smelting operations on his lands in Sussex. By about 1540 iron working had become more sophisticated with the introduction of the blast furnace and the finery forge. Besides the 'Iron Myll', property

transferred to the Darrell brothers included a couple of messuages and gardens, half a dozen cottages, 60 acres of land, 40 acres of meadow, 100 acres of pasture, 100 acres of heath and furze, 300 acres of wood and 80 acres of inland water, so there must already have been a going concern. There was also a forge at Leigh, conveyed to the Darrells in 1551, and for a while it was worked together with the furnace at Ewood. Later the two operations were combined at the Ewood site. The Darrells came from Scotney Castle in Kent but their name is believed to originate from around Airell, near St Lo in Normandy.

It is debatable whether Ewood was a good iron-making site. The nearest source of iron ore was the small outcrop of ferruginous gravel at Henfold Hill which in the sixteenth century was included in the Ewood estate, but later the ore had to be obtained from further afield. The iron masters were obliged by law to repair the roads, often using their own slag, so the area would not have been as impassable as it became in the eighteenth century. A plentiful supply of timber was certainly available. The third requirement was a good water supply to provide power, and in the absence of a permanent stream the pond had to be created.

The woodlands were treated as a valuable resource and the trees were carefully managed. Coppice, cut every seven to nine years, together with branches cut from taller trees ('top and lop') produced the charcoal for smelting whilst the larger timber was reserved for house building. An Act of 1558 forbade the felling of timber within 14 miles of the sea or of any navigable river, but in the county of Surrey, Charlwood, Ewood and Leigh were exempt, illustrating the importance of the industry.

The Darrell family were recusants, liable to fines, and were involved in the defence of Queen Mary Tudor at the time of Wyatt's Rebellion in the 1550s. Part of the manor of Ewood was conveyed to other parties and George died 'in reduced circumstances' in 1567. Christopher repurchased the remainder of the estate but he needed a loan from the Crown, to whose trustees he was obliged to convey all his interest. In 1580 came another Act forbidding the cutting of timber, but this time with specific exemption of:

*...: any woodes... standing or growing... upon any lands of Chris Darrell in the parish of Newdigate within the Weilde... which woodes... have... been by him preserved and coppysed for the use of his Iron Woorkes.*

A survey of Ewood was made by the Crown in February 1575 when:

*Robert Reynolds of East Grinstead (ironmaster) holdeth and occupieth the Capitall Mansion House... also the park of Ewood... with the stables stawles haylofts and other edifices... together with a little corte... an orchard and garden containing... in estimacion iiij acres. Also a brewhouse with divers brewing vessels... scituate west of the said Mansion House and adjoining to the iron-works there, late in the tenure of Christopher Darrell... Also one messuage or tenement there called The Old Lodge with pightelle [little enclosure], a garden plot and other edifices adjoining. The same Robert Reynolds also holdeth the Iron Mylle and works, a furnace, a forge and hammer and all the buildings... of Ewood otherwise Iwood Park with divers tools... also one great pond containing by estimacion 40 acres...*

Christopher Darrell died in 1581 and his will direct-ed that all his manors in Surrey and elsewhere be sold to pay his debts. The following year Queen Elizabeth I confirmed the lease of three quarters of the Ewood land and ironworks to Henry Darrell, another brother of Christopher, for £700, transferring a debt of £2,000 to Edmund Pelham with power to extract money from Darrell, but without seizing his property at Ewood. The land remained a royal pos-session until 1604. Henry married Margaret Gage of Firle, Sussex and after her death in 1616 he married Mary, the widow of Thomas Newdigate who had died in 1612. Henry died in 1618 and probably the ironworks closed soon afterwards.

In 1673 Ewood was referred to as 'a woody place where sometimes dwelt Henry Dorell or Darell gent.' By then, the pond was a fish-pond but still 'upon the bay thereof standeth a round mill.' In about 1662 Richard Morton, an ejected minister and physician, came to live at Ewood. The house had various descriptions; 'the capitall Mansion House' of 1575 became 'an ancient mansion and faire' and at the end of the eighteenth century it was called a 'large farm-house'. The present Ewood Farmhouse contains many reused timbers and was probably built at about the time of the demise of the ironworks. In the 1730s Richard Morton (possibly the grandson of the other Richard), not only had to pay a high rate of Poor Tax, but he was also obliged to pay Window Tax on 30 windows in his house at Ewood. Exact details of the 'capitall Mansion House' remain a mystery.

*Ewood Farmhouse with Victorian extension, now demolished.*

Very few Wealden ironworks survived past the mid-eighteenth century when coke furnaces began to replace charcoal for smelting and the industry moved north. The site at Ashburnham in Sussex was the last to close in 1803. However, the importance of Ewood in its heyday can be seen on an estate map of Greenings Farm in Charlwood, c.1560, where the road on the west (now Partridge Lane) is described as 'The way that cometh from Horsham to Iwod'.

# The Timber-Framed Buildings of Newdigate

Newdigate is blessed with many surviving timber-framed buildings which are now well maintained, cared for and loved. Joan Harding and Joyce Banks in their book *Newdigate – Its History and Houses* describe and illustrate each house in detail. The following descriptions are based on their work.

### Blanks Farm
Known as Cheesmans in the late-eighteenth and early-nineteenth centuries, this is a four-bay, central-smoke-bay house built in the late-sixteenth century. A distinctive range of high, narrow windows looking south-west on the first floor may have been intended to light a workshop, and a scratched symbol similar to a shepherd's crook may indicate a wool craft or trade. At the time of writing the house is undergoing major reconstruction work.

### Boothlands
This was originally a central-chimney house. Its timber frame was made almost entirely of chestnut, and has always been two-floored. Boothlands incorporated lands called Deanlands, Bachelors, Strideland and Bereland and was acquired by Daniel Booth on the departure of the Newdigates in 1636. A £100 endowment to the school in Newdigate by George Booth in 1681 provided for three more scholars. In the Tithe Award Boothlands was referred to as Rookery Farm. It was used as an officers' mess during the Second World War, after which time extensive repairs took place including the replace-ment of a damaged staircase with one from the semi-derelict Newdigate Place.

### Brooklag Farm
A four-bay medieval house from the late-sixteenth century. It became a laundry in the nineteenth century and gave its name to Laundry Hill just to the south.

### Chaffolds
Situated on the Sussex border to the west of Rusper Road, this property was built in two stages. The open truss of the two-bay open hall has a cut-down crown post, perhaps from an earlier building, and the braces are square in section which is an early feature.

*Chaffolds Farm in 1990 (formerly Eversheds Farm).*

*Rear view of Blanks Farm in 2000.*

Below: *Coombers Farm in the 1990s.*

Centre below: *The Elms (formerly Pancrass Rolls).*

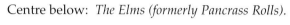

*Blanks Farm in 1920.*

**Boothlands in 1954.**

Above: *Brooklag Farm in 1990.*

Right: *Ewood Farmhouse in 1985.*

Originally there was a third floored bay to the east, which was gutted and used as a smoke bay. Later a large chimney occupied its space and a seventeenth-century parlour wing was built. In the eighteenth and nineteenth centuries the house was known as Eversheds after the family who occupied it.

### Coombers Farm

Formerly called Butts, this house dates from before 1600 when it was listed as a copyhold property of the manor of East Betchworth. William Cumber was the copyholder in 1679 – he and his heirs occupied the property until 1727. The oldest part of the house is the gable end which faces the road; the extension to the east is Georgian. After the Second World War it was described as 'a dilapidated old place'.

### Cudworth Manor

Located on a moated site, this manor house has grown around the core of a rare type of four-bay timber-framed building dating back to about 1500. There has been much alteration and restoration over the years which has disguised the original plan. This was a large farm occupied by substantial yeomen farmers although by 1872 it was described as 'run down'.

### Dean House Farm

This was a three-bay, two-and-a-half-storey wing, with the oldest part dating from about 1630, and a

*Cudworth Manor, c.1904.*

*Dean House Farm.*

jetty facing the church. There are traces of an earlier house behind this wing and at right angles to it. As far as is known this house is unique in Surrey as it has a double jetty at the west end and a single jetty at the east end. Traditions of secret passages to the church and the Six Bells public house have lingered in folk memory and could have been used for smuggling in the eighteenth century. The upstairs corner hearth is said to have been used for baking communion wafers.

### The Elms

Named Pancrass Rolls Farm before 1908–9, this was a late-sixteenth-century end-chimney house with two rooms upstairs and two rooms down. The name Rolls is from the Rolf or Rolles family whose lands in Newdigate and Charlwood covered a large area in the fourteenth century. Similarly, Pancrass comes from the family of that name. Blunden Shadbolt, an architect from Horley, enlarged and altered the house in the early-twentieth century into a 'gentleman's residence'.

### Ewood Farm

This building is neither old nor big enough to be the 'Capitall Mansion House' mentioned in the survey of 1575. It was probably built on the same site as the earlier house about the time that the ironworks declined, reusing old timbers in a very wide three-bay building.

### Gaterounds

A timber-framed house of two builds using many timbers from an older building, each of three bays; recent research suggests that the parlour wing was originally built in 1579 and that the house was probably jettied. It is likely that the name originates from Agnes, the widow of Robert Gawton who in a survey of Marshlands in 1591 held 'Okeleys and divers other lands'.

*Gaterounds Farm, c.1920.*

### Gosscroft

A timber-framed, three-bay hall house, probably dating from the early-fifteenth century. In the early-nineteenth century there were only two acres of land attached, which indicates that it was not primarily a

*Gosscroft in 1990.*

*A distant view of Harlings in 2002.*

*Greens Farm in 2002.*

*Home Farm – formerly Newdigate Place, the home of the Newdigate family.*

*Greens Farm showing outbuildings in 2002.*

*Hound House Farm in November 1989.*

Below: *High Trees House in 1990.*

*Halesbridge Farm in 1986.*

working farm. By tradition Gosscroft was once an alehouse called 'The Pussy Cat Inn'.

### Greens Farm

This is one of Surrey's finest hall houses. Parts of three bays remain, and various early features point to a date before 1300. The fine selection of outbuildings includes a detached stable or hayloft whose original purpose is much debated.

### Halesbridge House

Probably named after the Hale family as Thomas atte Hale was fined 3d. in 1396 for failing to repair Olfynhele. Hales Howse with three acres of land appears in the inquisition post-mortem of Thomas Newdigate in 1576.

### Harlings

Standing in a remote corner of Newdigate, only the centre part of the two-bay building is old, probably sixteenth century. There was a Harling or Hurling family living there in the eighteenth century.

### High Trees House

This building had a suspended floor over the smoke bay indicating a type of house in transition from an open hall. It was much modernised when the Tyler family were in occupation and many of the late-sixteenth- and early-seventeenth-century features were hidden.

### Home Farm

The manor house of the Newdigate family, which was gradually reduced in size and status. The remaining part was on the west side of the original house and includes a medieval crown post. There is close studding in some walls, indicating that this was an important house. It was originally called Newdigate Place, but the Herron family gave this name to their new mansion and the old house became Home Farm.

### Hound House Farm

Known as Twittenhams until the late-nineteenth century, much of the house was destroyed by a disastrous fire in 1981 that tragically killed the occupant, Henry Eggleton. It may originally have been an open-hall house but now very little remains of the old building.

### Innstead

Formerly Little Trees, this was originally built as two separate framed houses just a foot apart, and at times was occupied by three or even four families. It is now a single dwelling. In the eighteenth century there was reputedly a gunpowder factory situated to the rear.

### Ivy House

This is a medieval hall house of three bays with arch braces in the framing and a crown post roof, which was formerly called Cockmans. Its probable fifteenth-century date is confirmed by its mention in an indenture of 1497 when 'Cokemans' stood to the north of Gotwycksgrene in Rusper.

### Kingsland Cottages

Originally built in the late-sixteenth century as one large central smoke-bay house of four bays and two storeys, the chimney stack was added when the building was divided into two cottages. The west cottage, now called Bay Cottage, retains many old features as Evie Hopkins, who lived there for 70 years until her death in 1980, made very few alterations.

### Lance's Cottage & Nightingales

These homes are on the road to Parkgate, and were called 1 and 2 Lance's Cottages until about 1960. Lance's Cottage seems to be an earlier timber-framed building with two small bays and a chimney at the south end. Nightingales was added to this end. Ralph Lance lived in Newdigate around 1690 and may have built the cottages. However, although members of the Nightingale family farmed at High Trees in the mid-nineteenth century and later lived at Reffolds, they are not definitely linked with these cottages.

### Marelands

Originally a two-bay, timber-framed open-hall house of the mid-fifteenth century, this was one of the principal manor houses of Newdigate.

### Mill Cottage

A small, late-seventeenth-century, two-storey house of two bays, built from reused timbers. The ironworks closed in about 1610 so there must have been an abundance of timber for reuse as well as growing wood nearby. In the garden is a tall bank with two culverts marking the limit of the old pond.

### New House Farm

This may originally have been a hall house with the small bay converted to a smoke bay. It is also possible that it was built in the late-sixteenth century as a smoke-bay house of two floors throughout. The present house is a long, brick-clad building and is a working farm.

### Nyes Place

This property was once called 'Ducks Cottage', as they were the only occupants. It was probably built in the late-sixteenth century but when the Capel family took it over in the 1970s it was practically derelict. In 2002 it is a beautifully restored family home.

### Oaklands Park Farm Cottage

Formerly a farmhouse called Souters, this building had four bays, three of which were floored.

*Henry Eggleton of Hound House Farm with Allan (left) and David Trower on a wagon drawn by Captain.*

Above: *Hound House Farm after the fire on 22 December 1981.*

Above: *John Henry Eggleton (1904–81) at the Clock House looking towards Hound House Farm.*

Right: *Hound House Farm in 1906. Left to right: Susan James, Elizabeth Cooper holding Betty James, Kate Pelham, John W. James, Bertha Kempshall, Peter Mackrell and cousin Clara who was on a visit.*

Left: *Little Trees (now Innstead) in 1898.*
Left to right: *George Richard Johnson with his children Emily, Fanny and George.*

Above: *Lance's Cottage* (left) *and Nightingales.*

*Innstead in 1986.*

*Marelands in 2002, originally one of the early manors.*

Left: *Ivy House Farm in 1974.*

*Mill Cottage at Ewood.*

Left: *Kingsland in 1921.*

Right: *Old Beam Brook in 1989.*

Above: *New House Farm in the early-twentieth century.*

Right: *Olde Cottage in 2002 (formerly called Hasteds and originally part of Six Bells Cottages).*
Photo courtesy of Ricki and Colin Hughes.

Above: *Nyes Place in 1972.*

Right: *Nyes Place in the 1990s.*

Below: *Kingsland Farm and Old Kingsland Cottage in the early 1900s.*

*Oaklands Park Farm Cottage, formerly Souters, in 1974.*

*Six Bells Cottages in 1921 (now Olde Cottage and White Cottage).*

*Rolls Farmhouse (formerly Chinpegs), c.1903. The lady holding the baby is Lily Ann (Aunt Annie) Burberry (née Webb). The baby is Arthur Henry Robert Atkins (Bobby). His mother was Rose Harriet Atkins (née Webb) who was the sewing mistress in Newdigate School and died aged 34 in 1902. The identity of the other two girls in this picture is not known.*

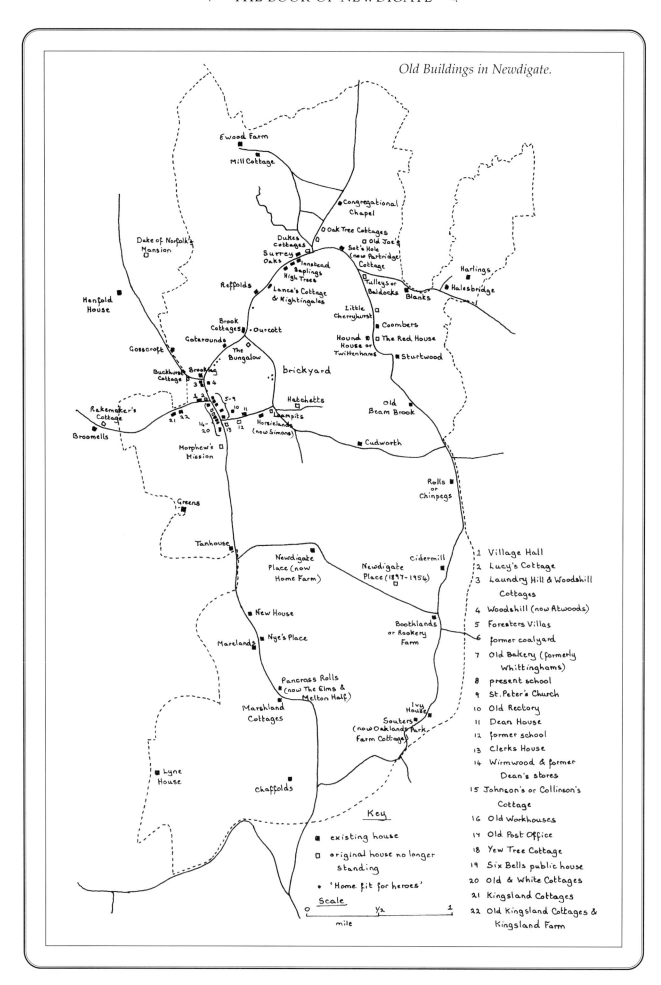

*Old Buildings in Newdigate.*

Ewood Farm

Mill Cottage

Congregational Chapel

Duke of Norfolk's Mansion

Oak Tree Cottages

Dukes cottages

Old Joe's

Sot's Hole (now Partridge Cottage)

Surrey Oaks

Innstead Saplings High Trees

Harlings

Halesbridge

Reffolds

Lance's Cottage & Nightingales

Tulleys or Baldocks

Blanks

Henfold House

Little Cherryhurst

Brook Cottages

Ourcott

Coombers

Gaterounds

Hound House or Twittenhams

The Red House

Gosscroft

The Bungalow

Sturtwood

Buckhurst Cottage

Brooking

brickyard

3   4

Hatchetts

Old Beam Brook

Rakemaker's Cottage

1  2

5-9

10  11

Loampits

21  22

14-20

13  12

Horsielands (now Simons)

Broomells

Cudworth

Morphew's Mission

Rolls or Chinpegs

Greens

Tanhouse

Newdigate Place (now Home Farm)

Cidermill

Newdigate Place (1897-1954)

1   Village Hall

2   Lucy's Cottage

3   Laundry Hill & Woodshill Cottages

4   Woodshill (now Atwoods)

New House

Boothlands or Rookery Farm

5   Foresters Villas

6   former coalyard

Marelands

Nye's Place

7   Old Bakery (formerly Whittinghams)

8   present school

9   St. Peter's Church

Pancrass Rolls (now The Elms & Melton Half)

10  Old Rectory

11  Dean House

Ivy House

12  former school

Marshland Cottages

Souters (now Oaklands Park Farm Cottage)

13  Clerks House

14  Wirmwood & former Dean's stores

15  Johnson's or Collinson's Cottage

16  Old Workhouses

Lyne House

17  Old Post Office

Chaffolds

18  Yew Tree Cottage

Key

19  Six Bells public house

■  existing house

20  Old & White Cottages

□  original house no longer standing

21  Kingsland Cottages

22  Old Kingsland Cottages & Kingsland Farm

●  'Home fit for heroes'

Scale

0                    ½                    1

mile

*Saplings (formerly Upton House and at one time a shop) in 1990.*

*Reffolds in the 1930s* (above) *and in 1990* (below).

**Rolls Farmhouse in 1990.**

Right: *Simons (formerly Horsielands) in 1990.*

Below: *A busy Six Bells in the early 1900s.*

*Six Bells in 1990.*

*The Surrey Oaks Inn in the 1950s.*

*George Butcher, landlord of the Six Bells,
and Charles Wood.*

*The Surrey Oaks Inn in 2002; the stump of the
second oak is just visible, behind the white posts.*

*The Surrey Oaks Inn, c.1900.*

*Tanhouse in 2001 when the garden was open for
the National Gardens Scheme.*

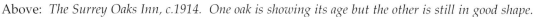

Above: *Tanhouse in 1903.*

Above: *The Surrey Oaks Inn, c.1914. One oak is showing its age but the other is still in good shape.*

### Old Beam Brook
A four-bay, central smoke-bay house built in the late-sixteenth or early-seventeenth century. By the late-nineteenth century the house was roofless and dilapidated.

### Old Cottage & The White Cottage
These cottages were condemned as unfit for human habitation before the start of the Second World War. Built in the mid-sixteenth century, for many years they were known as Six Bells Cottages and consisted originally of central four bays. The Tithe Award shows that part or all of The White Cottage was a public house called the Wheatsheaf.

### Old Kingsland Cottage & Kingsland Farm
Dating from the seventeenth century, these properties may originally have been a barn which was later adapted and divided. Old Kingsland Cottage, the western part, is 'black and white', whilst at Kingsland Farm several types of brickwork can be found. At the back was a sunken brewhouse with a side door where beer was sold.

### Reffolds
Originally a two-bay, continuous-jetty house of two storeys built in the early-seventeenth century, this type of house is uncommon in the Surrey countryside. The name Reffolds does not appear until about 1700 when William Reffill is assessed for Poor Rate.

### Rolls Farmhouse
This property probably acquired its name from the Rolfe family who lived in the area during the fourteenth and fifteenth centuries. In the nineteenth century it was known as Chinpegs. The building was originally an end smoke-bay house dating from the mid- to late-sixteenth century.

### Saplings
A 'suspended upper floor' house, probably built between 1550 and 1600. It is perhaps the earliest surviving house on this part of the 'road to Ewood'. By 1851 it was occupied by Robert Upton who was a beerhouse keeper, and the name Upton House lingered on for many years.

### Simons
This was the original Horsielands Farm and the name derives from 'Horse Eg' (derived from the Old English, meaning Horse Island, or land surrounded by wetlands). In 1241 it was La Horsie and in 1317 Horseye, but by 1576 it was Horsey Land. Simons was a medieval hall house and its land, together with Marelands, went to endow Henry VIII's new Trinity College in Cambridge.

### The Six Bells Public House
Formerly named the Five Bells, which corresponded to the number of bells in the church tower opposite. Although it has a central chimney, characteristic of the early-seventeenth century, the timber framing is not substantial and some of it is machine cut, indicating a later date. Mr Cheesman was landlord in the early-nineteenth century and supplied the Duke of Norfolk's household with ale in 1816. At the end of that century the last Manorial Courts of Cudworth met in the Bells.

### The Surrey Oaks
This property began life as a simple timber-framed cottage of two bays, probably built in the late-seventeenth century. The building contained a wheelwright's workshop into the nineteenth century but by 1851 it had become the Surrey Oaks Inn.

### Tanhouse
This was probably originally a three-bay house with two bays open and one floored over. It faced the Beam Brook which was widened and deepened for the tanner's use, and eventually became part of the Broadwood estate. In 1897 flooding occurred 26 times in 12 months.

### Wirmwood
This building started life in the late-sixteenth century as a central smoke-bay house. In the seventeenth century a one-bay house to the north was added. This was later used as a butcher's shop and the meat hooks can still be seen under the porch. A shop was already established in the early-nineteenth century and the Dean family developed it as a general store throughout the first half of the twentieth century.

### Yew Tree Cottage
Dating from before 1650 this was originally a symmetrical timber-framed cottage of two bays; the crosswing was added in 1966. There is ripple-stone paving outside and, as with many Newdigate homes, this was probably once also the internal flooring.

### Barns
In 1985 Barbara Capel and Brenda Daniel completed a survey of all the timber-framed barns in the parish and noted the poor state of repair of many of them. Since then the barns at Gaterounds and Mareland have been renovated and the barn beside the Six Bells, which had almost collapsed, has been saved and converted into a private residence. The barns at Greens are also undergoing renovation at the time of writing. During the 1990s Peter Hall recreated a beautiful barn at Gildings Farm, using local timbers and traditional building methods.

*Wirmwood in 1991.*

*Gildings Barn during construction.*

*The Six Bells, c.1960. The barn by the road has since been demolished. The other barn was moved backwards at some stage, and in 1996 it was converted into a dwelling called Six Bells Barn.*

*The renovated Marelands Barn in 2002.*

Right: *King John Barn, Cudworth, in August 2001.*

*Yew Tree Cottage in the 1920s. Fred Dean is in the garden.*

*Six Bells Barn in 1997.*

# Chapter 4

# Newdigate's Dark Ages

With the decline of the iron-making industry in the early-seventeenth century people moved away, and peace returned to Newdigate. For over 200 years the place declined as the timber-framed buildings, built during the period of prosperity, became dilapidated, damp and unsanitary. Farming was always difficult, although pigs were very important. John Aubrey in his *Natural History and Antiquities of Surrey* mentions a custom only known in Newdigate:

*They do not yoke their pigs, but thrust skewers through their nostrils which answers the same end. These skewers are about 2 to 3 inches long, and thrust through their tender noses, hinder their rooting up the earth or any plants.*

## Farming
### From an article by Robert Pols

Among those contacted by Surrey historian William Bray, when accumulating information about the county, was Thomas Duncomb, curate of Newdigate. This was a period of innovation in agriculture when new practices and techniques were being tried. The Board of Agriculture was set up in 1793 to encourage such experiment. Duncomb, however, reported 'the opinion and belief of many old inhabitants that the mode of husbandry has varied but little since time immemorial.' It was not that the farmers were unwilling to try new ideas, though Duncomb himself seems to have been no lover of novelty, but rather that the Wealden clay was firmly unresponsive to whatever was tried. The nature of the land was:

*... for the most part a poor clay, or a small hungry gravel – not admitting these improvements and that interchange of crops which have proved so beneficial to lighter soils.*

That same clay churned into a sticky mud which made it difficult to cart manure and travel to market for over half the year, so that the land was as difficult to move about on as it was to work.

Nevertheless there were those who tried out new ideas. The Revd Henry Jackson Close, rector of the parish from 1787 to 1789 who resigned over a dispute with parish officers and later farmed at Lyne, was a believer in the new technology. Duncomb reported that his 'drilling machines together with all his other new invented implements for husbandry are laid up as useless.' In fact, one of Close's new-fangled devices had not joined the rusting heap: a one-handled Suffolk plough was proving more economical than those used elsewhere. Attempts were made to drain the land; Mr Close dug deep ditches but his fields remained as wet as ever and the curate said that there were so many failures among speculative farmers in poor clays that he was no friend of experimental husbandry in these parts.

Conditions combined to make Newdigate 'the last place in the world' in which to farm and it was generally reckoned that the farmers, though 'very industrious', saw very little profit for their efforts. 'They kept a livelihood always partaking of the same humble fare as their servants', yet, in spite of this frugal lifestyle, seemed to be in danger of bankruptcy on a parish-wide scale. The farmers were largely tenants, and landlords seldom visited their estates. Cottages were 'in a very bad repair – most of them exhibiting a heap of ruins instead of the light and decent abode of the industrious labourer.' Families were often crowded several to a house, and new building was virtually non-existent, there 'having been but one house built in 40 years, and but two in the present century.' The two buildings referred to are probably Sturtwood Farm and Loam Pits, which was built on the site of the present-day Oakfield House.

Yet in spite of absentee landlords, poor roads and unrewarding soil, farming took place and some crops were produced. Only wheat and oats were normally grown for sale, though occasional small amounts of barley, peas and beans were sown for home consumption. Mr Ede of Cyder Mill tried the experiment of sowing ten acres of flax and met with some measure of success.

Due to the wetness of the ground, few sheep were kept, but oxen were bred and sold off at the summer fairs at two or three years old.

The general pattern of husbandry in the area followed a five-year cycle. In the first year the ground was broken up for the fallows in April, harrowed and rolled as required, and prepared in the autumn for wheat, allowing a kiln of lime or 50 cart-loads of manure for every three acres. In the second year wheat was grown and harvested. In year three oats and seeds were sown. In year four the seeds, presumably grass, were mown or pastured and oats were again grown in the fifth year. The following year the land was left fallow and dressed in autumn once more.

Farm servants, when taken on, were generally recruited at half-year hirings at Michaelmas and Lady Day and might receive between £6 and £7 over the year. The annual pay for maid servants varied between £1 and three guineas. Day labourers commonly earned 1s.6d. per day, being paid only for such days as the farmer required them and the weather permitted. Certain jobs such as threshing and reaping were paid on a piece-work basis.

Thomas Burberry, Steward to the Duke of Norfolk, kept an account of day labourers employed on the Duke's land at Newdigate from 1791. Among the occupations for males were ploughing, harrowing, thrashing, carting chalk and making and cleaning a road, whilst Jane Dolby, Rachel and Rebecca Bucket and Martha Humphreys were employed for two days in August and September in raking oats. Other occupations for females were haymaking, weeding and picking stones.

In 1801 Lord Pelham requested that the bishops of the Church of England should obtain from their clergy details of the crops grown in each parish. In Newdigate it was recorded that 463 acres were sown to wheat, 531 acres to oats, 56 acres to peas, 50 acres to beans, 8 acres to turnips and rape, 6 acres to potatoes and a single acre to barley. Although the printed form shows rye and tares there were none entered.

These 1801 returns give some interesting statistics but it is Thomas Duncomb's letter that brings Newdigate farming alive and shows it as a real, everyday occupation and a grim, unprofitable struggle in a parish where the 'rich' were poor and the poor were even poorer.

## The Struggle for Survival

Overseers of the poor were appointed to raise poor rates and to be liable for the poor and the sick. In 1725 an almshouse was acquired and almshouses are mentioned in the accounts for much of the sixteenth century.

At Workhouse Green there is a row of three cottages now known as Nos 1 and 2 Brook Cottages and Clairbrook Cottage. The original structure (half of No. 1 and all of No. 2) was built for the overseers of the poor in about 1796. It was built on part of a farm called Heath Land, to which was added the area nearest the road, enclosed from the waste of the manor. In the same year a contract was made for the care of the poor including the provision of 'a house to keep the poor in', replacing an earlier one near the church, in which Thomas Chart, the schoolmaster, took up residence.

In December 1800 a formal agreement was made between the parish officers and John Rooles of Witney in Oxfordshire that:

*... he should be paid at the rate of 12s. with board per week... to undertake the whole care of the poor... to instruct and teach all of them that shall be sent into this house, and others the officers shall think proper to send to him for the purpose of work in the Woollen Manufacturing Line from the space of 12 months from the date thereof.*

The overseers' accounts book, dated 1801 when Thomas Wonham junr and Henry Bridger were the overseers, has the following reference:

*1801 Feb 22 Carriage of wooll, cards and oil:*
*£0.2s.0d.*
*Mar 20 James Dalbey, a bill for woll: £2.5s.0d.*
*Mr Larkin, a bill for oil: £8.17s.0d.*
*Mr Foster, a bill for cards: £1.2s.0d.*

The manufactory made cloth for:

*Great-coats, Waistcoats, Blankets, Horse-collar Cloth, Yearn for Stockings etc, etc. The first garment, a waistcoat, that was made was for one George Weller, son of Peter Weller, price 4s. and ninepence and made by Thomas Chart, Vestry Clerk. The name of the cloth – Newdigate Frizzle.*

As there is nothing in the other parish records which suggests references to wool it can be assumed that this venture was short-lived.

Not all the poor were relieved here; many paupers were boarded out on a 'roundsman' system. The poor who were on relief stayed and worked for a certain length of time with one master and then moved on. It seems 27 people were relieved in this way in 1802 when £1,186.3s.2¾d. was spent on direct poor relief, not including the workhouse expenditure.

No parish wanted the expense of an unnecessary mouth to feed and the Newdigate Removal Orders show that John Dalby and his wife were examined twice in 1791 before being sent back to Reigate.

Mary Weller in 1786 and Ann Hole in 1790 were examined about the fathers of their illegitimate children, and their legal place of settlement was also looked into.

However, when the responsibility was clearly that of the parish, attempts were made to relieve suffering. When Joseph Tidy was buried at St Peter's Church in 1788 at the age of 28 he was described as 'poor'. His wife was carrying their fourth child and payments were made for the month prior to the birth, then a monthly sum paid to support her and the four children. The overseers also paid the rent for Joseph Tidy's house for a number of years both before and after his death.

*Newdigate Poorhouse (now Brook Cottages and Clairbrook Cottage) painted by John Hassell in 1828. He often made sketches but did not complete paintings until many years later; thus he cannot be relied upon for accuracy.*

*Brook Cottages and Clairbrook Cottage in 1990.*

In 1790 four successive entries in the burial register are followed by 'died of the smallpox', and the Poor Law expenses bear witness to this tragedy: at 'Waller's on moving of the people in the small pox 11s.6d.' Mrs Waller was the landlady at the Five Bells and later supplied 'liquor on the smallpox account'. Similarly, 'a boy going to the doctor on the smallpox account, 6d.' In the same year the overseers paid Dr Borer for inoculating 33 people.

In 1792 the overseers made an agreement with Dr G. Gregory in which he undertook to attend the poor of Newdigate resident within six miles of the Street, for an annual fee of five guineas, which covered physic and surgery, but excluded inoculations and midwifery (the former cost 5s.3d. each, and the latter 10s.6d.).

Even as far back as 1671 Newdigate had a medical doctor in the parish but he may not have administered to the poor. He was John Budgen, a member of the family that owned Newdigate Place from 1636–1807, and in his notebook he describes how a stone taken from the body of his father's (James) in 1671 weighed 2 ounces, 3 drachms and 31 grains!

Medical knowledge was poor during these times. On 9 December 1839, James Worsfold, aged 69, died suddenly in a field. The coroner's verdict was that he 'died by the visitation of God'.

Another way of looking after the poor involved putting children into care. The parish would place a child with a host family, paying something for food and, perhaps, clothing, leaving the hard-pressed parents with one less mouth to feed.

Benjamin, the son of James Lucas, labourer, and his wife Mary, was born on 16 January 1818. He was their sixth child, and two months after his birth the parish stepped in and arranged for the eldest daughter, Charlotte, to be taken into the care of Mr Hayler, a farmer at Dean House and Northlands. In the following year Ann was born so arrangements were made for a son, James, to go to Mr Thomas Burberry who farmed a total of 200 acres at Greens Farm and Kingsland. By 1820 both children had been moved on to other families.

Occasionally special payments were made; for example when bread was distributed to the poor in the snow and bad weather of 1786, and wheat was bought, ground, and the flour given away to the poor inhabitants in 1797.

The poor were also helped to a lesser extent by the Henry Smith's Charity but this was small in relation to the need: in 1786 £7.11s. was distributed amongst 32 recipients.

Women were paid by the overseers for spinning, weaving and making clothes for the parish, and we see that in 1789 Widow Tidy was paid for 'spinning half a dozen at 9d. tire (flax) – 4s.6d.' and Dame Hopkins was paid 1s.2d. for 'spinning a gound (gown) for Chart's girl'.

In 1829, the Church Commissioners stated after a visit that the area was 'wretchedly poor'. The Poor Law Amendment Act was passed in 1834 and Newdigate was one of the parishes that objected to the new law. At the beginning of the nineteenth century, apart from the newly arrived Broadwoods, the major landowners, including the Duke of Norfolk, Lee Steere Esq. and Trinity College, Cambridge were mostly absent. Thus, although the overseers were generally farmers, there was not a wide social gap between those who paid out relief and those who received it, and in a small population (519 in 1831) all were known to one another.

The overseers received a detailed questionnaire from the Board of Poor Law Commissioners which they diligently answered, but following a Vestry Meeting on 5 January 1836 they also resolved that the Vestry Clerk, John Chart, should send the following letter:

*Gentlemen,*

*Agreeable to your request we have returned answers to your several questions as correct as possible, and at the same time humbly beg to say we much regret that your enquiry of the expenditure did not extend to the current year as we have the satisfaction of seeing our Poor Rates gradually decrease and with all due submission to the Law and Government of our country, we cannot but express our heart sorrow and sincere lament, that there is now a prospect of the power being taken from us of distributing our own funds which we raise ourselves and expend as we think proper for the purposes of charity.*

| LANDOWNERS. | OCCUPIERS. | Number referring to the Plan. | NAME AND DESCRIPTION of LANDS AND PREMISES. | STATE of CULTIVATION. | QUANTITIES in STATUTE MEASURE. | | | Amount apportioned... |
|---|---|---|---|---|---|---|---|---|
| *[His] Grace the Duke of [...] (continued)* | *Hood James (continued)* | | *[Brought forward]* | *Brought forward* | 77 | 1 | 7 | |
| | | | *Helm Field* | *Arable* | 3 | 2 | 8 | |
| | | | *New House Farm house yards Garden Orchard and Buildings* | | 1 | | 4 | |
| | | | *Shaw Matt* | *Arable* | 2 | 1 | 24 | |
| | | | *Mellow Mead* | *Arable* | 0 | 1 | 22 | |
| | | | *Little Matthews* | *Arable* | 1 | 3 | 23 | |
| | | | *Great Matthews* | *Arable* | 3 | 2 | 22 | |
| | | | *Little Yethens* | *Arable* | 2 | | | |
| | | | *Great Yethens* | *Arable* | 1 | 3 | 14½ | |
| | | | *Upper Tice Acres and Row* | *Arable* | 3 | 3 | 3 | |
| | | | | | 114 | 1 | 14 | |
| | *Pullever James* | 21 | *New Wheelwrights Shop Garden and Orchard* | *Pasture* | 1 | | 24 | |
| | | 22 | *Copse at Packhart* | *Arden* | 1 | 2 | 24 | |
| | | | | | 2 | | 27 | |
| | *Taylor James, Barron Samuel* | 22 | *Six cottages and gardens* | | | 1 | 24 | |
| | *[...] Joseph this Space in Charge* | 21 | *Covered cottage* | *Wood* | 102 | 1 | | |
| | | 11 | *Park gate cottage* | *Wood* | 35 | 3 | 21 | |
| | | 22 | *New House cottage* | *Wood* | 21 | | 24½ | |
| | | 813 | *Rifields cottage* | *Wood* | 26 | | 2 | |
| | | 814 | *New House cottage* | *Wood* | 3 | | 22 | |
| | | | | | 152 | 1 | 4 | |

*[...] School Charles of Young Inn Renewal estate [...] School House*

A page from the Tithe Apportionment of 1843, including New House Farm (Nyes Place), the wheelwright's shop (now the Surrey Oaks Inn) and two cottages on Broad Lane. Reproduced by kind permission of the Surrey History Service.

*We have no doubt that the amended law may work well in large towns and manufacturing districts, but in parishes wholly agricultural like our own, we cannot perceive what benefits can be derived, as it has ever been our endeavour to manage the parish business in the most economical manner possible. We have not complained, nor should we do so if left to ourselves, but we cannot refrain from humbly stating our conviction, that if the proposed system is carried into operation, it will increase the expenditure without profiting the poor, and cause such dissatisfaction, as may endanger the peace, prosperity and property of the Country. We trust to be pardoned for thus expressing our opinions – they are founded on carefully watching the effects of the new system among our neighbours and should the consequences which we fearfully apprehend follow the introduction of the measure, we shall have the satisfaction of knowing that we are not the advocates of forming parishes into Unions.*

Thus began a peiod of more than 100 years during which the fear of the workhouse (The Union) was always present in the lives of working people; the fears of the overseers were not misplaced.

Among the Newdigate residents of the Union Workhouse, William Tidy is recorded as:

*... refusing to do any work when ordered to assist with the peeling of potatoes – he said that he was not sent there to work and therefore would not obey the Governor's order. By trade he was a shoemaker and might be very serviceable to the Union by repairing shoes.*

David Taylor and his two sons were allowed to go to Newdigate and return the following day. He was 'in liquor' on his return and he said that he had fallen over a heap of stones which caused his face to become scratched. In December 1836, he and his family were released and left 'the house in good health and spirits'.

Kezia Stone was admitted in 1837. She had already been mentioned twice in the 'bastardy papers' of 1828 and 1832, but where were her children? Had they died or was she forcibly separated from them?

In the eighteenth and early-nineteenth centuries gypsies and travellers were very much part of the landscape. The Newdigate Parish Registers have many entries such as 'a poor travelling woman, her name unknown, was buried on January 19th 1763.'

Children were still being born in appalling circumstances. In 1873 Melia, daughter of James Aldridge and Eve Johnson, 'tramps', was born 'by the roadside and privately baptised'. The census of 1841 lists 11 persons living in barns and sheds, etc. – a trend that was still true right up to the beginning of the twentieth century.

Mid-Surrey and mid-Sussex were great haunts of gypsies so it is not surprising that the Broadwood family of Lyne came into contact with them. In the early years of the nineteenth century, when old

customs were thought likely to be swept away, there was an interest in collecting folk songs before they became extinct. The Revd John Fowler Broadwood compiled a collection of these songs in 1843 and his niece Lucy Ethelred Broadwood brought out a revised edition of her uncle's collection in 1889 called *Sussex Songs*. In 1893, together with J.A. Fuller Maitland, Lucy compiled *English County Songs*, which included two Surrey songs sung by John Burberry, a gamekeeper who was employed by the Broadwoods and may have sung these songs to Lucy in his old age.

### A Wassail Song

James Shudi Broadwood wrote in about 1840:

*On St Thomas' Day (21st December) the poor families go round to their more wealthy neighbours to solicit assistance towards improving their housekeeping during the Christmas holidays in the ancient custom. On Xmas Eve and during Xmas holidays parties go round singing carols... and expect refreshment or a largesse in money.*

*A wassail, a wassail, a wassail bowl we sing*
*With cinnamon and peppermint and other spices in.*
*A wassail, a wassail with a jolly wassail*
*And joy come to you and to our wassail.*
*Good master and good mistress as you sit by the fire,*
*Oh think of us poor wassailers who trampsie*
*thro' the mire.*
*A wassail, a wassail, of holly napper ale,*
*And joy come to you from our wassail.*

*We'll wassail increase to thy store, we'll*
*wassail sheep and kine.*
*We'll wassail bees and apple trees and*
*everything that's thine.*
*A wassail, a wassail etc.*

*Hang out your silken handkerchief upon*
*your golden spear*
*And welcome we poor wassailers to taste*
*your Xmas cheer.*
*A wassail, a wassail etc.*

# Tithe Redemption

Until the Tithe Act of 1836 the rector of St Peter's Chuch was entitled to receive tithes from all the owners of land in Newdigate, but following an agreement with an independent valuer, the Revd John Young LLD received instead a rent charge amounting to £580.10s.0d. This annual income was sufficient to allow the rector, a Glaswegian, to live very well and to employ servants to look after his needs as a bachelor.

In confirmation of this agreement a map showing all the individual fields in the parish was drawn and a schedule produced, listing the owners and occupiers of each field, the acreage of these holdings and the rent-charge payable by each. The pattern of the fields has not greatly changed, although many of those fronting the highway have been taken up for house building, as has woodland such as Ewood. The whole quantity of land subject to the survey was 4,027 acres, of which 2,297 were arable, 854 meadow and pasture and 866 woodland. Considering the difficulties of ploughing it is surprising how much land was cultivated; it indicates the isolation of the parish from the outside and the need for the farmers to be mainly self-sufficient.

The cereal crops were mostly oats and barley, grown to feed the farm animals, but also some wheat, which reveals a change from Thomas Duncomb's letter 50 years earlier. There were five acres of common land, consisting of sundry strips of land by the side of the highways, known as manorial waste and used 'indiscriminately by the inhabitants of the parish as pasture land'; this was being enclosed piecemeal, with bits listed as orchards, gardens, and cottages, particularly along Broad Lane. Other small parcels of land throughout the parish, totalling 356 acres, were not subject to the new rent-charge, nor were the 74 acres of roads and wasteland.

Nearly all fields have names, some of whose meanings have been lost over the years. One of the most common is Church Field or Church Mead, found at Newdigate Place Farm (Home Farm), Gaterounds, Hatchetts and Horsielands; produce from such fields went to pay tithes.

Owl's Entry at Oaklands Park Farm Cottage is strongly suggestive of smugglers (colloquially called owlers) whose route from the South Coast lay through this heavily wooded country around Rusper and Newdigate.

Newdigate farmers were keen fox hunters and the name Fox Causeway appears at both Horsielands and Dean House; the many wide hedgerows in the parish were created to form a natural habitat for the foxes.

At various times there have been fields called Denchers (or variations) at Hatchetts, Jordans, Horsielands and Cowix. This is a corruption of the word Devonshiring, which was a method of treating the land, by which weeds and undergrowth were cleared by burning, leaving the ashes as fertiliser.

Kiln Fields and Sawpit Fields remind us of a time when farms had to be self-sufficient, and there are also Mill field names in Ewood and near Home Farm. Probably the oldest field names which survived until recently are Northeye and Southeye at Dean House Farm. 'Eye' is from 'eg', which is Old English for an 'island' or piece of drier land raised up from surrounding marshy land.

## Chapter 5

# VICTORIAN TIMES

According to the census return of 1851 the population of Newdigate was 605, with 212 under the age of 14 and 23 over the age of 70. Seven family names – Beedle, Burberry, Gad, Horley, King, Taylor and Weller – accounted for one third of the total population, the last name belonging to no less than 43 inhabitants. Most people were involved in agriculture, with 21 farmers employing 138 men as agricultural labourers or farm servants. Other people had occupations which depended upon the land – gamekeepers, wood reeves, gardeners, blacksmiths, grooms, wheelwrights, sawyers, rat-catchers, bailiffs, thatchers and cattle doctors. There were also bricklayers, tailors, shoemakers, grocers, dressmakers, carpenters, innkeepers, nurses, and teachers, as well as a fellmonger, a charwoman, a general dealer, a confectioner, a brick maker, a rector, a letter carrier, a laundress and a brewer. Newdigate needed to be self-sufficient, and this list shows the extent to which this was achieved.

The Broadwood family at Lyne House employed three house servants, a housekeeper, a bailiff, a groom and a brewer, all of whom lived in the house. In addition there was a gardener's cottage, a laundry and a farm cottage. None of the Broadwoods' employees were local.

In 1867, the London, Brighton and South Coast Railway opened a route to Horsham and a station at Holmwood was established. This made the area more accessible for newly wealthy people, who started buying up land from the established landowners and creating new estates. The Broadwoods had lived at Lyne since the end of the eighteenth century but now new families, requiring servants and labourers, started to come into the area. The population grew, and the church was renovated and enlarged to cater for the increased congregation.

The Farnell-Watson family, whose fortune emanated from the Isleworth Brewery, developed the Henfold estate which lies just outside the parish boundary, although they bought land within the parish as well. The Herron family, who were wool merchants in the City, bought the Newdigate Place estate from the Farnell-Watsons in 1887 and Sir Henry Tyler MP bought High Trees and much adjoining land in the 1890s. In 1880, Leopold Goldberg purchased Coombers Farm and built the Red House

in 1884. He later greatly enlarged his estate within the parish.

Thus over the course of about 20 years much of Newdigate had been sold to 'outsiders', who in different ways all greatly influenced the development of the village. No longer were the landlords absent. They needed staff and workers and they demanded loyalty and obedience. The villagers took up new occupations to cater for the needs of their new masters – and they were masters in every sense of the word. Older residents still recall doffing their caps to the 'toffs' when they passed through the village in their carriages.

## The New Landowners

### The Broadwoods
*By Bob Verner-Jeffreys – the grandson of Gerard T. Bray*

In 1799 the piano maker John Broadwood lent his son James Shudi Broadwood, who was then aged 27, £3,000 to buy Lyne Farm, a Georgian villa on the borders of Newdigate, Capel and Rusper. As the business grew he gradually acquired neighbouring land and farms to create one of the great Surrey estates. By the end of the nineteenth century his descendants had a sizeable holding in Newdigate, Capel, Charlwood, Ockley, Rusper, Kingfold and Warnham. Local farms included Greens, Tanhouse, Mayland (Marelands), Aldhurst, Mizbrooks and Temple Elfande.

*Henry Fowler Broadwood (1811–93) who rebuilt Lyne House in 1864.* Reproduced by kind permission of Bob Verner-Jeffreys.

4

| No. of House | Name of Street, Place or Road, and Name or No. of House | Name and Surname of each Person who abode in the house, on the Night of the 30th March, 1851 | Relation to Head of Family | Condition | Age of Males | Age of Females | Rank, Profession or Occupation | Where Born | | Whether Blind, or Deaf-and-Dumb |
|---|---|---|---|---|---|---|---|---|---|---|
| 13 | Village | William Harley | Head | Mar. | 36 | | Ag. Labr | Surrey | Newdigate | |
| | | Hannah D° | Wife | Mar. | | 42 | | D° | D° | |
| | | Emily D° | Daur | | | 11 | Scholar | D° | D° | |
| | | Henry D° | Son | | 9 | | D° | D° | D° | |
| | | Hannah D° | Daur | | | 6 | D° | D° | D° | |
| | | Frank D° | Son | | 3 | | | D° | D° | |
| 14 | Village | David Taylor | Head | Mar. | 64 | | Ag. Labr | D° | D° | |
| | | Elizabeth D° | Wife | Mar. | | 57 | | D° | D° | |
| | | Charles D° | Son | U. | 19 | | Ag. Labr. | D° | D° | |
| 15 | Village | James Francis | Head | Mar. | 58 | | Ag. Labr. | D° | Horley | |
| | | Mary Ann D° | Wife | Mar. | | 49 | | D° | Ockley | |
| 16 | Village | James Lucas | Head | Mar. | 78 | | Ag. Labr. | D° | Betchworth | |
| | | Mary Ann D° | Wife | Mar. | | 68 | | Kent | Bexley | |
| | | George D° | Son | U | 25 | | Ag. Labr | Surrey | Newdigate | |
| | | James Gad | Lodger | U | 19 | | D° | D° | D° | |
| 17 | One House Uninhabited | | | | | | | | | |
| 18 | One House Uninhabited | | | | | | | | | |
| 19 | Village | Thomas Baker | Head | Mar. | 32 | | Grocer & Baker employing 4 men | Sussex | Billingshurst | |
| | | Mary D° | Wife | Mar. | | 48 | | Surrey | Newdigate | |
| | | Mary Penfold | Neice | U. | | 21 | | D° | D° | |
| Total of Houses 15 U2 B - | | Total of Persons | | | 10 | 8 | | | | |

*Copy of a page from the 1851 census, listing six cottages along the edge of the Brocus (two uninhabited) and Wirmwood on Village Street.*

*James Shudi Broadwood (1772–1851) who together with his brother Thomas saw the company at its most successful period.* Reproduced by kind permission of the Broadwood Trust.

*Lyne House, the home of James Shudi Broadwood, c.1817.*

James Shudi Broadwood was High Sheriff of Surrey in 1835. He defended his estate against the new railway and against new roads; Newdigate's relative seclusion may have been reinforced by his efforts. He died in 1851 and was succeeded here (but not in the firm) by the Revd John Broadwood, a scholar and pioneer folksong collector (who in turn inspired his niece Lucy). On the death of John in 1864 a new force

arrived at Lyne in the shape of Henry Fowler Broadwood (1811–93), then head of the firm with a large and growing family. In 1865 he had Lyne remodelled as a neo-Elizabethan mansion at a cost of £3,445. His daughter Bertha (1846–1935), later renowned as a pioneer of village nursing care and cottage hospitals, helped with the planning. As Henry Fowler aged, Bertha took on the management of the estate. She studied land management in the agricultural depression of the late-nineteenth century, and encouraged local wealthy wives to support her healthcare ideas; she is still remembered.

The Broadwood family were said to have been 'Christened in Capel, Married in Newdigate, Buried in Rusper'. This may not be strictly true – John senior had ten children, James Shudi 16 and Henry Fowler 11, and they were frequently absent in London, Scotland and elsewhere – but the saying stuck. Certainly the dining-room at Lyne straddled the parish boundary – they could breakfast in Newdigate and dine in Capel.

The Broadwoods were considerable benefactors to Newdigate, particularly the church and school. The school was rebuilt in 1838 by James Shudi, and the Revd John Broadwood was a trustee, as were succeeding generations. Lucy taught the children singing. Henry Fowler spent £1,000 on rebuilding the rectory. St Peter's Church was restored and enlarged in 1876/7 and its spire renovated in the early-twentieth century, to all of which the family contributed.

When Henry Fowler's grandson and Bertha's nephew Evelyn Henry Tschudi Broadwood returned from the First World War, wounded but with a Military Cross, he took over

*Evelyn Joan Bray (née Broadwood) (1886–1972) whose husband Gerard was killed in Gallipoli during the First World War. She never remarried.* Reproduced by kind permission of Bob Verner-Jeffreys, Evelyn's grandson.

*Capt. Evelyn Henry Tschudi Broadwood at Lyne House. He was the last Broadwood to live at Lyne and to be involved in village activities.*

*Lyne House when unoccupied in the 1980s.*

Henfold House prior to 1970.

Henfold Cottages in the 1930s.

Right: Mrs Ellen Charlotte Janson of Newdigate Place.

Kenneth Chester Herron (1881–1916).

Inset: William Farnell-Watson senior of Henfold.

William Farnell-Watson with his gamekeeper at Henfold, by Thomas Musgrove Joy (1812–66). The picture is signed and dated 1854.

the firm and the estate. He never married, and on his death in 1975 the estate passed mainly to the Broadwood Trust, an educational and musical charity, while some of the outlying property passed to his nephew and nieces. The war memorial has no Broadwood name, but does include Gerard T. Bray and John A. Innes, both of whom married sisters of Evelyn; their children inherited some of the land.

Thanks to Evelyn Broadwood and the trust he established, the Surrey History Centre has a massive archive of the history of the firm and the estate, including plans and diaries, for those interested in discovering more.

His intention had been to preserve the house and estate as a centre for musical education. As those living nearby will appreciate, the Gatwick flight path together with the dilapidated state of the main buildings put an end to that dream. By one of those strange historical oddities, his mother's family, the Fuller-Maitlands, had a similar house at a village called Stansted.

Today, Broadwood pianos can still be found throughout the world and Lyne House has been restored and converted into apartments.

### The Farnell-Watsons

William Farnell-Watson had amassed a fortune through his ownership of the Isleworth Brewery. When he died in 1879 he left this fortune to his son, also called William, although he created a charge on the estate by leaving his widow £3,000 per annum – at that time a farm labourer's annual wage was probably £40.

William junr had purchased Henfold in 1868 and acquired a number of properties previously owned by the Duke of Norfolk, including the Newdigate Place estate, with over 1,600 acres, for which he paid £51,000. Later purchases included many of the houses in Village Street and the fields which are now the Brocus. Landowners and farmers in the parish were responsible for maintaining the church fence according to the amount of tithes paid, and by 1878 William junr owned so much land that he was assigned 146 feet, a third of the total length of the fence.

William married Evelyn Colvin and they had four sons, but after a scandal his wife obtained a divorce. He then married Bessie Catherine Coles, by whom he had four more children. F.E. Green wrote in *The Surrey Hills* that 'a romance is attached to Henfold House, for the second wife of Mr Farnell-Watson was a beautiful village girl of humble origin.'

In 1886 William transferred shares worth £100,000 into the names of trustees to provide for the annuities under his father's will. He also sold many of his Newdigate properties by auction, including the Newdigate Place estate which was purchased by George O.M. Herron, though he continued to live at Henfold.

As substantial landowners in Victorian England

the Farnell-Watsons were able to live extremely well and indulge their many interests. William was fond of hunting and shooting, and was Master of Foxhounds. He maintained his own cricket ground, playing matches against Surrey Club and Ground and other guest teams, for which he employed a professional bowler, Frank Golding.

The family was generous in relieving the hardship of the ordinary parishioners. In the Women's Institute scrapbook of 1955 an elderly lady wrote that:

*... most of the land belonged to the gentleman at Henfold... who in his gardens, fields and woods employed many of the people, building cottages when they were needed, and letting them to workpeople for 2s. a week.*

The Henfold Cottages are an example of where the rent-charge was very low.

In 1885, Mrs Farnell-Watson gave clothing such as suits, dresses, stockings, and Welsh capes to 98 children attending Sunday and day-school. They also made a special gravel path for the dozen children who had to walk over the fields to get to school from Ewood.

William died suddenly from a brain haemorrhage just before Christmas in 1897, at the young age of 44 years. One of the newspaper reports of his death said:

*The loss to Newdigate is a very deep and lasting one. Mr Farnell-Watson was a good and generous neighbour and to the poor was a true and generous friend. They will sadly miss him.*

Practically the whole village attended his funeral and he was interred in a new vault in Newdigate's churchyard. A memorial window was installed in the church and this can be seen in the north aisle.

His widow Bessie preferred to live in London, and consequently Henfold House remained empty for many years. She did not forget the village, and in 1901 had a Village Hall built as a memorial to her husband.

The last part of the estate was sold in 1945, when the Brocus was purchased as a memorial field for the village. Mrs Farnell-Watson died on 5 February 1950, a widow for over 52 years.

### Mrs Janson & the Herron Family of Newdigate Place

From about 1890 to 1940 Newdigate benefited greatly from the influence of Mrs Ellen Charlotte Janson on many aspects of village life.

The daughter of Frederick James Chester, Mrs Janson was born in 1848. It was said that her family could be traced back to the reign of Edward III in the fourteenth century. The family seat was at Poyle Park at Seale, near Farnham.

In 1869 she married a widower, George Oliver Mellick Herron, a wool merchant in the family firm of G.R. Herron & Son. He already had two small sons,

*Newdigate Place (as seen from behind), c.1913.*

*Newdigate Place, the home of Mrs Janson.*

*Mrs Janson and Clifford Parker displaying a pair of bellows made at the woodcarving class.*

Above: *Ockley Lodge, c.1907, part of Newdigate Place estate.*

*Mrs Janson feeding her fantails at Newdigate Place.*

Right: *Haymaking for Mrs Janson at Newdigate Place Farm, c.1920.*

Left: *One of the pew ends carved by a member of Mrs Janson's woodcarving class.*

Herbert George Whitby, who later served in the Indian Civil Service and became under secretary to the Viceroy, Lord Curzon, and Robert Douglas who died in the Boer War whilst serving with the Queen's Bays. His son Cyril also died, aged 19, in France in 1915.

The Herrons had six children, two of whom, Walter Fitzroy and Kenneth Chester, were killed in the First World War. Walter, aged 44, was killed instantly when a defective grenade exploded while he instructed some men in grenade shooting; Kenneth, aged 37, served as an observer in the Royal Flying Corps, and died when a stray bullet pierced the fuselage of his aircraft. All four of the Herron war dead have memorials in Newdigate church.

The family came to the town in 1887 when George Herron purchased the Newdigate Place estate from William Farnell-Watson. Ten years later he built a new and spacious mansion on a site east of the old Newdigate Place, which he then renamed Home Farm. Mrs Herron personally supervised the architectural side of the building work under the architect J. Hatchard Smith, and the house had a much-admired staircase and fine panelling, which were the work of Mrs Herron herself and her elder daughter Julia.

George Herron died on 23 December 1902 at Brighton and in 1904 Ellen married John William Janson, a direct descendant of James II. She erected the chancel screen in the church to her first husband's memory, and when her second husband died in 1906 she had a cross (since removed) placed on top of the screen.

Mrs Janson was a practical agriculturalist who made a profit from her farming activities. She brought in many Welsh sheep each year, and among other animals she kept two emus and about 100 fallow deer in her park.

She was a churchwarden, chairman of the Newdigate Women's Unionist Association (her first husband had been a Liberal Unionist), trustee of the Newdigate school and chairman of the Nursing Association, but her great love was woodcarving.

She started a woodcarving class, with Mr Hackwood's assistance, at Newdigate Place because she noted that the young lads had 'nothing to do except loaf about, and hang around Mr Dean's shop window for the sake of the lamplight.'

The pews in the church were suffering from dry rot so Mrs Janson purchased new pews from Wippel & Sons of Charing Cross and 54 pew ends were carved by the class, which consisted of: Percy Weller, Joe Sanders, Luke Gadd, John Rusbridge, Henry Hackwood, Ralph Beedle, Gilbert Trow, William Broughton, Alfred Thomas, Arthur Rusbridge, Arthur Monk, William Andrews, Harry Standing, Albert Freeman, Fred Drewery, William Wyatt junr, Henry Pilbeam, Raymond Potter, William Wilkins and Mrs Janson herself. The litany desks were carved by Joe Sanders, the lectern stool by Albert Freeman in memory of Mrs Cooper, and the angels on the choir stalls by William Broughton.

When Mr Hackwood died in 1915, the Lady Chapel altar was erected in his memory and carved by Joe Sanders, William Broughton, Albert Trow, Arthur Beck and George Horley. Their names can still be seen on the side of the altar.

Mrs Janson was a women of many talents and the banner depicting St Peter's Keys, by the entrance to the church, was worked by her. When one enters the church, the influence of Mrs Janson can be seen everywhere although the family have not lived in the village since the mid 1900s. She died on 9 October 1941 at the age of 93 and a memorial window depicting a carpenter can be seen in the church. Her daughter, Lillian, died in 1944.

Newdigate Place was occupied by Canadian troops during the Second World War and left in a dilapidated state. The house and estate were sold in 1954 by auction and the house went for just over £1,000. It was promptly demolished and the building materials used elsewhere. A bungalow, also called Newdigate Place, now stands on the site.

Kenneth Vernon Chester Herron, the son of Kenneth Chester, continued the wool business into the 1960s, when he sold it and bought a fruit farm in Spain. The company ceased trading a few years later. Kenneth later returned to England and in 2002 was living in Oxfordshire aged 94.

### The Tylers of High Trees

Sir Henry Whatley Tyler, his wife Margaret and their family came to Newdigate from Pymmes Park in Edmonton in the mid 1890s. They had a London home at Highgate and made their new country home

*Coronation celebrations at Newdigate Place, 1911.*

Left: *Capt. Sir Henry W. Tyler, d.1908.*

Right: *Dr Margaret Lucy Tyler, physician at the London Homeopathic Hospital in London. She died in 1943.*

Above: *High Trees Stables with George Horley.*

Right: *High Trees House in 1986.*

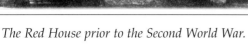

*The Red House prior to the Second World War.*

Right: *The Red House before the rebuild in 1950.*

at High Trees; they eventually owned land along Parkgate Road right up to the village.

The Tylers had three daughters – Margaret Lucy, Madeline Georgina and Amelia Charlotte – and eight sons, amongst whom were John Charles, Edward Ernest, William Pastey, Henry Edward, Arthur Malcolm and Alfred Henry.

Sir Henry died on 30 January 1908 aged 81, and in his will he left effects to the total value of over £162,000. The will mentioned that Woodlands Farm was owned by John Charles Tyler and the farm at High Trees by Margaret Lucy and Madeline Georgina. He left Linden House in Highgate to John Charles with the proviso that his wife should continue to live there with an income of £400. His wife had the organ installed at St Peter's Church in her husband's memory, and a brass plaque nearby commemorates this gift.

Three of the Tyler family were killed in the First World War and during this time Margaret was a doctor at the London Homeopathic Hospital. She was a remarkable woman, working at the hospital during the day, while in the evenings organising the collection of sandbags to go out to the Front. In 1915 she wrote the following moving piece to the people of Newdigate:

*Newdigate is amazing! 1700 bags. I will send your letter to France to my brother. He was down every Sunday at High Trees last autumn when waiting for his Brigade to arrive from India. It seems years ago. I have not been down to Newdigate since he went out to the Front. Certainly not since sandbags. I simply work at them, writing for them every moment. I can't get away from Hospital till late at night, or late next morning rather, and all Sunday. I comfort myself that to labour is to pray. It is to save life, and we have the Divine sanction here. I think we are doing what he would have done. We should have been proud had we raised and equipped a Regiment. We should be more so for having saved one! Suffering and death and bereavement averted. Lives, the bravest and best of the Nation preserved. The Germans fight over sandbags. They turn their machine-guns on to them. Thank the people of Newdigate. We do belong to them and they to us. My father did love the little farm, and my mother too. So many memories are there! I was never reconciled to their passing on till this war. Now I thank God they have been spared all this.*

*Of ours at the Front, so far three are killed and one wounded and long ago back in the worst of it. Three more to go – perhaps five. What will be left when it all ends?*

There was a desperate need for sandbags at the Front and women in Newdigate volunteered to make them at specially organised parties in the Village Hall. The finished articles were sent to Margaret at Linden House and she wrote the above in appreciation.

After the war Margaret Tyler continued to visit Newdigate; she was met at Holmwood Station by Sid Burberry in his pony and trap. Mrs Barbara Hall, the daughter of the late Revd J. Ward, a past rector of Newdigate, recalled that on one occasion Miss Tyler took the Ward children to the theatre to see a 'promising young actor' called Laurence Olivier.

Margaret was first registered as a doctor on 30 July 1903, at the age of 46, although she had graduated as MD in Brussels in 1893. By the First World War she was the Assistant Physician at the London Homeopathic Hospital where she worked for over 40 years.

The out-patients' department, she declared, was the happiest place of her life and she always looked forward to meeting her friends, as she termed her patients. She had an able pen, though she declared that she wrote with difficulty and much correction. Her *Drug Pictures*, published in 1942, dealt with homeopathic remedies culled from every possible source; it was a storehouse of information and became standard reading for students. She died on 21 June 1943 at the age of 86 and Sir John Keir KCVO wrote in her obituary notice:

*Behind the physician was the woman who was deeply imbued with the ultimate religious values of life. In that spirit she did her work, trusted and respected by many, for her fine character, personal integrity and complete lack of all selfish ambition. She will rank with that good Victorian company in which we honour the name of many richly endowed adventurous souls who saw 'the future in the instant' and clung to their faith and, for right or wrong, brooked no interference in their concept. Despite failing health she worked to the very end, and died in service. It is typical that almost her last quotation was: 'At the end of life we shall not be asked how much pleasure we have had in it, but how much of service we gave to it, not how full of success, but how full of sacrifice, not how happy we were, but how helpful we were.'*

### The Goldbergs of the Red House

Leopold Goldberg came to Newdigate in 1880 when he purchased Coombers Farm for £1,620 and then acquired the adjoining farms of Sturtwood, Blanks and Hatchetts. On the southern-most four fields he built the Red House, and a stable block which is now the Clock House, and used Coombers to house the farm bailiff.

A City of London solicitor of Prussian origin, Leopold had a London house in Cadogan Gardens, but like many successful Victorians wanted a country estate as well. He, his wife Louisa and their four sons and four daughters moved into the Red House in 1884, but their happiness was short-lived as Louisa died in 1888, aged 38. Two daughters married, and the two remaining Miss Goldbergs took an active part in many of the village and church activities. They organised a soup kitchen for the schoolchildren long before a school canteen was established, purchasing sacks of peas, beans and lentils for the purpose. The soup was delivered by pony and trap daily, except in snowy weather when the food was carried a mile across the fields by a man using a shoulder yoke. The sisters entertained the children at Christmas time by providing a bran tub. They also formed the Girls' Friendly Society within the parish.

Little is known about two of the sons but the other two are commemorated on the war memorial, as both lost their lives in the First World War. The eldest of these two, 2nd Lt Herbert Walter Goldberg, was born in 1880 and went to Charterhouse and University College, Oxford where he gained a first-class honours degree in jurisprudence. He was a barrister in the Inner Temple and author of *Politics for the Pocket*. He contested the Reigate Division of Surrey in 1910 as a Liberal and in 1914 he married Angela Vernon Sanderson. In 1915 while serving in France he was injured in the arm and leg by shrapnel. He wrote to his father to say that he expected to lose an arm but was looking forward to being invalided back to England. He never recovered and died from his wounds. His brother, 2nd Lt Frederick William Goldberg, was born in 1882, also educated at Charterhouse and University College, and became a barrister at the Inner Temple. He was a fine sportsman and played hockey for England against Ireland in 1904 and tennis at the championships in Wimbledon. He was killed in 1916. The rector at the time said that:

*Entrance hall of the Red House in 1926.*

*The Red House after the rebuild.*

*... another brilliant career has been cut short and England has lost one of her most promising lives. In spite of his achievements he was a man of great modesty and his disposition was charming in its gentleness, childlike simplicity and unselfishness.*

In 1924, Leopold Goldberg died and his obituary notice in *The Times* reported that he had practised as a solicitor for nearly 60 years, briefing as juniors many who became leaders of the Bar. He was connected with numerous famous cases, was an authority on international law and author of several works on legal subjects. In spite of his strenuous life in London he found time to be a successful farmer and was for many years a magistrate in Surrey. A man of great intellectual refinement, he had wide and varied tastes and sympathies and retained to the last his acute brain and clarity of judgement. On his death, the Red House and estate were sold, and his daughters moved to Cornwall.

At the time of the Second World War the house was owned by the Crump family. It was commandeered by the East Surrey Regiment and later occupied by the Dental Corps of the Canadian Army. By 1945 the house and estate were in poor condition; the roof lead had been removed, which meant that rainwater poured in, there was wet and dry rot everywhere, and the vinery and greenhouse were derelict.

The compensation from the Government was insufficient to rebuild the house so the Crumps pulled it down, leaving only a small section, and sold much of the material. A new design was drawn up utilising the existing foundations, and with the help of local builders such as George Trower, the Crumps, father and son, did the rebuilding, using salvaged timbers and bricks laboriously cleaned off. Some items were put back to their original purpose, including the front door, but others, such as window frames, had to be completely remade. Dudley Crump sold the house with its eight acres of ground and moved into the Clock House. He later sold the fields to Henry Eggleton of Hound House Farm. His son, David, made the church altar and lychgate, and later moved to Cornwall.

# The last years of Queen Victoria's reign

Technology was coming to Newdigate, and in April 1884 the parish magazine commented upon the state of the roads:

*We may note as a condition never before experienced at this time of year since roads were made hard, the absence of those beds of loose stones which were enough to 'shake our bones out of our garments' and over which we were accustomed to plod painfully to ourselves and our horses, with the risk that with a stumble they might:*

*All headlong cast us down,*
*and on the rugged stones beat forth our brains.*

*Now thanks to that strong yet obedient puffing monster which 'in a fine frenzy rolling' appeared amongst us about Christmas last, and which 'rolls, and rolls, and rolls' we 'run smoothly in an even road'. All horses, if not all their owners, must surely rejoice at the change wrought in the condition of our highways by the new method of repairing them, the full benefit of which will not be reached until after a year or two's time.*

Henry Hackwood was the headmaster at Newdigate school. He had been there since the new building was first opened in 1872, and still subscribed to traditional values. He used a quill pen and wrote the old fashioned *ſs* instead of *ss*. His pupils, known as scholars, came mostly from the surrounding cottages and farms, and had little expectation beyond following their parents onto the fields or into service in one of the larger houses.

Mr Hackwood would have noticed changes over the previous ten years or so, but he could not have anticipated the fundamental changes that the generation born in the 1890s would experience, starting with the arrival of the railway and the development of the new estates. He had witnessed the growth in population and seen new houses being built throughout the parish to house new residents. He had seen his classes getting bigger, and experienced for perhaps the first time the involvement of the new landowners in the running of the school as governors and benefactors.

No one could have imagined that by their old age those small boys and girls would have experienced two world wars, motorised and air transport, telephones, electricity in homes, radio, television, refrigeration and great advances in medicine and public health. They even witnessed man walking on the moon in 1969. Perhaps no previous generation has experienced or future generation will experience such fundamental changes as did these youngsters.

During the 1890s Britain basked in the glow of Empire. Since Trafalgar in 1805 the Royal Navy was undefeated and sailed to every port on the globe. The great review at Spithead displayed a confident if not complacent Navy. The Army was operational in theatres as far afield as Africa, China and India and the heart-rending soul-searching of the Boer War was still to come. The docks were full of ships exporting and importing goods and heavy industry and the textile mills and mines represented the powerhouse of the economic wealth of the nation. Great Britain was at the heart of the world's industry, and the public buildings and town halls in the country's great industrial cities reflected just that.

Victorian wealth had spawned a new middle class, which Newdigate became aware of as larger houses were built. But there was still much poverty, and many of the cottages were overcrowded and insanitary. There was a place for everyone and everyone knew his/her place. The men worked hard with long hours and low pay, and the poor doffed their caps or curtsied to the rector and the wealthy.

There would have been a silence which we would not recognise today. The main sounds would have been human voices, iron-shod cartwheels and horse-powered machinery, as well as animals and birdsong. A man standing in the centre of the village would know that Mr Horley of Parkgate was mending his fence because he would have heard the hammering. People's voices would have carried much further than today. At night when there was no moon, it would have been pitch black, broken only by the occasional light from a window.

In 1891 there were 681 people living in the parish of Newdigate in 142 dwellings, 27 of which had fewer than five rooms. Little Cherryhurst, the home of George and Jane Jenkins, had only two rooms.

Mr Hackwood's pupils would have spoken with a distinct Surrey/Sussex border accent which today has disappeared except amongst those older residents who have lived in the village all their lives. Nevertheless, even in the 1890s the villagers were becoming aware of other influences and strange accents. At Lyne House, the dairymaid had come from Hexham in Northumberland and the housemaid and kitchen maid were both from Gloucestershire. The footman was born in Germany. At Oaklands Park the coachman came from Radnor and the cook from Liverpool. At the time of the 1891 census there was even a visitor from Australia. James Black, the bailiff for the Red House estate who lived at Coombers Farm, came from Ireland and his wife Maggie from Scotland. The evangelist, Gabriel Woodward, who lived at The Manse in Broad Lane, was from Oxfordshire. The rector, the Revd Lancelot Studdert Kennedy, was also from Ireland. So the young people would have heard at first hand about other places and cultures. Small wonder that in 1914 so many of them rushed to join the Army as a means of escape and adventure.

Many of the families had lived in the village for generations – Lucas, Taylor, Beadle, Voice, Pratt, Gadd, Horley, Weller, Worsfold, Monk, Trow and Collinson. A number of houses were known by other names – Marelands was Marshlands, Holly Tree Cottage was Normans Cottage, The Elms was Pancrass Rolls Farm, Oaklands Park Farm Cottage was Souters, Partridge Cottage was Sot's Hole and Simons was Horsielands Farm. The smaller cottages were often known by the person who lived there. Whole areas of land that are now used for housing would have been open fields or woodland. On one side of Parkgate Road there was no house between Lance's Cottage and the church, and on the other side no houses between Reffolds and Workhouse Green. In Cudworth the only buildings were the manor and its farm. There were only two houses in Ewood: Mill Cottage and Ewood Farmhouse. Partridge Lane (then called the Back Road or Old Rusper Road) and Broad Lane were empty except for the old farmhouses and a few isolated cottages.

The majority of the male population worked on the land, and the others were mostly craftsmen who provided service to the community, such as carpenters, bricklayers, shoemakers and tinkers. The women were employed as domestic servants to the big houses and farms. At times farm work was considered more important for the children than education, which was certainly an irritation to Mr Hackwood.

Gardens were used for growing vegetables and fruit, and often a pig was reared for bacon. However, the results of the annual horticultural show indicate that gardens were also used for pleasure and flower growing. At one show, J. Broughton, trug maker of Kingsland, won first prize for the best-kept cottage garden and W. Greenfield, harnessmaker of Parkgate and later Foresters Villas, and J. Young, the farm bailiff at Hound House Farm, came second and third.

Savings Clubs were established to help with yearly finances. It seems 37 subscribers paid a total of £18.10s.0d. to the Coal Club, which earned a bonus of £4.18s.6d. This meant that each subscriber was able to receive half a ton of coal. A similar system existed for clothing – money was collected, a bonus paid, and clothes were distributed. Jumble sales were also a useful way for the working man's family to obtain cheap clothing and implements for the house. The proceeds from a typical jumble sale would be about £6 or £7.

People also subscribed to the Nursing Association, the subscriptions paying for a nurse to be on call throughout the parish. To reduce abuse of the system, the practice of people joining just before calling the nurse had to be stopped. Nurse Elderson made her calls by bicycle from 9a.m. to 1p.m. and 4.30p.m. to 8.40p.m.; she had a half day on Tuesdays and one month's annual holiday. Subscriptions cost 3s. for widows and widowers and 4s. for labourers. Non-subscribers would be helped for a fee of 5s. (widows) and 6s. (labourers).

*Village Street in the 1890s. The Brocus is on the right; on the left is Glebe Meadow, now the site of the school and Glebe Cottages.*

*Village Street looking north in the 1890s.*

In 1913, 1,336 visits were paid, and for this Nurse Elderson received a salary of £50 per annum and £5.5s.8d. for her uniform. Funds then were so low that there was talk of disbanding the Association, but it continued at least until 1922.

A highlight of the year for the children was the annual school treat, held on the rectory meadow, the site of the present school. This consisted of games and a tea, supervised by the rector. Boys were encouraged to sing in the church choir, and were rewarded with an annual excursion involving a train journey from Holmwood to the seaside at places such as Brighton. The boys' choir was also invited to cricket and tea at Stanhill. There was a boys' class at the rectory for instruction in vocal and instrumental music. The members of the adult choir were treated to an annual choir dinner by the rector.

The Girls' Friendly Society, run by the Misses Goldberg, attended an annual festival in Dorking, where they were entertained at Sondes Place by the Misses Bovill. They also had a stall, on which they displayed examples of their needlework and knitting skills. Some girls received a reward of 5s. for faithful service.

For the adults, the cricket team played in the field opposite the Surrey Oaks Inn, and there was a cookery class whose members were examined in Dorking. The Mothers' Union and Sunday school were also popular.

Other entertainments were provided. Magic lantern shows depicting places of interest in London were enjoyed, and the Surrey Bee-keeping Association visited, bringing a van and tent to the rectory meadow where they gave lectures on the skills of bee-keeping. An annual tea was held for about 100 adults on New Year's Eve, when carols were sung. At the same time a bountiful tea for over 100 children was given by the Misses Goldberg – a Christmas tree was lit up and each child received a bun and an orange.

Generally the church services were well attended, particularly at Christmas and Easter, and the church was always decorated with flowers, often from the hot houses at the larger homes.

So Newdigate slipped into the twentieth century.

# Chapter 6

# THE FIRST HALF OF THE TWENTIETH CENTURY

Just over a year into the new century, Queen Victoria was dead, the Boer War was over and the telegraph came to Newdigate. This was a period of optimism with apparently long, warm Edwardian summers.

*Village Street, c.1911. Foresters Villas are on the right.*

*Mrs Sophia Wood at Brocus Cottage, c.1910.*

*The Knowle, c.1928.*

However, poverty was never far away, and in 1900 a council surveyor inspected Beanbrook (sic) when Henry Burrows was the occupier. Of the two bedrooms, one of 993 cubic feet was occupied by a man and wife and three children. Its walls and ceilings were foul, and there were foul holes in the floor and through external walls. There was a fireplace but no stove. A smaller bedroom of 840 cubic feet was occupied by four children aged 13, 11, 9 and 3. This also had foul walls with holes in them and just the thatched roof as a ceiling. Only one of the bedroom windows could be opened. Downstairs there was just a living room and a wash-house, the former paved with stone slabs, the latter with brick, in both cases defective. Here too, only one window would open, there were no drains and the closet was just a seat with a wooden roof on four poles.

When people became ill the old traditional potions and cures were used. Mr Baker was well known for his ointment, which was a real cure-all. He would never divulge the recipe but he made small quantities which he sold cheaply to parishioners. Before his death he passed the recipe on to Mrs Dinnage, and her daughter, Mrs O. Hollands, remembered that her mother continued making the ointment until the 1930s and sold it at 4d. per pot. The recipe was as follows:

*2oz Best Yellow Beeswax*
*2oz Rosen*
*2oz Frankincense*
*½oz Venus Turpentine*
*4oz Sweet Oil*

All the ingredients were simmered for a day over a fire, strained off into an earthenware pot and then put into jars. It was used for 'broken breasts' (possibly cracked nipples), cuts, wounds and chilblains.

## The Newdigate Spa

In the *History and Antiquities of the County of Surrey*, written about 1814, Manning & Bray said that Aubrey spoke of a medicinal spring, in the eastern part of Newdigate parish, which possessed the same quality as that of Epsom.

In the parish magazine in 1906 it was reported

that Mr Beetham Wilson, a chemist from Dorking, had sent the following account to the rector under the heading, 'Will Newdigate some day become a second Epsom?':

*About two years ago I first heard of the existence of a mineral water spring at Newdigate... locally known as 'Chilson's Well'. It is situated a little to the east of Beam Brook, about 208 feet above sea level, Lat. 51° 10' N, Long. 0° 15.5' W, and was described as being a deep and always clear spring... held in repute for the past 100 years as an eye lotion and a cure for sprain and bruises, a reputation which the analysis of the water fails to justify.*

*When I was first shown the position of the spring on the grass covered road-side, the only evidence of it was a small shallow hole which did not seem to be the spring at all, but the removal of a few spadefuls of turf exposed the 'well'... The water had a slight smell... but settled quite clear.*

*A preliminary analysis showed it to be a saline aperient spring, not uncommon throughout the country, but certainly unfit for internal use.*

*Since the well has been dug out I have made repeated analyses of the water and have found its saline constituents – and impurities – of constant strength. Its composition is not unlike that of the Carlsbad waters, which are described as being beneficial for affections of the liver, rheumatism, etc.*

*The presence of ammonia indicates that the water is totally unfit for consumption and as I find the yield of the spring is only about four gallons an hour I doubt if it is worth the trouble of properly protecting it.*

The name Chilson may possibly have come from Henry and Mary Chelsam, who buried their children at Newdigate in January 1618 and January 1619.

# The Small Holdings Association at Cudworth

On 12 December 1902 The Small Holdings Association Limited purchased for £4,500 a freehold farm in Cudworth from Benjamin Stretton, who had himself bought it from the Lee Steere family of Ockley in 1891. It comprised about 345 acres of land, which was largely permanent grassland but with some fields sown to oats, swedes and mangolds for animal feed. There was also a wheat field. The Beam Brook flowed through the centre of the farm, and the only woodland was 14 acres known as Cudworth Copse. It included Cudworth Manor, then described merely as a farmhouse, and the farm buildings now called Cudworth Farm. The only other building was a dilapidated cottage in Partridge Lane which today is the Grade II listed Old Beam Brook; by 1919, if not before, it was roofless.

The Small Holdings Association was formed on

Socialist principles to provide working men with 'a few acres and a cow'. The land was sold at £20 to £30 an acre to deserving working men on a ten-year system of payment. The object was to promote the repopulation of the land by the provision of small farms in a district where very little was grown and fruit, vegetables, poultry and other such staple goods were expensive.

Each purchaser of land had to accept certain conditions imposed by the Association. Permission was required before a building could be erected, and its use was generally restricted. There were also restrictions on the type of vehicle which could use Cudworth and Burnt Oak Lanes.

The public were attracted to the scheme and all the lots were purchased, but the Association apparently did not survive, as a document dated 1912 contains the signature of the liquidator.

In 1904 the author Frederick Ernest Green spent £230 on a five-acre plot on the south side of the lane and another of three acres on the north side, where he built his house, Baringsfield. He later bought two further plots. He described his purchase:

*The situation charmed me, for from this hilltop holding, horizoned by trees save where the long line of the Downs stretches across the skies like greyhounds 'in full career' as George Meredith says, I could gaze at Leith Hill throned amongst them like a queen, sometimes robed in blue, sometimes in purple, and at times shrouded in gossamer mist or of brooding clouds which, when uplifted at the call of the sun on an early spring morning, reveals herself radiant in the vivid emerald of the larch.*

His farm prospered and he also became a prominent letter writer, boldly criticising the agricultural policies of succeeding governments whilst staying aloof from all political parties. He wrote a book entitled *A Few Acres and a Cottage,* which described his work on the farm and his newly developed apiary.

During the war he received a telegram stating that his son, David, had been killed. It is not hard to imagine his reaction when shortly afterwards another telegram was received stating, 'Please cancel my telegram respecting 2nd Lt D. Green. Error has been made in this office.' David survived the war and was awarded the Military Cross in 1918.

F.E. Green spoke in Newdigate at the first meeting of the Workers' Union on 1 December 1917 when he pointed out the startling facts in relation to the employment of boy labour and the low wages in the neighbourhood. He wrote prolifically, producing such works as *The Tyranny of the Countryside, The Smallholding, The Settlement of Ex-Servicemen*, and *History of the Agricultural Labourer 1870–1920.* Through his letters and books he became nationally known and contributed much towards the creation of a new agricultural atmosphere. He sold the farm in

1921 and died a year later aged 55 years.

For others life was much harder. The Hawkins family bought a smallholding at what is now called Oulton and William Walter Hawkins helped his father with the venture.

William's father was a village carpenter and joiner who took a smallholding at the age of 46. He paid a deposit of £27 on a 10-acre holding which left him only £20. He put up fencing, planted fruit trees and spent every spare hour erecting his farm buildings. After two years he had exhausted every penny of his earnings on the outbuildings and borrowed the hard-earned savings of his two daughters, one of which was in service and the other was teaching in the village school. Enough money was raised by a mortgage to complete the six-roomed cottage, leaving enough over for the purchase of stock – two heifers, a pig and some poultry.

Soon after the cottage was finished he set out to earn money to pay off various debts contracted. The fierce midsummer sun beat down pitilessly on his head, and from scaffolding around a building where he was working he fell to the ground, and died in two days. No sooner had the dream of his life been realised than death claimed him.

His son William was in the Royal Flying Corps during the First World War and when peace came it was a major task to get the smallholding back into shape. In 1925 he and his wife and four children decided that they had had enough, and emigrated to New Zealand.

## Lady Abdy & the Aircraft Factory

The *Dorking Advertiser* published on 3 March 1910 ran the following story:

*The announcement that Lady Abdy is to devote £50,000 to the promotion of aviation has aroused considerable interest and in an interview with the press, Lady Abdy has stated that she is going to establish a factory, build aeroplanes and get airmen to fly them for her. Asked where her Headquarters would be Lady Abdy said, 'My headquarters will be my own property, The Elms in Newdigate'. She continued, 'I shall there build a factory for passenger aeroplanes to go from London to Paris. The factory will be named the Abdy Aviation Factory.*

This scheme, however, came to an end with the death of her husband on 9 August 1910 after little more than a year of marriage.

Lady Florence (Fanny) Abdy was the third wife of Sir William Neville Abdy and was, apparently, quite a feisty character. For example, she insisted that her chauffeur should drive her to Holmwood Station in exactly four minutes – the journey time in a modern car is eight minutes!

Just prior to her husband's death she was involved in a flying accident at Brooklands and *The Times* reported as follows:

*There was keen competition to obtain the privilege of making the first passenger flight with Mr C. Graham White on Saturday, but Lady Abdy who secured the right was not to be envied her experience, for through the engine not working well, both she and the airman were thrown to the ground, though fortunately neither was hurt. Seats for rides in the aeroplane were sold by auction and for the first ascent there was spirited bidding up to fifty guineas, when the issue lay between Lady Abdy and Miss Pauline Chase. By five guinea calls it went to 110 guineas which was offered to Miss Chase, but Lady Abdy added ten guineas at which the first seat was sold. After Lady Abdy had taken her place in the aeroplane the machine was started, but it rose only a few feet in the air. The motor was not firing properly, and it became evident that unless the engine would pick up, the machine would have to be brought to the ground. The airman described a half circle and just cleared the river Wey, but had scarcely done so when the opposite bank was struck and the machine badly damaged. One of the blades of the propeller was broken off and the right foreplane was damaged.*

She later married a Mr Grant and was known as Lady Abdy Grant and although she tried to sell the Elms in both 1910 and 1911 it was not finally disposed of until 1917.

The Elms was called Pancrass Rolls Farm before 1908–9 and was part of the Broadwood estate. Blunden Shadbolt, an architect from Horley, enlarged and altered the house in the early-twentieth century and it was divided in the 1950s. The northern part, the Elms, embraced the old Pancrass Rolls and the other part was named Melton Half.

An unsubstantiated rumour has persisted that the Elms was used by Edward VII for one of his dalliances. We shall never know if this is true.

## The First World War

On 5 August 1914 at two in the morning, Tom Boult the village policeman left his home at Hillside and strode towards the centre of the village. He could smell baking bread in the warm air as he approached the general store. Walter Carpenter was busy removing loaves with his peel from the oven when Tom knocked at the bakehouse door. 'I've just had a telephone call – we are at war with Germany.' The baker tapped at Alfred Dean's window with the peel and the three men sat up the entire night reminiscing and predicting the future.

Next morning, on the field called The Glebe or Rectory Meadow, now occupied by the school, a meeting was held for the purpose of recruiting young men into the Army. There was no shortage of

*The Small Holdings Association Ltd, Cudworth.*

*William Monk, Helen Monk and Albert Monk haymaking at Baringsfield.*

*Capt. Evelyn Henry Tschudi Broadwood.* Reproduced by kind permission of Bob Verner-Jeffreys.

*F.E. Green's apiary at Baringsfield.*

*John Alfred Innes (1881–1918).*

*Newdigate's war memorial shortly after it was erected.*

*Sidney John Burberry and Arthur Henry Monk in 1914.*

volunteers and no lack of advice and encouragement from the older generation. Here was a chance of travel, glory, excitement and widening horizons.

The rector, the Revd H.G. Bird, wrote:

*Never in our time has England been called upon to face such a terrible trial as she has at the moment and there are various ways in which we can help. The young men of the parish should enlist in the Regular Army or join Lord Kitchener's Force. What stories some will tell their children and grandchildren 50 years hence of what they had witnessed abroad.*

Stirring news soon started coming in from the Front concerning local people. A bullet had passed through Lt Evelyn Broadwood's cap and another through his leggings without touching him. Captain Nicholson was saved after being in the water for three hours. 'We must increase our Army as greatly and speedily as possible', wrote the rector in October 1914.

Lt Broadwood later wrote about his experiences in France:

*With the bullets now flying all around, we got over another wall and as we ran away I remember – as an instance of the stupid things one does in moments of excitement – my little hair-brush jumped out suddenly from my haversack and I ran back five or six yards to pick it up, and risked my life for a hair-brush.*

The lieutenant was soon lying grievously wounded in a hospital in Boulogne having been shot through a leg close to an artery. He survived.

Then in December came the sombre news of the first death in the village – Sidney John Burberry of Laundry Hill Cottage:

*Poor Jack, a lad in the flower of youth – sacrificed on the alter of that vile monstrosity, that demi-god, the German Kaiser. On the battlefield of life he only ranked as an ordinary soldier, just doing his bit, but in death he ranks with the highest officer in the Army who shared his fate.*

April 1915 saw the landing at Gallipoli and 2nd Lt Gerard T. Bray was killed whilst rescuing a comrade. He had married Joan Broadwood in Vancouver and at the onset of war had travelled back to his mother country and settled his family at Greenings with his sister-in-law, Audrey Innes (née Broadwood) and her husband John Alfred Innes.

*Wilfred S. Bird in 1913.* Reproduced by kind permission of Ludgrove School, Wokingham.

In the same year the rector wrote:

*Some will be interested in reading the following account of my son's last moments as sent from an officer to the editor of the* Malvernian: *'He was ordered to lead his men out of the trenches across an exposed 300 yards and was killed instantaneously by machine-gun fire whilst cheering them on. Every officer in the charge was either wounded or killed!*

Further losses were reported in the village and the changing attitude of the rector became apparent. He wrote:

*We must find our own faults and those common to the nation and repent of them, and we must pray as we have never prayed before – the National Mission of Repentance and Hope is a call to repent, not because we believe that we are guilty of provoking this war, but because we have failed to learn to live together as a Christian family.*

The first day of the Battle of the Somme – the much-anticipated 'Big Push' – was 1 July 1916. A distraught rector reported how Sapper William Wyatt of Kingsland left behind a large family, how deeply Mr and Mrs Harber of Myrtle Cottage felt the death of their youngest son, Stephen, how William Hopkins was progressing favourably until blood poisoning set in and his leg had to be amputated, how Leopold Goldberg of the Red House lost his second brilliant and cultured son, and how although Corporal Arthur Monk had survived Neuve Chappelle, Festubert and Loos, he had been knocked insensible at Aubin's Ridge by a German (who broke his rifle in the act) and shortly afterwards met his death at Fleurbury. He was a Newdigate bell-ringer and never lost an opportunity whilst in France to take a rope.

A major offensive was launched at the end of July 1917. Sir Douglas Haig wrote:

*The low-lying, clayey soil, torn by shells and sodden with rain, turned to a succession of vast muddy pools. The valleys of the choked and overflowing streams were speedily transformed into long stretches of bog, impass-able except by a few well-defined tracks, which became marks for the enemy artillery.*

Such was war in Flanders.

The final push of spring 1918 exhausted itself and with the impact of the American forces, the Germans sued for peace – but not before Newdigate suffered the loss of further loved ones.

John Alfred Innes took his car to the Front in 1914 and served at Ypres and Verdun, carrying wounded troops from the battlefields in Red Cross convoys. He was awarded the Croix de Guerre by the French and survived until September 1918 when he contracted appendicitis and died in a field hospital in

Rouen. Mrs Gadd, of Church Cottages, lost her second son, Ernest Weller, when he was killed in France on 4 November 1918, just one week before the Armistice.

Finally the great guns were silenced and the surviving men returned home. The people who would have inherited the estates of the Herron, Goldberg and Tyler families were all dead, and the families in the smaller cottages also suffered most grievously.

A memorial was erected in the churchyard showing the names and ranks of all those who lost their lives. It was designed by J. Hatchard Smith (who was also the architect of Newdigate Place), and made by the Dorking builders Gilliam & Sons.

After the Second World War, the names (without rank) of those who died in both conflicts were engraved on plates which were placed over the original inscriptions.

*The war memorial with the one plate removed revealing the original names, complete with rank.*

## Roll of Honour: Men of Newdigate who died in the First World War, 1914–19.

*Pte George H. Ackland, 32610, came back from Australia to fight in the war and died on 8 February 1919 aged 29, in the room where he was born at Brooklag Farm. He served with the 14th Battalion, Royal Warwickshire Regiment and is buried in St Peter's churchyard.*

*Pte William Beedle, 4125, was the son of Frank Beedle of Cyder Mill Farm. He served with the 9th Battalion, East Surrey Regiment and died on 16 August 1916, aged 28. His name can be seen on the Thiepval Memorial.*

*Lt Wilfred S. Bird was the son of the Revd Henry G. Bird, rector of Newdigate. He was educated at Malvern College and gained a cricket blue at Oxford in 1904. He played 11 matches for Middlesex CCC and Wisden honoured him by stating that he had 'proved himself an admirable wicketkeeper'. In 1913 he played for the MCC. He had been assistant master at Ludgrove for eight years and regularly brought a team to Newdigate to play against the local side. He joined the 5th Battalion, King's Royal Rifle Corps and was killed by machine-gun fire whilst leading his men out of the trenches across an exposed 300 yards. His name is on the memorial at Le Tournet.*

*2nd Lt Gerard T. Bray was the son of His Honour Judge Sir Edward Bray and the husband of Evelyn Joan (née Broadwood). He travelled from Vancouver to serve his country and whilst with The Queen's in Gallipoli he was reported missing. He died on 9 August 1915 aged 30 and his name appears on the Helles Memorial in Gallipoli.*

*Pte Sidney John Burberry, L/10692, was the son of Sidney and Harriett Burberry of Woods Hill Cottage and was the first son of Newdigate to die in the war on 21 November 1914. His name is on the Ploegsteert Memorial in Belgium.*

*L/Cpl Benjamin Burrows, 43461, was the son of Henry Burrows of 1 Oak Tree Cottages, Broad Lane. He served with the 1st Battalion, Middlesex Regiment and was killed on 23 October 1918. He is buried at Englefontaine British Cemetery in France.*

*Pte William Charles Chatfield, 5/18013, was serving with the 13th Battalion, Royal Sussex Regiment and died on 8 September 1916 following an accident. He was aged 30 and is buried at Couir British Cemetery in France.*

*Lt William Edward Worsdale Cottle was the son of Walter Herbert Cottle of Melton Half on Rusper Road. He died on 31 July 1917 whilst serving with the Grenadier Guards. His name appears on the Menin Gate at Ypres.*

*2nd Lt Herbert Walter Goldberg was the son of Leopold Goldberg of the Red House. He was a barrister in the Inner Temple and author of* Politics for the Pocket. *Whilst serving with the 3rd Battalion, The Queen's in 1915 he was injured in the arm and leg by shrapnel. He died from his wounds on 31 July 1915 at No. 2 British Red Cross Hospital in Rouen and is buried at St Sever Cemetery in Rouen.*

*2nd Lt Frederick William Goldberg was Leopold Goldberg's second son and like his brother was a barrister at the Inner Temple. He played hockey for England in 1904 and tennis at the championships at Wimbledon. He was with the 3rd Battalion, The Queen's attached to the Royal Dublin Fusiliers and was killed on the Doiran Front in the Balkans. He is buried at the Struma Military Hospital in Greece.*

*Pte Roy Frederick Goldsack, L11236, served in the 6th Battalion, The Queen's and was the grandson of Frederick Goldsack of Redhill although he lived with the Trow family in Newdigate. He was a sniper and died on 30 June 1918 aged 20 and is buried in the Dernacourt Communal Cemetery in France.*

*Pte Stephen Charles Harber, G/440, died on 14 July 1916 during the 'Great Push' in Flanders. He was serving with the 7th Battalion, The Queen's and has no known grave although his name can be found on the Thiepval Memorial. He had been a member of the Newdigate Rifle Club and was in the Territorial Army where he had a reputation as a 'good shot'.*

*Lt Walter Fitzroy Herron who served with the 4th Dragoon Guards, was the son of G.O.M. Herron and Mrs Ellen C. Janson. He served in the Imperial Yeomanry in the South African War and was managing director of the family firm. He died on 3 April 1916 whilst demonstrating the use of the rifle grenade. He is buried in the Etaples Military Cemetery in France.*

*Lt Kenneth Chester Herron received a commission in the Essex Yeomanry and was the youngest son of G.O.M. Herron and Mrs E.C. Janson. He transferred to The Royal Flying Corps as an observer in August 1917 and was hit by a rifle bullet whilst flying low over German lines in Viller-Brettoneux, dying instantly. His pilot was uninjured and flew back to the nearest British ambulance, so he did not fall into the hands of the enemy. He is buried at Vilacourt British Cemetery, near Amiens. A stained-glass window in his and his brother's memory can be seen in the south aisle of St Peter's Church.*

*2nd Lt Cyril Douglas Herron served in the Queen's Bays and died in action on 13 May 1915 aged 19. He was the son of Captain Douglas Herron who was killed in the South African War. He is buried in the Potijze Chateau Grounds Cemetery in Belgium and the memorial to both father and son is in the north aisle of St Peter's Church.*

*L/Cpl Cecil Thomas Hills, 316, was the son of Arthur and Emma Hills of Coombers Farm who had emigrated to Australia. He died of his wounds on 3 November 1917, aged 25, whilst serving with the 12th Australian Light Horse and is buried in the Beersheba War Cemetery in Israel.*

*Rfn George Charles Howson, R/17362, served in the 16th Battalion, King's Royal Rifle Corps and died on 12 October 1918 aged 21. He was the son of Charles E. and Dorcas Howson of Charlwood Place, Charlwood and his memorial is at Vis-en-Artois in France.*

*Pte Aubrey Hudson, 1986, was born in Ifield but his family lived in Rusper Road. He died on 28 July 1916 and his memorial is at Thiepval, France.*

*John Alfred Innes was married to Audrey, née Broadwood, and lived at Greenings in Charlwood. In 1914 he joined a Red Cross Motor Ambulance Convoy with the British Expeditionary Force and was mentioned in Lord French's despatches, and held the 1914 Star. He was with the French at Verdun where he was awarded the Croix de Guerre. He died in a field hospital in France on 9 September 1918, aged 37, following an operation for appendicitis.*

*2nd Cook's Mate Westley Johns, M16918, died on 20 January 1916 and is buried at St Peter's Church.*

Pte John Kempshall, G6925, was the fifth son of John and Alice Kempshall of North Barn Cottage, Newdigate. He was 21 years of age when he was reported missing and then officially reported as being killed on 13 July 1916. His name appears on the Thiepval Memorial.

Cpl Arthur Henry Monk, 10697, was the son of George Monk and a member of the family who had the brewery in Kingsland. He went to France in December 1914 and was engaged at Neuve Chapelle, Festubert, Loos and at Aubin's Ridge he was fiercely hit over the head by a German who broke his rifle in the act. A keen bell-ringer, he met his death at Fluerbury on 3 September 1916 whilst serving with the 7th Battalion, The Queen's and his memorial is at Contay British Cemetery in France.

Pte Benjamin Taylor, G/6060, was the eldest son of Joseph and Emily Taylor of Broad Lane. He was wounded whilst fighting in France in 1916 and was in hospital in England for some time before rejoining the 1st Battalion, The Queen's Royal West Surrey Regiment. He was killed on 14 April 1918 and is buried at the Canadian Cemetery No. 2, Neuville-St Vaast in France.

Maj. Alfred Henry Tyler, Royal Engineers, died on 14 November 1914 and his name is on the Menin Gate, panel nine.

Lt Albert Tyler, Royal Engineers, died on 12 November 1914, aged 21 and his memorial is also on the Menin Gate, panel nine. He was the son of Mrs H.E. Tyler of Chester Lodge, Sandown and the late Col H.E. Tyler. Thus a son and grandson of Sir Henry and Lady Tyler of High Trees Farm were killed within the first few months of the war. 'The best of two generations.'

2nd Lt John Collett Tyler of the Royal Field Artillery was the son of Col J.C. Tyler and Mrs F.M. Tyler of Colchester and died on 18 April 1915 aged 31.

Pte Ernest Weller, G11989, was the son of Mary Gadd (née Weller) and the late Mark Weller of Church Cottages. He died of wounds on 4 November 1918, aged 42, just seven days before the armistice. He served with the 2nd Battalion, Royal Sussex Regiment and is buried at Le Rejet-de-Beaulieu Communal Cemetery in France.

Pte George Weller, G6934, was serving with the 11th Battalion, The Queen's when he was killed on 7 June 1917, aged 32. He was the son of Frederick and Agnes Weller and his name appears on the Menin Gate.

Pte Percy Frederick Weller, MZ/202311, died of heatstroke at Basra, aged 34, whilst with the 783rd M.Y. Coy., Royal Army Service Corps. He was the brother of Ernest and was married to Nellie. He was a member of the choir and conductor of bell-ringers at Newdigate. He is buried at the Baghdad War Cemetery in Iraq.

Rfn B. Whitehouse, 44595, died on 7 June 1917 whilst serving with the 12th Battalion, Royal Irish Rifles. He is buried at the Lone Tree Cemetery, Spanbroekmolenn in Belgium.

Cook's Mate Alfred Edward Victor Wooltorton, M22723, was the sixth child of George and Margaret Wooltorton. He worked at Dean's Stores and was a member of the Rifle Club. He was serving on board RNHM Trawler Garth, when it was torpedoed and sunk. He was rescued but died of pneumonia in hospital in Edinburgh on 24 July 1918. He is buried at the Seafield Cemetery in Edinburgh.

Spr William Wyatt, 139570, was a mason and bricklayer from Kingsland. He left 14 children when he was killed on 14 July 1916 and is buried at the Basra War Cemetery in Iraq. His widow, Ann Selina, lived a further 59 years, dying on 27 May 1975 at the age of about 105.

Sources:
The Recorder, Charterhouse School, Godalming; The Malvernian, Malvern College; Newdigate's Parish Magazine; Dorking Advertiser; War Graves Commission; Curator of the MCC.

Above: *Alfred Edward Victor Wooltorton worked as a baker's boy for Dean's Stores.*

Left: *Pte Roy Frederick Goldsack.*

## Homes Fit for Heroes

The Government had promised the returning soldiers 'homes fit for heroes', and consequently many small bungalows were erected in Newdigate. Local builder, Mr Peckover, who lived next to the forge, built each house's footings and chimney, while the walls and roof were supplied in sections and erected on site.

One such house was called Our Cott and it was situated on the site of the present-day Casa Mia. The Hopkins family lived there for a number of years but during the Second World War it was the home of the Barnett family. In 1944 the mother went to Dorking on the bus with her young son Bill, to collect her husband's wellington boots after repair. He had gone to meet the butcher, and their daughter was at the village school, so the house was empty when a VI doodlebug exploded nearby, demolishing all but the front of the building. The family were rehoused and the cottage was later rebuilt.

There were two bungalows opposite Grove House in Parkgate Road which were owned by the Misses Tyler. Jim Munn and his bride Edie (née Trow) moved into one of them, called Ridsdale, in 1932. The rent was 7s.6d. (37.5p in modern money) per week and Jim, who was a gardener at Baringsfield, earned 35s. (£1.75) per week. Other bungalows included Wilcuma, Little House (demolished in the 1990s), Leith View, Anwil, Cranleigh, Southview, Chitterling and Mile Oak. Almost all have now been replaced by larger houses.

Samuel Savidge was a shoe repairer from Camberwell and had been a despatch rider in the Signal Service. In about 1930 he purchased 1¼ acres in Hogspudding Lane, the site of the present Lansdown and adjacent undeveloped plot. Once

again, the footings and chimney were built by Mr Peckover and the frame and roof reputedly originated as a workman's hut from the Woolwich Arsenal. Sam and his mother set up business as poultry farmers and he called the house The Bungalow.

He was short and slim in build, with a cheeky grin and a sense of humour. His mother died in the 1950s and he lived alone until he moved to a nursing home just before his death in 1985.

Unfortunately, by this time The Bungalow had fallen into disrepair. A dark passage led to the living-room where a wood burner provided heat, and there were gas lights; the mantles had disintegrated, so flames leapt out, scorching the walls. Sam used to sit by the fire in an armchair, which had been covered with a succession of old blankets. Over the fire a line held what looked like drying socks, but they had been there so long they turned to dust at a touch. The sitting-room was in a very poor condition and was very damp. Part of the ceiling had collapsed and was resting on an old but once beautiful chesterfield. On the floor, green with mould, was a leather-bound bible and a photograph album with pictures going back to the 1880s. Sam's bedroom contained only his large brass bed and a small chest of drawers where he kept his clothes. He said that he had not been in the spare bedroom for some time. The door was difficult to open as a bag of chicken feed had fallen behind it, but on the back of the door hung his Home Guard uniform where he had left it in 1945. There were piles of china, tied together with auctioneer's lot number tags, apparently left there by his mother who enjoyed going to auctions; the legs of a chair turned to dust and collapsed when he leant on it.

After Sam died, the contents of his home were piled into a skip and taken away but the Newdigate Society was able to save his wooden box containing

Left: *The Old Post Office in the 1920s.*

Below left: *Little House, Parkgate Road, in 1990. The house built on the site at a later date is called The Hawthorns.*

Below: *Harold Hopkins with his father William in the 1930s at Our Cott.*

*The Bungalow, former home of Sam Savidge (1893–1986).*

*Luke and Sarah Gadd outside Luke's workshop in the garden of Lucy's Cottage.*

*Miss Levitt of Woods Hill.*

Left: *King John Barn where Col French made condiments and a lethal cider.*

photographs and documents from his days as a despatch rider.

Sam always had a soft spot for Maudie Hopkins from Homelea and they often had tea together; the relationship could not blossom because Maudie had to look after her brother Edgar. In death, however, they are together, as they are buried in adjoining graves in St Peter's churchyard.

## Colonel French & his Chutney & Cider Factory

Colonel Herbert French earned his rank whilst serving with the Royal Army Medical Corps during the First World War. He was a doctor and a consultant at Guy's Hospital and lived at Cudworth Manor. He set up a manufactory in the King John Barn and employed ex-servicemen who initially made crab-apple jelly. He then developed his 'Peppery Chutney' which was said to be the hottest in Britain, and was eventually mixing and bottling up to 3 tons per week. He made other condiments, including 'Gaffers Sauce' which was very similar to a modern-day brown sauce, and later became famous for producing an absolutely lethal cider!

The flagstaff in St Peter's churchyard was made from one of his own trees and erected in 1947 by Colonel French in memory of his wife. His daughter, Nancy, remained in the village after the Second World War and was active in a number of village activities.

## Life in the 1920s & 1930s

### Memories of the village
### By Peter Monk

There were far fewer houses in the village in the 1920s than there are at the start of the twenty-first century and a number of interesting ones amongst them have since been demolished. Of course, the pace of life was much slower back then. Sunday was the quietest day of the week, when all shops were closed, although not the Six Bells public house.

There were two general stores – Whittingham's and Dean's. Each had their own bakery, wood fired with faggots supplied by Henry Horley's woodyard adjoining the Surrey Oaks Inn at Parkgate. Dean's shop included the Post Office which he had recently taken over from Michael Dean, the postmaster at the Old Post Office next to Yew Tree Cottage. Both shops delivered bread, groceries and many other items daily, as did Roy Peters the butcher at Foresters Villas next door to Mr Greenfield, maker of harnesses and other leatherwork. Adjoining was the coal yard of Messrs Cutler and Jackson. Neither gas nor electricity had yet reached the village, so coal was in great demand. The ring of the anvil could be heard from Bradshaw, the blacksmith at the Forge in Rusper Road, and the amiable Luke Gadd repaired footwear, working from a small wooden shed in the garden of what is now called Lucy's Cottage. At Woodshill (now Atwoods) Miss Levitt sold sweets and, during the summer, fruit from her garden. Further along, next to Lucas the builder's yard, lived Ernie Ockenden. He cycled daily to Holmwood station to collect the newspapers and delivered them throughout the village and as far as Norwood Hill. Ben Wood of Brocus Cottage, just beyond the Village Hall, supplied many wood products and occasionally a coffin. At Kingsland, Bill Fuller ran a taxi service with his Model T Ford. Bill Monk of Kingsland Farm and Harry Winfield of Brook Farm in Cudworth delivered milk daily, ladling it from a milk churn into the customers' jugs. Also at Kingsland, Bill Broughton supplied new bicycles and motorcycles and performed all kinds of repairs. At the far end of Trig Street lived Joe Edwards, known as the 'rakemaker', turning out rakes of all shapes and sizes, mainly for use by farmers. The nearby woods were his source of chestnut, with which he made walking sticks. In the early 1920s medical attention was administered by Dr Wakefield from his surgery at Norwood Hill – quite a journey in an emergency – and the District Nurse, Miss Elderson, had to cycle from Coldharbour.

A familiar sight was the muffin man walking through the village, ringing a handbell with a tray of muffins balanced on his head. A fish van called once a week, as did The Home and Colonial & International Stores from Dorking. The East Surrey Omnibus Company ran a service from the village to Redhill using an open-top bus with solid tyres, and a coach ran from Newdigate to Ewhurst – an enjoyable, scenic journey.

*The Fuller family outside No. 4 Kingsland, c.1910.*
Left to right: *Emily, Kate, Leonard and William.*

The church, school and Village Hall were the dominant features in the village. The provision of leisure facilities was fairly adequate considering that most people worked longer hours each day over a five-and-a-half-day week. The Village Hall provided for a wide variety of interests. Harry Whittingham organised socials, dances and whist drives, which were well attended, and games such as billiards could be played there. Tennis was played on a court in a field opposite the hall (now Winfield Grove). For cricketers, the field opposite the Surrey Oaks Inn provided a good pitch, with plenty of liquid refreshment across the road. At one time the school was used by members of the Rifle Club. The Six Bells public house was a popular venue and had a large number of regulars.

The school was very fortunate in having three dedicated teachers – Mr Brackley the headmaster, Miss Archer and Miss Dynes. Extramural activities included swimming lessons for the older pupils in the top lake of Newdigate Place. Boys aged 11 to 14 were given a plot of garden, which was judged for a prize at the end of the summer term. A carpentry class was held in the Village Hall. Of course the majority of pupils walked to school but a few had bicycles. Many who could not return home at midday for lunch enjoyed hot soup provided daily by a benefactor and brought to the school. Annual school concerts given by senior pupils were another of the many features of school life.

At St Peter's Church the Revd John Ward drew large congregations from afar with his forceful sermons. Apart from the spiritual benefit, the financial result allowed treatment of the woodworm in the roof. Mention of St Peter's must include the many activities of George Horley – churchwarden, bell-ringer, village postman, etc. He undertook the regular mowing, by hand mower, of the entire churchyard.

A centre was established at Dean House Farm by the owners, Miss Darbyshire and Miss Lovell, to enable women students to continue their practical studies for a career in agriculture. Livingstone Haig

ran an aquatic nursery at Beam Brook in Partridge Lane, growing and supplying everything concerned with water life. It was another source of employment and became a thriving business.

In general there appeared to be enough work for everyone. Those who worked in the towns or the City cycled to Holmwood station to catch their train. The brickworks at Newdigate and Beare Green also provided local employment. Although farming was in decline, a farmer only tended to do routine jobs on a Sunday. During this period, there were signs of a quicker pace to come as tractors were slowly replacing horses. One man with his team could plough an acre a day, but a tractor could do three.

Nearly every village has its characters and some certainly lived in Newdigate. Jim Pratt would never alter his watch to summer time, Bob Rowland always boiled his new boots and Fred Hopkins the gravedigger, on his way to the churchyard, spade on shoulder and wearing his bowler hat, would greet people in a loud voice from afar. A Miss Alexander from Faygate occasionally drove her four-in-hand coach, complete with post-horn, through the village.

The roads were very safe places to walk or cycle along, with few vehicles to worry about. Repairs to the roads involved a steam roller first tearing up the surface, then replacing it with hard stones; these were consolidated and then sprayed by hand with a layer of hot tar.

The 1920s were a quiet, steady period, with Newdigate recovering from the loss of young men in the First World War, unaware of the 1930s depression to come or the build-up to another war in 1939.

### A Personal Account
*By Joan Charbonneau (née Brett), the last daughter of Robert and Florence Maud Brett, born in the upstairs bedroom at New House Farm. Joan's father was the farm bailiff and worked for three generations of the Crutcher family. He had a horse and cart and as a special treat he would drive young Jean along Rusper Road on a summer's evening to hear the nightingale sing.*

*Doris Voice and I started school on the same day when we were four. We immediately became bosom pals and were always together. Our teacher was Miss Dynes, a very kind and gentle lady. She wore hand-knitted suits, mostly of emerald green. I think she taught kindergarten and grade one. By the time we left her room we could read, spell and knit. It was a rude awakening to graduate to the next room. Miss Fanny Archer was very different. She was a stern little women, quite rotund, but I always admired her beautiful hands.*

*The next room was headed by the schoolmaster, Mr Brackley. We were in awe of him. After Miss Archer had drummed the 'times tables' (up to 12) into us, he taught us long division. One day he got so frustrated with us that he threatened to jump over the piano.*

*Joe Edwards, rake maker.*

After school he would walk with us across the fields to Janson's lake (the top lake of Newdigate Place) and teach us to swim.

Then a new teacher, Miss de Voil, came as head-teacher. She was a big-boned (not fat) maiden lady, who lived with her parents in the house by the school.

Previously I had hated history and geography, but Miss de Voil made them so interesting that they became a joy. I remember she would have us draw 'still life', and bring to class a dish with cut-up oranges, apples and bananas. She never knew how my mouth watered, or that we had oranges only at Christmas. Miss de Voil was great for music, and one year our choir competed at the Leith Hill Musical Festival. We walked away with all the prizes.

Once a week the older girls would walk to the Village Hall for cookery classes. An elderly lady came by bus to teach us how to make bread, pastry and cakes.

Each year the school voted for a May Queen and in 1932 I was chosen. I wore a powder-blue ankle-length dress with a train and a garland of flowers in my hair. The crowning was held on the rectory lawn and there was dancing around the maypole.

In the school grounds there was a soup kitchen. Mrs Parker made the soup each day and I believe we paid a penny for a bowl, which we ate at our desks. We got a slice of bread too – it was very good. Mrs Parker was a very motherly person and would button us into our coats to walk the mile home, often through floods by what is now Tanhouse Farm. Sometimes my father would be waiting with the horse and trap ahead of the flooded road.

Newdigate was very fortunate to have great benefactors like Mrs Janson and her daughter, Miss Herron. The whole school was taken to a garden party at Newdigate Place and every child given a shilling. Mrs

Route S26 in 1924. Arthur Dennis is the driver and Chris Lucas the conductor.

East Surrey AEC bus, route 29, to Dorking via Parkgate and Brockham in 1929.

Janson would also send someone to the school, when we all stood on our seats to have our socks and shoes inspected. Those who had no socks or worn-down shoes received new ones. Another benefactor was Miss Levitt of Woodshill. Every Christmas there was a party at the school with a large decorated tree and every child received a present. We would be shaking with excitement when it was announced 'Santa Claus is coming'. I believe this was paid for by Miss Levitt.

My father was a great campanologist and with other bell-ringers rang the bells at St Peter's. Every year they rang in the New Year. There was great imbibing in the back room of the Six Bells; I would hide in the corner with bread and dripping given to me by Mrs Grinstead.

Like my sisters, I sang in the church choir. Mrs Toon was the organist and once a week I was allowed to cycle to the village for practice. This marked the beginning of boyfriends. The boys would chase us after choir practice, but they could never find me, as I climbed up a tree in the churchyard.

Dances and whist drives were held at the Village Hall, which was looked after by Mr and Mrs Vine. Billy O'Dare played the piano so fast for dancing that we couldn't keep up with him. He had very bad asthma. There were lots of special events in the village, like flower shows, jumble sales and fêtes. The Women's Institute was a wonderful outlet for local housewives.

A great fascination for me was the blacksmith's shop on Rusper Road. It was a delight to watch Mr Bradshaw and Len Smith pump the fire into sparks and hammer the red-hot horseshoes.

My father often gave me a penny for sweets, and sometimes one for Doris too. We would press our noses against Mr Whittingham's window to choose our penny's worth. Eight aniseed balls cost a penny.

Left: *Demonstration to Labour MPs, 28 July 1927. William Schermuly explaining the pistol rocket line thrower he is about to fire.*

Below: *Demonstrations to Naval attachés in April 1926 showing a 6lb rocket in flight.*

Left: *Aerial view of the Schermuly factory.*

Below: *William Schermuly with his three sons in 1924. Left to right:* Conrad, Alfred and Charles.

Above: *Capt. C.D. Schermuly about to fire a pistol during a demonstration to Naval attachés in April 1926.*

*My best friends were Doris Voice (Tanner), Alice Whiffen (Melville) and Audrey Dennis (Clear). At last the day came when my school-days were over and I had to earn a living. As the years go by I am grateful for the basics of education and of living that was given to me in the country school by dedicated teachers. They were the good days!*

Modernity as we now know it came to Newdigate during this period. John Ede from Winfield Grove tells us that on 26 March 1923 the first regular bus service (route S26) to the Six Bells started, running five times each weekday to and from Redhill via Parkgate, Leigh and Reigate. The vehicle, operated by the East Surrey Traction Co. Ltd, was kept overnight in the coal yard in the centre of the village. Often a double-decker was used for the service. This caused some concern and one lady motorist, a comparative rarity in 1923, was incensed enough to write to the local newspaper stating how alarming it was to meet head-on a large and unwieldy double-decker bus in the narrow lanes around Newdigate. As a consequence the company substituted single-deck vehicles.

Gas and electricity were first installed to parts of the parish in 1933. Mains drainage came to the village in the 1970s and to Cudworth in 2001/2, but even in 2002 there are some houses that have not been connected.

# The Schermuly Pistol Rocket Apparatus Co.
### By the late Alan Warman

In 1933 a company based in Cheam applied to the Home Secretary for a licence under the Explosive Act of 1875 to build and operate a factory in Newdigate. The application was duly advertised for the statutory three months and the licence was granted on 8 January 1934. Thus, on a 14-acre field to the west of Mill Lane, construction of timber-framed, corrugated-iron-clad buildings commenced.

The first buildings were near the entrance to the site and averaged about 1,000 square feet in area. Subsequently 24 sheds, each of less than 100 square feet, were set out further into the site in a symmetrical pattern. These identical sheds were well spaced and screened from each other by a grid of masonry walls, so they were called the 'walled city' by those who worked on the site when explosive processing began.

The factory became known as 'SPRA Works' – SPRA being Schermuly Pistol Rocket Apparatus. The company owed its existence to William Schermuly. After serving several years before the mast in the Merchant Navy William gave up seafaring in 1880 and set about improving the abysmally low standards of safety at sea. In 1897 he founded the firm to manufacture the world's first viable ships' line thrower of his own design. In 1921, William patented the vastly improved pistol rocket line thrower.

On New Year's Day 1929 an Act of Parliament made it compulsory for all British-registered ships of over 500 tons to carry line-throwing apparatus. Regrettably William died less than three weeks after the Act became law, but his son Conrad was already in the business, and the company was geared up to meet the upsurge of demand, boosted subsequently by other countries implementing similar legislation.

By 1933 housing developments around the factory at Cheam encroached on prescribed safety distances, hence the need to move to the green-field location in Newdigate.

The company continued to expand, developing and producing a complete range of pyrotechnic distress equipment, and its reputation for inventiveness and quality led to contract work for the Government. In the early months of the Second World War, work of this nature increased, and when the 'phoney war' of 1939 developed into the 'blitzkrieg' of 1940, Conrad, usually known as 'the Captain', and his brothers Alfred and Charles, directed the company's resources to finding speedy answers to some of the problems besetting the country's Armed Services.

Prominent among the wartime products designed and made in the Parkgate factory were the PAC rocket which carried a steel cable to a height in excess of 500 feet as a defence against low-flying aircraft, 'Skymarker' and target indicator bombs for the RAF's Pathfinder force, 'Snowflake' illuminating flares for nocturnal U-boat hunting, and line-throwing grapnel rockets for assault troops.

Design and production of marine and aeronautical distress equipment also continued on a rising scale. These included rockets throwing buoyant lines that automatically fired when a lifeboat entered the sea. These provided a means whereby survivors in the water could gain access to the boat. There was also a rocket-launched kite-supported aerial which significantly increased the range of radios in inflatable dinghies, liferafts and lifeboats.

The factory had already been extended into an 18-acre field to the north of the original site. In June 1940 the company acquired a further 109 acres of land on either side of the northern limb of Ewood Lane, including a number of houses. Some of this land together with Ewood Old Farmhouse was actually conveyed to Conrad, who farmed there, although subsequently the company acquired title to the whole area. A further portion was used to extend the factory to about 60 acres in all. The remainder served as pasture and doubled up as proof fields in which equipment was tested. The labour force also increased until at the peak of wartime production there were some 1,400 employees.

In the summer of 1942 an explosion occurred in the charging shed with very serious consequences. A local man named Bob Rowland lost his life and two other people were seriously injured. Mrs Grace Fowler, who lived at the Duke's Head in Beare Green, received extensive burns, and Eric Wickens suffered extensive injuries. They survived thanks to prompt action by the local GP, Dr R. Gordon Fear, and Marjorie Smith (née Trow) who was a nurse. The casualties were bandaged from head to foot and taken directly to the hospital at East Grinstead where thanks to the expertise of the staff both Grace and Eric recovered from their frightful burns.

After the end of the war there was a massive reduction in output, leading to a reduced labour force. A large number of buildings were removed and others were let to outside users, the last of whom vacated the site in 1967.

Meanwhile, in 1963, the land to the east of Ewood Lane, 36 acres in all, was sold to Judge Stock of Shellwood Manor. In return two fields on the west side of Ewood Lane, totalling 27 acres, were purchased from him, so the company owned all the land west of Mill and Ewood Lanes. Some of this land was leased to Shellwood Manor, which also retained grazing rights on the fields sold to the company.

Conrad gave up farming and retired from the company, which under his leadership had achieved world-wide renown in less than 30 years. His brother Alfred remained as technical director, but he in turn retired soon afterwards. He was succeeded by his son, another William, who was then living in Ewood Old Farmhouse. The last of the second generation of Schermulys in the company, Charles, continued as works director until he too retired several years later. Some years prior to Conrad's retirement the Charterhouse Group had invested venture capital in the company and when Conrad retired the company became a fully owned subsidiary of Charterhouse. New technological advances also presaged a change from highly labour-intensive to automated processes.

Over 350 people were still employed in the factory when the family relinquished its financial interest. By 1973, when ownership passed to the Wilkinson Sword Group and the company was amalgamated with its chief UK competitor, Pains-Wessex, there were fewer than 250 employees, although turnover had been enhanced. Eight years afterwards the industrial slump necessitated transfer of all activities to the Salisbury factory of Pains-Wessex; when redundancy struck in 1981 there were just 146 people left at the Newdigate site.

Of the second generation of Schermuly brothers, only Conrad was a Newdigate resident, although a married sister, Blanche, also lived here. Conrad was a remarkable leader; during the First World War he joined the Army at the age of 19, was awarded the Distinguished Conduct Medal, mentioned in despatches and demobilised with the rank of captain, the title by which he was generally known. In Newdigate he took an active part in village affairs and is remembered particularly because he underwrote the cost to the community of buying the Brocus field. He was also the motivating force in setting up two memorials to members of the family there – the drinking fountain on the east side and the adjacent blue cedar tree.

Both the sons of the third generation, William (better known as Bill) and Jimmy, went to the village school, but tragedy struck the family hard when the younger boy met his death accidentally while climbing a tree outside his home, Ewood Old Farmhouse. Young Jimmy was buried in St Peter's churchyard and his death was perhaps a contributory factor to Bill's own untimely death.

Hugh Richards, from Ewood Farm House, recalled that in the 1970s there was a substantial security alert when the name Schermuly Ltd was found in an IRA terrorist flat in London, presumably because Schermuly was assembling rubber bullets. A security fence was hastily erected, dogs patrolled the perimeter and there was a high level of police and Army activity both day and night.

At about the same time, by way of an emergency training exercise, it was assumed that two passenger aircraft had collided and crashed in the proofing field and the adjoining woodland. Two lorry loads of bent and broken aircraft bits were scattered around the woods, and 50 realistically made up 'victims', some carrying additional false limbs, arranged themselves. Then a succession of fire engines, ambulances and police cars arrived with their sirens wailing to find the site of the 'disaster'. On questioning the senior fire officers afterwards about the usefulness of the exercise they replied that they had learnt that it was inadvisable to drive fully laden fire engines into waterlogged clay fields as the first three had stuck fast and blocked the access.

## Cudworth Holiday Camp

Charles Lancaster Almond and John Aitchison both wanted to buy the same plot of land at Cudworth. As they were of the same political persuasion they agreed to share the land. John Aitchison also had the house. He started a holiday camp on the site just

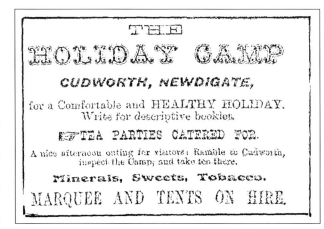

before 1910, and Charlie and his wife Nellie would come down for the weekends to see their children who lived there for the benefit of their health. Charlie had a bakery in Battersea and would cycle to Newdigate on a Friday night and back again on Sunday evenings whilst his wife travelled by train.

Charlie had strong Socialist political views, was well read in the classics and was a poet. He built a wooden bungalow, called The Hut, on the site of the house which is now called Almonds. Next door was the Aitchisons' house and behind this a small building which served as a shop where campers could purchase many of the goods they required. They could also buy sandwiches, for which the village bakery made special 4lb loaves, twice the size of a normal loaf.

Above: *Cudworth Holiday Camp in the 1930s.*

Left: *Cudworth Holiday Camp in the 1930s with campers dressed in their Sunday best.*

Below: *Cudworth Park in 1988.*

Behind the shop were a common-room and dining-room lit by acetylene lamps. Rhoda and Nan Rochester, nieces of Mrs Aitchison, used to serve the food. The trestle-tables were cleared away each evening and communal games were played.

The campers were normally left-wing Socialists, because John Aitchison advertised the camp in the *Lansbury Gazette*, a left-wing periodical. The Labour League of Youth used the camp and the Russian violinist Soernos stayed and gave recitals.

Charlie was not above a little poaching, and one day he was walking home with his daughter and with a pheasant tucked into his poacher's pocket. It was getting dark as they came from Spark's Field and they met Mr Boult, the policeman. They chatted together for a while as they walked homewards. They turned into Burnt Oak Lane and had said 'Goodnight', when Mr Boult suddenly said, 'Mr Almond'. Charlie looked round. 'Tuck those feathers in, will you?' 'Alright! Goodnight!', chuckled Charlie as he continued home with his daughter.

The camp must have given people many happy memories as the following verse, written by A.B. Elsbury in 1925, testifies:

*When your nose is all in pieces*
*And your forehead seems all bumps;*
*When the horse-flies and the skeeters*
*Biting hard, give you the jumps;*
*When your poor feet feel like turnips*
*After coming from a tramp,*
*Then you write home to your mother,*
*'Dear Mum, it's lovely at the Camp'.*

*When the hungry ants have suppered*
*On the limbs you call your own*
*And the breakfast bell rings loudly*
*As you're sleeping with a moan;*
*When you need a rest so badly*
*and sit on the grass that's damp*
*'Dearest Ma' your pen writes glibly,*
*'It is splendid here in Camp.'*

*But when the fortnight's over*
*And you're at your work again*
*Do you think about the skeeters,*
*All the 'sorrow' and the pain.*
*No! You show your brown complexion*
*To your best young man – the scamp*
*And look forward to next season*
*When he will write you at – The Camp.*

The site developed first into a caravan camp and then into a landscaped area of park homes called Cudworth Park. This has become very much a community and even has its own mini bowling green.

## The Orphans of Hatchetts & Brick Making

On 5 October 1920 Miss Marion Martha May Leighfield purchased Hatchetts Farm and 33 acres from Leopold Goldberg. She had a long-standing close friend named Mrs Caroline Aspland Jones, a clergyman's widow, who also came to Newdigate when she purchased other land nearby. Together they

*Hatchetts, c.1930.*

*Newdigate Brickworks in 1986.*

*Peter Higgs in the early 1990s.*

set up house at Hatchetts, with a housekeeper, a cook, two maids, gardeners and a bailiff. Both were the epitome of Victorian ladies and had great respect for each other. One favoured a lorgnette (eye glasses held by a long handle) and in her later years, when her hearing deteriorated, Mrs Aspland Jones used an ear-trumpet.

Mrs Aspland Jones' brother was Frederick William Lawrence (1871–1961) who in 1901 married Emmeline Pethick and together they took the name of Pethick-Lawrence. From 1902 to 1905 he was part owner and editor of the London newspaper *The Echo*, for which Mrs Aspland Jones provided some of the capital. In 1906 the couple joined the Women's Social and Political Union and became prominent within the movement, editing the magazine *Votes for Women*. In 1897 Frederick built a house in South Holmwood (on the present A24) to a design by Edwin Lutyens, which was named The Mascot, but since 1924 has been called The Dutch House. In addition, in 1904, they built The Sundial, just along the road, as a holiday home for poor London children and single mothers. Sylvia Pankhurst was known to be a regular visitor to The Mascot. By 1912 the suffragettes had become very militant and the Pethick-Lawrences were sentenced to a period in jail, during which time they were able to reflect upon the effectiveness of the campaign. They announced their opposition to further attacks on property and following a trip to Canada found that they had been expelled from the WSPU by Mrs Pankhurst.

It is not known whether Mrs Aspland Jones or her friend were suffragettes but it is known that two of Miss Leighfield's sisters were active in the movement.

The two ladies brought up five orphans at Hatchetts: Charles Edgar Parish, William Ball, Florence Sutton, and Frederick Corroyer and his sister, Mary.

Charles Parish recalled staying with the Pethick-Lawrences and being taken to a Parliamentary function. He also claimed that he travelled in a small open train around the Wembley Exhibition of 1924 with George V, and a grainy film of the period does show a boy in a grey flannel suit in the front seat.

The Corroyers were related to Mrs Aspland Jones and as Mary was also given the names Aspland Lawrence it is assumed that they were her nephew and niece. Mary loved horses and was often seen driving a pony and trap around the village. She had an accident and later contracted tuberculosis; she died in Dorking Hospital in September 1942, aged just 28. Mrs Aspland Jones died on 12 July 1937.

Frederick Corroyer was described as cheerful, likeable and full of enthusiasm, and a keen sportsman, playing in the local football and cricket teams. His first attempt at starting a business was during the General Strike of 1926. Timber logs were fetching a high price so he installed an engine and a saw bench and gave work to local men who cut up cordwood which he delivered to London.

He then thought that he would try his hand at brick making. By this time, about 1928, the two ladies had transferred four fields, including a lake and the 'New Barns', which were to become the brickwork site, into Fred's name. They also gave him the house near Hatchetts Farm, which was then called Kingston, but is now Killips, and he and Mary moved there. Mrs Aspland Jones also left legacies to Charles Parish, William Ball and Florence Goodings (née Sutton).

Fred asked builder Frank Lucas to make some moulds and to get a mill working to process the clay. On one occasion he took the village blacksmith, Mr Bradshaw, down to Bristol and back in a day in his Bentley, an open tourer, to see an engine. Upon his return Mr Bradshaw climbed out white and shaken, never having travelled so fast in all his life.

The brick making got off to a good start and gave employment, at a time of depression, not only to local skilled brick makers but also to less skilled clay diggers and general yard workers. During the Second World War the brickworks were closed down. Fred joined the Army and was posted to North Africa. When in 1946 he left the Army as a Lt Colonel he sold the business and went to live in Kenya.

Miss Leighfield continued to live at Hatchetts until her death in 1942 when the house became a Women's Land Army hostel until the end of the war.

The late Peter Higgs worked for over 30 years at the nearby Beare Green Brickworks and he described the life of a maker of hand-made bricks:

*The clay was excavated after the top soil had first been removed. It was then left to weather, allowing the salts in the clay to be washed away. (Many modern buildings today can be seen with salt staining in the bricks – caused either by insufficient weathering or sometimes by salts being absorbed from the ground on the building site.)*

*The clay was spread on to pans and griddled, then passed through two crushing rollers and into a skip. The skip travelled on rails and its contents were spread into the soaks by the 'hommicker' – this word is used by the old brick workers at both Newdigate and Beare Green – who used a hoe for the work. Water was poured over it and left to soak in. Finally breeze, a finely ground coke, was smothered over the entire length of the soak, unless red bricks were required, when sand was substituted for breeze. The hommicker then continually placed the clay into a steam-driven mill which worked like a giant mincer. The clay was now ready for brick making.*

*The brick maker worked from 7a.m. till 5p.m. with a 15-minute break at 10 o'clock and 45 minutes at one o'clock.*

*The ready clay was placed on a bearing-off table and, using a cockle, the brick maker cut a lump to the approx-imate size of a brick. He rolled it into a mould called a wort which fitted over a base with a raised centre, placing it carefully and skilfully, and taking care to expel*

*any trapped pockets of air. The base was called a 'frog' and bore the initials of the works – N for Newdigate and BG for Beare Green. The brick maker dusted the mould with sand to stop it from sticking, and every so often he washed it out and cleaned the frog. (The pan man put a tin of barium in the pan to take the scum out of the bricks.) He pulled a bow across the mould to remove the surplus clay and then used a strike for smoothing the surface of the brick. He placed a pallet on top like a lid and swiftly turned the whole upside down, extracting the mould, but leaving the pallet underneath. Having produced 30 bricks he then placed them on a trolley.*

*Two people would take a fully loaded trolley to the drier where the 'green' bricks were laid out for three weeks under a tunnel which had a slatted cover. The dried bricks, 25,000 per firing, were carefully placed into a kiln, and hardened off in a temperature of around 2,200°F (1,200°C). At Newdigate clamps were used, which explains the variation in colouring, caused partly by the brick's position in the kiln.*

*A skilful brick maker could produce up to 2,000 bricks per day and was paid by the number of bricks he produced.*

*A number of houses within the village were built from bricks made at the Newdigate works. Homelea, Sundown and Ferneyfield are examples of such houses built in the 1920s and '30s.*

## Jubilee Day, 1935

The Silver Jubilee of King George V took place on 6 May 1935 and Newdigate celebrated in style. The following newspaper report was pasted into the Rangers' notebook at that time:

*Newdigate is not likely to forget its Jubilee celebrations for many a long day, and particularly will they remember their enormous bonfire, which stood 30 feet high and contained 600 bundles of faggots. In the morning there was an impressive service in St Peter's Church, conducted by the rector (the Revd J.W. Ward), and the actual festivities began in the afternoon. The procession, which started from the School Meadow, proceeded through the gaily decorated main street of the village to Hogspudding Lane, and thus completed a circuit of the village. With the celebrations was combined the annual ceremony of the crowning of the May Queen, and a prettily decorated wagon, in which the May Queen elect, Violet Beadle, the retiring May Queen, Joan Peters, and their attendants, headed the procession. The wagon, which was pulled by a farm horse, was kindly decorated and lent by Miss Darbyshire and Miss Lovell. Following was an old-fashioned brougham lent and driven by Mr Jackson and decorated by a willing band of helpers. The occu-pants were dressed in period costume. Other decorated vehicles and bicycles followed and the children who were taking part in the sports completed the procession.*

*The procession dispersed on its return to the School Meadow and maypole dancing and sports started and*

*the side shows and stalls were busy. Over 500 teas were served in the school by the Women's Institute.*

*As it grew darker, Mr Schermuly, of the Newdigate Rocket Factory, presented a spectacular display of the rocket life-saving system. The huge bonfire was lit several fields away and community singing was directed by Mr H. Cooper and at 8.00p.m. the King's speech was relayed by Messrs S.J. Clear & Co.'s amplifying equipment.*

Left: *Celebrations to mark the silver jubilee of George V in 1935, showing Foresters Villas and Whittingham's shop (now the Old Bakery).*

Below: *Silver jubilee celebrations, 1935.*

# The Second World War

War once again visited Britain, and as in 1914 the young men of Newdigate rallied to the cause. Many of the 32 men from Newdigate who lost their lives in the First World War came from families who had lived in the village for generations. Of the ten who died in this war only one, Arthur George Brett who was the son of Robert Brett the farm bailiff at New House Farm, was actually baptised at St Peter's. This illustrates a fundamental change that had occurred over the previous 20 years with the coming of many new people into the village and the old-established families leaving.

Although far fewer villagers lost their lives, the village itself felt the effects of this war far more directly. Bombs fell right across the area, troops were stationed in some of the big houses, and the local Home Guard actively patrolled the lanes and fields.

Mr ffinch Mitchell and family lived at Gaterounds and he worked for the War Cabinet as a materials specialist. One of his responsibilities was to develop materials for the Mulberry Harbour and he worked in the barn, which was strictly 'out of bounds'. An air-raid shelter was built nearby. It was strongly constructed and designed to withstand a nuclear attack. Food supplies for three months were stored in the shelter and Herbert Morrison came down from London to inspect it.

### Wartime Memories
Some people who lived in the village share their reminiscences:

*The late Vere Wallis*
Vere Wallis of Reffolds was Captain of the 1st Newdigate Rangers and on 25 September 1939 she wrote to her girls:

I am talking to you in my garden, with our tame robin singing a cheery Autumn song to me – just above my head. It is difficult to realise not very far off, thousands of poor Polish people are suffering, that the London Parks are full of military activities and trenches, that men and women everywhere are all ready for whatever un-nameable frightfulness may come upon them – ready with First Aid knowledge and preparations, ready to be used in whatever ways they may be called upon. Nursing, the WVS (Women's Voluntary Service), the WAACS (Women's Army Auxiliary Corps), the WATS (Women's Auxiliary Territorial Service), the Riverside Emergency Corps and all the other sections of active service on the Home Front.

Other women are sacrificing their home-life, sending their children into the country for safety, giving up their homes and flats to go into the country with the boys and girls, to teach them in strange schools, where they are obliged (cheerfully enough, as I know from having three teachers, one the head-mistress, billeted at 'Reffolds', from the Sydenham Secondary School) to share the new schools with the teachers and children already living there.

Life is rapidly changing everywhere, but some things NEVER change: loyalty to the best we know, as Rangers; love towards our 'neighbours', be our neighbours German people, Polish, French, Russian, Indian

The Girl Guides filling palliasses at the farm,
in readiness for the first evacuees, 1 September 1939.

Armistice Day Church Parade, 1941.

*Newdigate Auxiliary Fire Service 1929–45.* **Left to right, back row:** *Roy Peters, Bert Martin, Steve Pescud, Peter Monk, Jack Fane, Gilbert Monk, Jim Pratt;* **seated:** *Fred Buckman, Chub Taylor, Cecil Monk, Tom Smith, Fred Taylor and Lew Horley.*

or English; and a sense of humour and the gift of laughter, both of which are essential to our lives.

Like the flame of the camp fire, warming us and rising to the starry sky, so our hearts must be lifted up on these difficult days, to warm the lives of others, and our prayers must rise up to the great heart of God, that He will forgive men their cruel and needless ways, that Peace may come again.

### Pearl Moore (née Jones)

In 1939 my family were living at Sturtwood Farm in Partridge Lane, where my father was farm bailiff. We were an incredibly happy family, the house was always open to friends and neighbours. The orchard and fields were a perfect playground for us and we felt this idyllic life would go on forever. The farm was owned by Mr and Mrs Coxon, who lived most of the time in London, although they had now built Sturtwood House, and they would spend frequent weekends at the farm.

There were six children in the family but by 1939 only the youngest son, Ron, was left. I was 15½ years old and worked as a nanny for Dr and Mrs Fear.

I remember so clearly the first air-raid siren, on Sunday, 3 September, shortly after war had been declared. It was a false alarm, but it caused a great deal of fear. My second brother Ken was already in the Royal Air Force, stationed at Cranwell and training as a wireless operator/air gunner. Early in 1940, my sister Ruby joined the Women's Auxiliary Air Force.

During the Battle of Britain we had many disturbed nights with aircraft overhead and frequent dogfights in the area. The Fears had their dining-room at Grove House reinforced with wooden supports to the ceiling and sandbags surrounding the walls and in front of the windows, and we all slept there. Apart from feeling safer, the sandbags helped to cut down the noise.

One evening about this time we were all alarmed to see what appeared to be half the sky illuminated in vivid oranges and reds in the direction of London. Many people turned out to watch this rather awesome sight, feeling that the whole of London must be ablaze. The following day it was revealed that there had indeed been a long and sustained attack on the East End, with severe damage to the docks. The newspapers showed

Sturtwood Farm in 1940.

horrific photographs of the devastation and it took the firemen days to quench the flames.

By this time British troops had appropriated the Red House, a short distance from the farm, and there were constant movements of troops and vehicles. My mother was given the option of taking either pregnant mothers from the danger zones or army officers and their wives. She opted for the latter; having reared six children, I guess she felt she had seen enough of babies! Night and day the front door of the house remained unlocked in case it was necessary to recall the officers at a moment's notice in an emergency.

One day I was spending an evening at home when totally out of the blue there was an enormous explosion, windows were blown out, doors blown open and plaster was falling in all directions. Mrs Tilly, an officer's wife living with us, found the pen she had been writing with across the other side of the room. We later discovered an enormous crater in the field just behind the house. A bomb weighing 1,000lbs had fallen, just missing the buildings. My brother Cyril was on night duty at Schermuly's and came dashing home fearing the worst. After this most nights were spent in the Anderson shelter in the orchard.

Shortly after this Cyril was called up and joined the Royal Navy, and my elder brother, who was working as secretary for Mr and Mrs Haig at Beam Brook Fisheries, joined the Royal Artillery.

After my 17th birthday in 1941 I applied to the East Surrey Hospital in Redhill and was offered a vacancy to fulfil my lifetime ambition to become a nurse.

One of the difficulties was the blackout, both in homes and on vehicles. It was extremely awkward riding a bicycle with only the dimmest of lights, particularly when there was no moon. On one occasion, returning from choir practice on a particularly dark night, I suddenly hit someone. I had heard him but hadn't expected him to be staggering along the middle of the road. I came off my bicycle and he fell to the ground, the bottles clanking in his pockets. He had obviously just left the Surrey Oaks Inn a little worse for drink.

The year proceeded with either one or the other member of the family on leave as by now all except Ron were serving their country.

At the end of 1941 Cyril informed my parents that he had volunteered for the submarine service. As Christmas approached I recall our distress that there was no news and no Christmas card from Cyril. The bombshell came when a telegram arrived from the War Office stating that A/B Norman Cyril Jones was missing, presumed killed. In April further news arrived stating that the submarine H31 had been torpedoed on Christmas Eve in the Bay of Biscay, with all hands lost. Cyril was 19 years old.

Only days later, on 18 April 1942, another telegram arrived, this time from the Air Ministry. Flight Sergeant Kenneth John Jones had been killed on active service. Although he had served for some time with Coastal Command on this occasion the Wellington bomber was on a test flight over Salisbury Plain when it crashed. All the crew were killed as it burst into flames on impact. I was summoned to the telephone in the hospital and was given the news by the rector, the Revd Albert Stone. Ken's body was brought home and he was buried with military honours in the churchyard. He was 22 years old.

Sturtwood Farm and its buildings were painted white and considered a landmark for the Germans. Painters were brought in and the whole place camouflaged.

As the war progressed the British troops moved out of the Red House and the Canadians moved in. My mother no longer accommodated the officers but instead we had a family with one baby evacuated with us.

Ron, like the other boys, was keen to join the forces and in 1944 he was accepted for the Army. He enrolled in the 3rd Battalion of the Coldstream Guards and was stationed initially at Caterham. This pleased my father greatly as he had served in the very same regiment and battalion in the First World War.

### Dr Bill Wheeler

In August 1938 my father bought lots 1 and 2 of the old Rolls Farm, giving him an area of 50 acres, and in August 1939 he started to build the house which is now called Toogoolawah. This was finished about Easter 1940 and cost him £1,100.

One of my earliest memories of living there was the presence of many Canadian soldiers in the area. At the time of the threatened invasion after Dunkirk, among the many places guarded by the Canadians was the bridge over the Beam Brook, just outside our gate, on what was then called Back Lane or the Old Rusper Road, but is now Partridge Lane. What they were guarding that bridge for I cannot imagine, but the nights were made hideous by their shooting water voles with revolvers and rabbits with both Bren guns

and Boyes anti-tank rifles. There wasn't a great deal left after they hit one!

Newdigate had its fair share of bombs, including flying bombs after the invasion of Northern Europe. On the night of the 15/16 June 1944 the first flying bomb landed on Newdigate, knocking down the first two cottages on the right as one goes down Broad Lane from Parkgate. The roof of Kiln Cottages was blown off and Spring Cottage and Pear Tree Cottage had their windows blown out. This bomb had a radio transmitter on it so that the Germans could tell where it landed for ranging purposes.

On 21 July a flying bomb landed in the field behind our house at 9.30a.m. The bomb blew a hole 30 feet across and 10 feet deep, about 10 yards from the house. Most of the windows were blown out, but apart from some damage to the bedroom nearest the explosion and the garage and large portions of the roof, the house was not really badly damaged. The only casualties were a slight glass cut on my mother's forehead and my twisted ankle. The propulsion unit was blown over the house and landed in the road outside. It slid across into a bit of woodland near Beam Brook Cottage.

At 8.15p.m. on 24 July another flying bomb landed just in front of Baringsfield in Cudworth, at the base of a large oak tree which it demolished, leaving just the stump. By the time we got there the Home Guard was patching up the roof and the windows. The ARP (Air Raid Precaution) people were there, and the fire brigade. The house was badly damaged. PC Ryder subsequently arrived on his bicycle. He propped it against the stump of the oak tree, took out his notebook, gazed round at the devastation and said 'It's alright everybody, it's gone off.' This astonishing piece of deduction was greeted with the sentiment it deserved. There was only one casualty – a lady who had superficial cuts including a cut lip, which Dr Fear stitched up. She was taken to Dean House Farm, and the people from Baringsfield to Simons in Church Road.

I was in the Home Guard at Farncombe, near where I was studying at St Thomas' Medical School, and when I came home I was expected to make myself available in the local Home Guard. I was interested in communications and I wired a telephone from the local Home Guard HQ, a room at the back of the Six Bells, to Lieutenant Down's house in Ewood Lane. As I remember it he was a manager at Schermuly's rocket factory.

### Eileen Funnell (née Weller)

I was nine years old when war broke out and living at No. 1 East Lodge, in Partridge Lane, a cottage on the Newdigate Place estate which my father, James Weller, rented from Mrs Janson. I stayed at Newdigate School until I was 14 because the new school at Beare Green had been taken over by the [students of] Westminster Technical College who were evacuated from London.

In September 1939 a number of children were evacuated from London to the village and they

A Doodle.Bug
coming too near, —
Made us scramble
right under the table;
But nobody showed
any fear,
And the "Bump" was
soon muffled in
BABEL !

*A sketch taken from the log book of the 1st Newdigate Guides, showing a doodlebug and people hiding under a table, 24 August 1944.*

attended our school. They were billeted in various houses and we had one – Jean Stone from Shirley near Croydon. She stayed only about nine or ten months before returning home.

Troops occupied Boothlands Farm, and after Mrs Janson's death in 1941, also Newdigate Place. At Boothlands, Mr and Mrs Cripps ran the NAAFI canteen and did the cooking. My brother and I, and other children who lived nearby, like the Beedles, were allowed to go there to see the film shows. Lots of Nissen huts were erected in the fields of Boothlands Farm to house the troops and after the war they were used to provide housing for many people, some of whom moved to Winfield Grove when that was built. At first the troops stationed here were British, but later various regiments of Canadians, who had previously been under canvas, moved in. I know that one Canadian regiment were Highlanders. They sometimes wore kilts and they used to walk up the road playing bagpipes. Mother hated bagpipes!

We children got on very well with the Canadians, who gave us sweets and chocolates. We knew many of their Christian names. They got lots of food parcels from their families and once mother received one, with dried fruit in it, which she made into a cake. Mother did the laundry for the officers and sometimes at weekends she would put up the wives of British officers.

The troops had sentries at each end of Dukes Drive – at East Lodge and West Lodge – and we all had to have passes so that we could get through to school. At first we had to keep showing these, until the soldiers got to know us. Later we changed our route and went via Partridge Lane and Cudworth. The guards were necessary because ammunition boxes were piled up under the sycamore trees on either side of Dukes Drive from East Lodge as far as the lakes. After the war we found many cartridges lying around from boxes that had broken open.

At the time of D-Day the troops suddenly went without warning – one morning they had all gone. They had done a lot of damage to Newdigate Place, for instance chopping up some of the furnishings for firewood. A lot of the lovely panelling was damaged. It was a bit of a wreck after they left and was never lived in again.

Several of the girls married soldiers. I remember cycling up from Newdigate Place with my mother to see the double wedding of Alice Whiffen and Nellie Burrows in September 1941 to two sergeants in the 12th Lancers – Joseph Melville and James Baker.

In 1940 we used to watch the Battle of Britain dogfights overhead and we collected spent cartridges and shrapnel from the garden and the fields. Once a German aircraft was shot down near us and the Army sent out soldiers to take prisoner the pilot who had parachuted to safety near Glovers Wood. Later, German prisoners of war were brought by lorry to do farmwork for various farmers. I don't know where they came from and we didn't have any contact with them.

Often bombs and incendiaries were dropped and I remember going down to see the big bomb crater near New House Farm.

One day a German aircraft began to [fire its] machine-gun along the road as we were cycling back from Charlwood, and we had to jump into a ditch. We could hear the bullets on the road – it was very frightening. I don't remember the air raids ever interrupting our schooling, but sometimes the siren would sound as we were going home. We had to go to the nearest house of people that we knew and wait there until the 'all clear'.

We had an Anderson shelter in the garden and later a Morrison shelter in the house, but during the raids, when father was on duty, the soldiers would collect us and take us to the big underground shelter which the Army had built opposite Fir Tree Bungalow.

In 1944 the V1 bombs started and one of the first fell in Broad Lane and completely demolished the row of cottages where my brother and I were born. The motors of the bombs often stopped when they were overhead. I remember on one occasion, whilst we were picking wild strawberries in Glover Wood, one stopped and we watched it crash somewhere the other side of the village.

There was a sad time when my parents told me that Johnnie Frankpitt, who had been a gamekeeper at Newdigate Place and was in the RAF, had been killed. He lived with his sister, Mrs Monk, at Fir Tree Cottage.

### Rhona Farrin (née Davy)

It was in 1941 when I arrived in Newdigate as a 17-year-old, having just left school, naïve and rather apprehensive.

Through The Women's Farm and Garden Association I began my one-year farm training at Dean House Farm together with a school friend, Margaret Worsfold.

Miss Darbyshire owned the farm with Miss Lovell – only a name to us, as we never met her. She owned a herd of pedigree Guernseys. Buckman the cowman lived in the cottage opposite, and Charlie the carter looked after the two big shire horses and the old pony, Jimmy.

Betty Caspers was in charge of the dairy and there was another girl called Felicity. My first effort at hand-milking Floss was not very successful and we never milked the heavy milkers, Jan and Buttercup. At the end of the cowshed was a stall for the goat who ran with the herd.

The milk was weighed and poured into 10-gallon churns. In the dairy we filled half-pint, pint and quart bottles and fitted the cardboard disc caps ready for the milk rounds. The surplus was collected by the milk lorry. Another necessary job was washing bottles and sterilising all the milking buckets, strainers, etc. Miss Darbyshire and Betty drove a little green van to deliver the milk and Margaret and I harnessed Jimmy to the trap for deliveries to Cudworth.

It was an early start each morning to call the cows in from the field opposite. 'Come along, cow, cow...' Each knew her own stall and went straight to it to be chained up and washed before milking. There was a large Guernsey bull kept at the back of the barn. The servicing of cows was not something we young girls should witness! Buckman was injured once when the bull went mad and it had to be destroyed. We helped feed the calves in another shed.

After milking and mucking out we had a welcome breakfast in the big dining/living-room, seated round a long oak table. There was a large productive garden and several outbuildings at the back of the house and in one shed we were taught how to kill and pluck chickens.

Being wartime we each had to do a spell of fire-watching in a small room attached to the Village Hall, but in spite of rationing we lived very well on home-grown produce.

### Diana Salisbury (née Green)

I was two years old when the war started so memories of that period are a little dim, but I do remember how my father cut a hole through the wall in the down-stairs cloakroom so that we could all sleep under the stairs. My sister, born in 1940, was put to bed in a box on top of the closed toilet and pulled through into our cubby hole whenever there was a raid.

We lived at Hanjague in Mill Lane, and did not have a shelter until after our house was bombed in February 1944 – one of the last big bombs before the doodlebugs. That night we had returned to our beds when my father realised a dogfight was going on and quickly got us downstairs and under the kitchen table, just in time before the bomb landed in the garden, demolishing the garage and making a crater large enough to put a house in. The whole house moved sideways and it took six months to make it safe to live in. Two family friends staying upstairs were badly injured and one of our cats was killed. My guinea pig escaped, never to be seen again.

We were taken to the small hospital at the Schermuly factory. I clearly remember being carried down the road by Mr Dearden – a very tall man he seemed to me – and noticing how clear the sky looked through the bare trees. Anne Schermuly gave me a doll to cheer me up! We went to live with my grand-parents at Brockham until the house was repaired and I went to Brockham school. We seemed to spend most of our time sitting in the shelters singing songs like 'One man went to mow' or diving into the ditch as a doodlebug went over or crashed into the side of Box Hill as we went to and from school. One day we were given a handful of chocolate powder each – a gift from the Canadian soldiers.

Some of these soldiers camped in a wood opposite our house in Mill Lane for some time before we were bombed, by which time they had moved elsewhere. They used to keep us supplied with meat in exchange for hot baths. Apparently there was a notice in Mill Lane: 'No swearing – children live here', but I am not sure this was entirely necessary as my parents have said how kind they were, especially keeping an eye on us when father was away.

### The late George Green

Following the fall of France and the evacuation from Dunkirk in June 1940, and with the imminent threat of invasion by German forces, civilians were mobilised into the new Local Defence Volunteers, which later became the Home Guard. Having failed a medical to join the Royal Navy, I joined the Ewood squad which was attached to the East Surrey Regiment.

Members of the Timber Corps stationed at Ewood during the Second World War.

*The Home Guard parading at Whiteoaks in Ewood Lane.*

*Bomb damage, February 1944, at Hanjague (now Woodcote) in Mill Lane.*

## Ewood Squad

| | | |
|---|---|---|
| Sargeant T.H. Dupere | White Oaks, Ewood Lane | Accountant |
| Private G.C. Green | Hanjague, Mill Lane | Insurance Official |
| Private N. Jenkins | Leith View, Mill Lane | Proprietor of Honey Mfg |
| Private L. Luckman | Hanjague, Mill Lane | Storeman (evacuee) |
| Private R. Devonald | Axford, Broad Lane | |
| Private H. Horley | Rambler Cottage, Broad Lane | |
| Private A. Minns | 2 Oak Tree Cottages, Broad Lane | Gardener |
| Private A. Turner | The Spinney, Broad Lane | Woodsman |
| Private F. Patmore | Tanglewood, Broad Lane | Businessman |
| Private L. Jones | Woodbury Cottage, Broad Lane | Accountant |
| Private H.A. Penkeyman | The Coppice, Broad Lane | |
| Private B. Nicholls | Little Dwelling, Broad Lane | Colonial Office (retired) |

We were issued with uniforms and .303 Lee Enfield rifles, and were responsible for guarding an area from Broad Lane to the railway line at Lodge Farm. Arms training took place in Sergeant Dupere's home – in the kitchen – where we learnt to strip down and maintain our rifles. We practised on a .22 range on the site now occupied by Furzefield Copse, but had to go to the North Holmwood brickyard to practice with the larger .303 rifle. Once someone accidently fired over the wall of the Butts; fortunately nobody was there.

We marched and exercised along the country lanes. On one occasion, as we marched down Broad Lane, the joker of the squad, Leonard Jones, said in a barely audible whisper 'Look out lads, we're being followed.' It was our leader, Sergeant Dupere, a portly, short man of about 60 who had trouble keeping up with us.

During this early period I recall a scare when someone reported hearing foreign voices. After investigation, these proved to be French Canadian troops stationed nearby.

Early one morning at about 3a.m. we stopped a car for routine checking and found it full of 'brass hats'. With some trepidation we asked for their passes which they duly showed us. Having never before seen Army identification documents we assumed that they were OK and allowed the car to pass. It later transpired that the Army were conducting manoeuvres in our area without notifying the Home Guard.

On the night that the doodlebug fell in Broad Lane we had just met another patrol, where the Ockley road goes down to Forest Green and Coldharbour, when we heard a strange noise and had our first sight of a flying bomb. Not knowing if our families were safe or not it seemed a long journey home after our night of duty.

### Bill Tanner recalled an incident in 1940

In the early days of the Home Guard, a colleague and I were guarding the telephone exchange in Rusper Road. At about 2a.m. in pitch darkness footsteps could be heard coming towards the village, and a challenge being made, we found them to be those of a young lady. She had walked from Aldershot, searching for a Canadian soldier believed stationed at Home Farm. She was taken to the rectory to spend the rest of the night and later to Dorking to catch a train home. Judging by her condition it was considered that the population of Aldershot would soon increase by one, thanks to the unknown Canadian soldier.

**Ann Baldwin**

*Throughout the war my mother and I lived with my father's parents at Newlands in Broad Lane, the house that grandfather built in 1932. My father was in the Army and we only saw him when he came home on leave.*

*We had an underground air-raid shelter in the garden, equipped with two camp-beds and a chair. Duckboards were necessary on the floor as there was always water covering it. It smelt damp and clammy, and cooking on a primus stove and lighting by paraffin lamps made everything seem tainted. At first when the sirens sounded we used it, but later decided not to as it was so horrid. So when the air-raid warning went we moved into the hall and bathroom. With the doors of the sitting-room and two bedrooms shut, and a blanket and heavy curtain over the front door, we felt safe from flying glass.*

*My mother hung a little bag on a string around my neck during the day. I didn't understand why, but she showed me a picture of a man with a very cross face and a tin hat, and said that if a man like this came, I was to throw the bag into his face and run away. I didn't know where I was supposed to run to, but years later she told me the bag had pepper in it. She must have been so frightened, with her husband away, two ailing parents-in-law, and the Germans just across the Channel.*

*We watched 'our boys' going over in formation during the Battle of Britain and saw many of them coming back. The lady next door had a son in the RAF and several times he flew over, leaned out of his plane and waved to us – such excitement!*

*Grandfather went up to London for two days most weeks to open the family upholstery and soft-furnishings business and to check for bomb damage. It must have been very difficult with all the materials rationed, and I often wonder how the family managed.*

*Our milk was delivered in a pony and trap from Dean House Farm by Miss Darbyshire or one of her Land Army girls. They used two oval buckets on a yoke, with measuring ladles hanging around the edge. We had clean jugs and net covers with bead weights ready for when they came. The weekly grocery order came from Whittingham's (now the Old Bakery) and the meat from a butcher in Holmwood. If we were out the door would be left unlocked and the money on the kitchen table; our supplies and change would be there on our return.*

*There was 'ration swapping'. Next door the lady was a great tea drinker, so we exchanged our tea for her sugar. My grandmother could then make preserves from hedgerow and garden fruits. The cloth for straining jelly was made from an old nightie or from butchers' muslin, tied to the legs of an upturned chair and with a bowl underneath to catch the drips. This was left for 24 hours.*

*As a special treat I was allowed to stay up to listen to 'Monday Night at Eight', and 'ITMA' (It's That Man Again!) on Thursdays. Daytime listening was 'Workers' Playtime' from some war-work factory at lunch-time, and at teatime there was 'Children's Hour' with Uncle Mac, Uncle David, Toytown and Nature Parliament.*

*On VE day we were in the front garden when Olive Cloke came running down the lane from the farm – 'The war is over, it's on the wireless.' Grandfather went up into the loft and brought out his big Union Jack, which he had hidden under the eaves for years, and like many other* [village residents, we flew the flag] *proudly from the roof of our house.*

**Peter Monk**

*From the first sound of the air-raid siren on Sunday, 3 September 1939 until late spring 1940 war slowly changed village life. Items such as footwear and clothing were hastily bought in expectation of coming shortages. Members of the Home Guard, AFS (Auxiliary Fire Service) and ARP (Air Raid Precautions) were more in evidence, and a number of evacuees arrived from the London area. The expanding workforce at the Schermuly factory drew men and women of all trades from the surrounding villages and towns, travelling by bus, coach, cycles and a few cars. By early 1940 various units of the Armed Services were being stationed around the locality, including the 48th Highlanders of Canada (with bagpipes), who*

GREETINGS

'E' COMPANY. 7TH BATTALION
SURREY HOME GUARD

arrived in Timpson coaches. They encamped around Cudworth Copse, Acorn Wood and out towards Dukes Drive. A sentry was posted at Cudworth Manor's entrance close to the barn where Dr French produced a rather potent cider. Not surprisingly perhaps, cider and Army life were not good companions, and the barn was 'out of bounds' to the Canadians.

During the Battle of Britain in 1940 the first squadrons of enemy aircraft were seen on their way to bomb Croydon and London. One momentous day was 30 August, when a Heinkel bomber came down at Swires Farm in Henfold Lane, in a field beside the drive entrance. Remaining bombs on the aircraft exploded, causing damage to the farmhouse and an Army convoy which had taken cover in the drive. Some members of the crew baled out and drifted towards Capel, pursued by the Canadians.

The Blitz on London began in September that year, and almost every evening at about 6 o'clock the sirens would warn of another air raid, which continued well into the night, or until morning. I lived at the Old Brewery then. One night a string of explosive and incendiary bombs fell around Greens Farm, and the house was damaged. During the following months there were many noisy nights and some bombs fell in the parish. The anti-aircraft guns defending London caused doors and windows to vibrate, and after a fire raid on the City in December burnt ash fell on parts of the village.

The effects of the war gradually became more evident. There were no signposts, and military convoys passed through the village preceded by an odd-looking vehicle which we now know as a jeep. In the drive for food all uncultivated and spare land was taken over by the Surrey War Agricultural Committee, and fields that had not been ploughed in a lifetime were cultivated. Everyone was encouraged to rear a pig to help the food production, but one became attached to it and parting was very emotional.

### Audrey Spinks (née Boorman)

My father, Cecil Edmund Harold John Boorman, was born in Redhill on 9 January 1897. His father was a Regimental Sergeant Major in India, and brought his family up to be intensely patriotic and loyal to 'The Regiment', The Queen's Royal West Surreys.

Aged 15 he ran away from home and joined the Army as a drummer boy. In 1915 he was gassed and wounded in the fighting around Hill 60 and after a spell in hospital in England he was shipped back to France. He was again badly wounded in July 1916 after the attack on Delville Wood. Gangrene set in and he was asked by the French surgeon to sign a consent form allowing him to amputate his leg, but he chose to take a chance and the leg was saved. Then followed a number of operations at the Royal Metropolitan Hospital when over 40 pieces of shrapnel and a number of bullets were removed.

After the war Cecil met and married Primrose

Enticknap of Newdigate and moved to London to find work. His wife hated city life, and returned to her parents' home at Park House whenever she could. When her third child was due in November 1926, she came back to Newdigate to be cared for by her mother. I duly arrived safely, but 16 days later my mother died. Everyone was devastated and Cecil was inconsolable. We children were cared for by our grandparents, but four years later Cecil married one of his sisters-in-law and we were all brought together again. We lived in Middlesex, but in 1937 Cecil expected another war to break out and decided we had better move to the country permanently.

When war came he joined the RAF, who were pleased to take him on – a trained engineer – in spite of his age and a slight limp.

He served at a number of stations repairing bombers, but on D-Day he was diagnosed as having cancer. After much suffering he died on 5 November.

He is buried in Newdigate churchyard.

### The late Alice Melville (née Whiffen)

I first met my husband, Joseph Robert Melville, when he was stationed by the Army at Newdigate Place in 1940 to rest and recover after the evacuation from Dunkirk. He was a regular soldier, who had enlisted at the age of 15 and been trained as a bandsman, but the war changed that and he became a fighting soldier in the 12th Royal Lancers, being promoted to the rank of Sergeant. The regiment then trained for service in the Middle East, finally moving shortly after we were married at St Peter's Church on 6 September 1941.

Within a short while of him becoming involved in the desert fighting, I received a telegram saying that he was missing, assumed dead. Several months went by. I carried on working at the Schermuly factory, not knowing whether he was alive or dead. I received no letters, but finally heard that he was in a prisoner-of-war camp in Italy. He was allowed only a well-censored postcard or lettercard once a month to give me news of his well-being.

Italy capitulated on 8 September 1943. My husband took the opportunity to escape before the Germans could take over. Again there was a long period during which I had no news at all. Friends and my two sisters were receiving letters from their loved ones, but I could only carry on and be brave. At Christmas 1943 I had a breakdown. I finally heard in January 1944 that he had reached Allied lines and would be home for six weeks' leave before being sent to another theatre of war. He was not able to rejoin his regiment, which was still fighting in Italy, because if he was recaptured by the Germans he might be shot as an escaped prisoner. He was given two other choices – to go to the Far East, or join the British section of the Palestine Police.

Although he was born in Yorkshire, he grew up in Palestine from the age of three, when his parents settled in Haifa after the First World War. They were still there. He would be posted near to them and *maybe I would be able to live with them until our own house was ready. So he chose to go to Palestine.*

*Being in the Palestine Police Force was a dangerous job because of the Jewish terrorists. Two weeks before the war in Europe ended I heard that he had been killed on duty. He died on 18 April 1945, aged 30, a true brave soldier, full of life and humour. Two weeks later I received a letter written by him saying that he had [received] permission for me to stay with his parents.*

*I do not recall VE Day at all or anything about the celebrations. It was a dreadful time and I was ill on and off for the next three years. I came home from convalescence to find that my father was ill, and he died suddenly the next day. That is how my mother and I came to live together for the next 43 years until her death in hospital at the age of 102.*

### John Williams of Mississauga, Ontario

*In the summer of 1943 we were stationed at the Red House in Newdigate. We were a very small head-quarters staff of about 40 men, who supported and serviced 21 dentists individually attached to different regiments. Altogether we were known as a dental company. There was a company attached to each Canadian Division and Canadian Corps. The dental companies were equipped with mobile surgeries, able to treat any aspect of tooth or gum disease. We had portable generators to power motors, electric lights and so on.*

*In October 1943 we left Newdigate and embarked from Liverpool for Sicily, and later crossed over to Italy. In late 1945 and early 1946 our unit was disbanded and returned to Canada.*

*I remember the kindness and hospitality of Newdigate – also the visits to the Six Bells!*

### The late Lawrence Eric Wheeler

Husband of Connie Wheeler of Eureka in Hogspudding Lane, Lawrence served as a radio officer with the Royal Engineers and saw action on D-Day in Normandy. This poem is taken from a selection of his poetry entitled *Brown Bulls*:

*People say, 'Weren't you afraid?'*
*It comes again from so many years ago.*
*Afraid! My God! I was terrified.*
*But that didn't matter so long as my mates*
     *didn't know.*
*They probably felt the same,*
*Only none of us liked to give terror a name.*
*I think I must have died a hundred times or more,*
*Just wading ashore.*
*I remember thinking 'What's it like*
*When a bullet stops you and makes a hole in soft flesh.'*
*And naturally I thought of personal and tender parts;*
*Not heads and hearts*
*That bring swift death,*
*But searing pain going on and on.*
*I remember that my stomach didn't seem to be*
     *part of me,*
*But floating away – away.*
*And yet my brain held the briefing.*
*The briefing that was forced into me.*
*Word by word over and over again.*
*Yes I knew*
*Exactly what I had to do.*
*Contact Canadians. Find them. Get them.*
*Poor devils. They were brave.*
*First wave.*
*They met the hail. So many of them went down.*
*But they took the town.*
*Saving us so much.*
*I didn't dare to touch*
*The piles of clothes that once were living men.*
*But French children were already there*
*Robbing the dead and the dying*
*Where they were lying.*
*I remember thinking, 'God what a place'.*
*Some of the dead had only half a face.*
*On that day nothing made much sense.*
*The whole thing seeming just one pretence.*

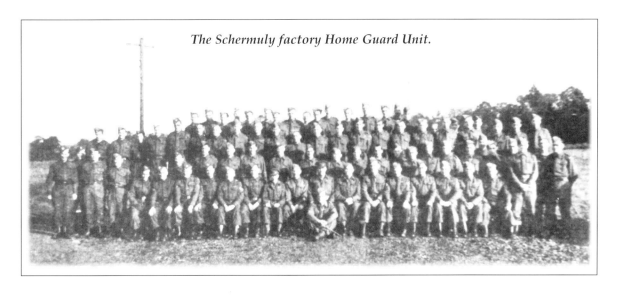

*The Schermuly factory Home Guard Unit.*

# Roll of Honour: The Men of Newdigate who died in the Second World War, 1939–45.

*Sgt Ronald Theodore Ainsworth, 551745, joined the RAF at the start of the war and was killed whilst serving with 12 Squadron on 14 May 1940. His stepmother, Bertha A. Ainsworth, ran a small private school at Woodlands on the Newdigate Road in Beare Green. He is buried at the Pouru-St Remy Communal Cemetery.*

*Charles Edmund Harold John Boorman was born in Redhill in 1897 and after an eventful career in the Army during the First World War he joined the RAF and served at a number of stations repairing bombers. He died from cancer on 5 November 1944 and is buried in the churchyard at St Peter's Church. His name also appears in one of the memorial books at St Clement Danes in London.*

*Arthur George Brett was the son of Robert Brett, the bailiff of New House Farm, and his wife Florence Maud. He was a pilot and was killed in 1939, three weeks after his posting to the Middle East.*

*LAC John Richard Frankpitt, 1187969, lived at Fir Tree Bungalow (Boothlands) and was an Air Gunner in the Royal Airforce Volunteer Reserve. He was killed on 14 March 1943 and his name is recorded on panel 171 on the Runnymede Memorial.*

*F/Off. Malcolm Goss Grant was born in Croydon in 1915 and worked for the family department store, Grants of Croydon. He married Amy Marie Plumpton in 1939 and lived at Old Beam Brook. He joined the Air Transport Auxiliary, ferrying planes from factory to airfield, and was killed on 28 August 1942, aged 28, whilst delivering a Boston from Prestwick to Cambridge. There was an emergency and he crashed in a wood at Bassingbourn and is buried at the cemetery at Golders Green crematorium.*

*Sgt Philip S. Hammond served in the 156 Squadron of the Royal Airforce Volunteer Reserve and was killed in action over Holland whilst flying in a Wellington on 14 September 1942, aged 19. He was the son of Dudley Victor and Simone Marguerite Hammond and is buried at Gramsbergen General Cemetery in Overijssel.*

*Flt/Sgt Kenneth John Jones, 550677, served with 224 Squadron Bomber Command and was killed on 18 April 1942, aged 22, when his aircraft crashed at Garston, having gone into a dive which could not be corrected.*

*Ord/Sig. Norman Cyril Jones, C/SSX34101, like his brother was a member of the Jones family from Sturtwood Farm. He died on 24 December 1941 whilst serving on the Submarine H31 which was lost off Cape Finisterre. His name is remembered on the Chatham Naval Memorial.*

*Sgt James Robert Melville, 3473, died 18 April 1945, aged 30, whilst serving in the Palestine Police Force. He is buried in plot Q20, Ramleh War Cemetery in Israel.*

*Charles Percival, it is believed, came from 1 Woodside Cottages in Broad Lane but further information cannot be found.*

*Sources:*
*The War Graves Commission and the memories of June Taylor, Mollie Posner, the late Betsie Sawtell who was Malcolm Grant's cousin, and R.W. Stevens, whose brother-in-law was Philip Hammond.*

# Chapter 7

# THE POST-WAR YEARS

## The Newdigate Community Centre & The Brocus
### By George Green

Plans to remember the fallen of the First and Second World Wars were under way even before the D-Day landing. In 1944, following a discussion of the Parish Council, a 'Newdigate Recreation Ground Committee' was formed. Its first meeting was on 28 March at Dr Fear's house – Grove House, Parkgate Road – and the doctor was appointed chairman. At this meeting reference was made to the 'Bookers' being more suitable as a recreation ground than another possible site in Hogspudding Lane.

At a meeting on 27 April 1945 it was suggested that a suitable site for a recreation ground should be purchased as a war memorial. Dr Fear later reported that the Rural District Council had zoned the Brocus field partly as a residential and shopping area but this would not preclude its development for recreational use. It was decided to pursue its purchase.

The 1841 Tithe Map shows the Brocus as three fields: East and West Buckhurst, and Buckhurst Meadow nearer to Trig Street. The surviving oak trees grew on the boundaries between these fields. A postcard from the early-twentieth century calls the field Bookhurst, but after the first meeting of the new committee, it was referred to in minutes as the Brocus. The origins of the name are obscure, but Brocus may be a corruption of Brookhurst, meaning 'the copse by the brook', or Brockhurst, 'badger's wood'.

The field formed part of the remaining Farnell-Watson estate, which was put up for auction on Monday 3 July 1945 at the Red Lion Hotel in Dorking by the trustees. The auctioneers were Messrs White & Sons, and of particular interest to the parish was lot

*Bookhurst Meadows (now the Brocus), c.1920, with the Village Hall on the left and Brocus cottage on the right.*

12, an enclosure of 12.589 acres, stated as being particularly suitable for development or as a recreation and sports ground. The rent was apportioned for the purpose of the sale at £10, and the tithe at £1.18s.0d. When the auctioneer asked for bids for lot 12 an offer of £1,250 was immediately made by W.L. Dean on behalf of the parish, and just as quickly the auctioneer's hammer fell. The Brocus field belonged to Newdigate.

A trust deed was completed on 3 July 1946 setting up an association to be known as the 'Newdigate Memorial Recreation Trust' – the field to be a memorial to those who lost their lives during both world wars. The original trustees were H.M. Trouncer of Henfold House, Dr Fear, W.L. Dean of Sylvan Lodge, Beare Green (formerly proprietor of Dean's Stores which was sold at the same auction), and Captain Conrad D. Schermuly.

The £1,250 required was found by way of a bank loan at four per cent interest, but this was largely paid off very quickly through fund-raising activities including a fête, a gymkhana, waste-paper collections and a number of donations. A meeting held on 17 July 1946 elected the first committee, consisting of the rector (the Revd Bruce-Walker), two members appointed by the Parish Council, two by the trustees, five by the donors of £50 or more and five as elected members. The first decisions of the committee included arranging for the erection of children's swings and allowing Mr Hickman to use the field for grazing at a rent of £10 per annum. It was reasoned that this grazing would assist with the initial upkeep of the field.

A Sports Committee was appointed, the football club adopted the Brocus as its ground, the cricket club transferred from its ground opposite the Surrey Oaks Inn, and the tennis club moved from its court in what is now Winfield Grove. The first organised bonfire

# NEWDIGATE BALLOON ASCENT

JUMP BY THE
BRITISH PARACHUTE CLUB

• • •

## NEWDIGATE
### near Dorking

# SATURDAY, 13th JULY, 1968
11.30 am to 5 pm

Programme 6d.

Proceeds in aid of Local Charities

---

# TRACTION ENGINE
## AND
## HISTORIC
## COMMERCIAL
## VEHICLE
## RALLY

### SATURDAY, 21st MAY, 1966
### BROCUS MEADOW, NEWDIGATE

## DISPLAY BY 10th BATTALION
## THE PARACHUTE REGIMENT (T.A.)
(by kind permission of Lt. Col. J. W. Lloyd, M.C.)

Proceeds in aid of Village Hall and Brocus Meadow improvements.
Organised in conjunction with the Worthing Historic Commercial Vehicle Group

## PROGRAMME

### PRICE 6d.

The dedication of the water fountain on the Brocus in 1951.

Mrs Vine on the tennis court opposite the Village Club, now part of Winfield Grove.

Newdigate Horse Show, 1948. Fred Collinson is receiving the cup.

1   Pavilion
2   Cricket Table
3   Bowling Green
4   Garden of Remembrance
5   Grass Courts - 6
6   Hard Courts - 2
7   Swings, See-saw, Roundabout
8   Club
9   Institute
10  Brooklag Farm

*The original plan for the Brocus.*

Medieval Tournament in 1967.

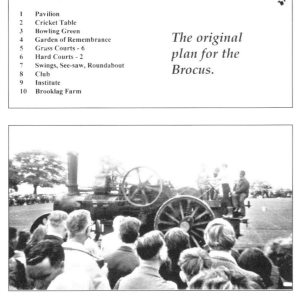

Traction engine rally on the Brocus, 21 May 1966.

**West View Cottages, Rusper Road, 1990.**

# MEDIEVAL TOURNAMENT

## NEWDIGATE, near Dorking

### SATURDAY, 3rd JUNE, 1967

11.30 am to 5 pm

Proceeds in aid of National and Local Charities

Programme 6d.

---

# NEWDIGATE GALA
AND
# DONKEY RACES

SATURDAY, 18th JULY, 1964
BROCUS MEADOW, NEWDIGATE

OPENING AT 2 p.m. by

JOHN TREGORRAN of 'The Archers'
by kind permission of the B.B.C.

First Race 2.30 p.m. Donkey and Horse Race Betting by B.P.A. members on the Course

★ ★ ★ ★ ★ ★

Parade of the Surrey Union Foxhounds
by Courtesy of the Master

Crowning of the Gala Queen
SEPARATE RING WITH

British Legion Tug o'War Competition

Gatton Sea Cadets Display

Childrens Dancing    Horley Band

Dog Obedience Display, etc. starting at 3 p.m.

★ ★ ★ ★ ★ ★

| SIDE SHOWS | COUNTRY MARKET | Light Refreshments |
| TRADE STANDS | CHILDRENS CORNER | and Licensed Bar |

★ ★ ★ ★ ★ ★

ADMISSION 2/6    CHILDREN (under 14) I/-
Car Park 5/- and 2/6.    Ringside 10/-
Proceeds in aid of Village Hall and Brocus Meadow improvements

## Twelve Acres of Fun — Come and Join Us!

*David Neil & Company Dorking Surrey*

and procession took place in November 1950 and various other organisations such as the Youth Club, Brownies and Horticultural Society became regular users. The grazing rights were soon discontinued.

A magnificent feature of the Brocus is the 'Jackson' oak, situated between the cricket square and the bowling green – so called because beneath its branches Thomas William Jackson courted his lady, Lillah Lucas, in 1895–6. Mr Jackson was the coal merchant and carman in Newdigate for many years, working from the site now known as Inglenook Yard. They lived at Myrtle Cottage, and before the First World War served teas in their garden to many a passing cyclist.

In addition to being a war memorial, the field contains other memorials to Newdigate residents. On the patio of the Village Club is a seat donated by the Dorking District Independent Order of Odd Fellows in memory of Bro. H.T. Whittingham, proprietor of the grocery shop which is now a private house called the Old Bakery. There is also a plaque on the wall here to George A. Treadgold, treasurer of the Village Club from 1966 to 1972. In the south-west corner of the field was a maple tree (Goldsworth Purple) commemorating the 1971 Golden Jubilee of the British Legion. This was removed during construction at the bowling club but will be replaced. The cricket sightscreen is a memorial to Vic Cloke, carpenter and husband of the late Olive Cloke, and the north gate remembers Roy C. Wheatland who was treasurer of the Community Centre until October 1980.

To the east of the ground is a blue cedar (*Cedrus atlantica glauca*) planted by Mrs C.D. Schermuly to commemorate the presentation of the field to the village on 27 July 1947. There is also a seat to the memory of A. McGuiness of Newdigate's OAP Club. Susan Schermuly, the wife of William, is commemorated by the drinking fountain which was presented by her children in 1951. The oak lych-gate, recently renovated by Chris Dare, remembers Blanche Hilda Darbyshire (d.1955), a former owner of Dean House Farm and founder of the Newdigate Women's Institute.

During the 1960s, when the Community Centre Committee was headed by Dr Bill Wheeler and George Green was the secretary, a number of ambitious events took place to raise money. In 1966 a traction-engine rally attracted a crowd of nearly 5,000 people and raised the princely sum of £900. Queues were reported as being half-a-mile long and the village was brought to a standstill. In later years there was a balloon ascent, a Countryman's Fair and a medieval tournament.

Today the Village Hall and the adjoining Brocus are in constant use. Two of the biggest events, when villagers turn out in force, are the annual Village Day and the bonfire night. The entire area is managed by the Newdigate Community Centre, which is a registered charity, the trustees of which represent every organisation using the Brocus facilities.

One other memorial on the Brocus has not been mentioned: a chair, made by Les Fidler from an oak that came down in the great gale of 1987. It sits under the trees that divided what was once East Buckhurst from West Buckhurst, and is in memory of the writer of this piece about the Brocus, George C. Green.

## Building Developments

As early as 1902 the Rural District Council talked of building houses and although in April 1914 Newdigate Parish Council thought that 'six workman's cottages would be enough', it was not until 1922/3 that four at Parkgate (Kiln Cottages) and four at Newdigate (West View Cottages) were finally built.

At a Parish Council meeting plans were submitted for new houses to be built opposite the Sports and Social Club, and in 1947 an estate of 60 houses was built and named Winfield Grove after Mr H.G. Winfield of Brook Farm who was chairman of the Parish Council from 1934 until 1946. Later, bungalows for old people were added. By 1961, these developments had brought the total number of houses in Newdigate up to 450, with a population of 1,400 people.

There was a large influx of young people from the suburbs in the early 1970s. They moved to Newdigate for two reasons: it was a nice environment in which to bring up children, and houses were cheap. Many of them still remain in the village, having seen their children grow up and, frequently, move away because of the high property prices during the late-twentieth and early-twenty-first centuries. Most new-house building that took place in the 1970s was infilling existing plots, but during this decade permission was granted for a number of detached houses in what became Woodpecker Lane, and at the end of the 1990s an estate of large detached houses called Becket Wood was built on the Schermuly site. Another estate, The Mulberries, with an element of affordable housing, is being developed in 2002 on the site of the old Newdigate brickworks. Encouragingly for the village, a number of residents from these estates are taking an active part in community affairs.

*Flats in Winfield Grove, 1990.*

Left: *Newdigate brickworks and lake in 1986, now the site of the Mulberries housing estate.*

Below: *Collinson's or Johnson's Cottage, before it was demolished in 1959.*

Below: *The site of the Duke of Norfolk's mansion.*

*Lucy's Cottage during the floods of September 1968.*

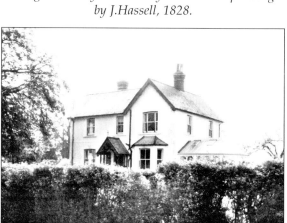

*The Clerk's House and the Six Bells with the village stocks by the churchyard. From a painting by J.Hassell, 1828.*

*Lucy's Cottage in 1973.*

*Oakfield House in 1990, formerly Fairholme, on the site of Loompits.*

# The Lost Houses of Newdigate
## By Jane Lilley

Over the centuries, many houses must have been built in Newdigate which have since vanished. Of the earlier ones, most have left no trace except perhaps a name in a document. We know a little more about some of the houses which were lost in the nineteenth and twentieth centuries. The most recent are recorded in photographs, but even when photography became common, few pictures were taken of the more ramshackle buildings, which were regarded as squalid hovels rather than interesting or picturesque dwellings.

One of the most impressive houses was the Duke of Norfolk's mansion, built in the early-nineteenth century but never completed. In his book *Surrey Hills*, F.E. Green describes the remains of the mansion, situated in the damp hollow opposite Henfold House, where alders and willows grow. The house was only built as high as the roof by a former Duke of Norfolk, but during the building work, he died (1815), and it seems that his successor did not want the new house; it was left abandoned and roofless, and the materials were gradually used elsewhere. By 1915 only moss-covered stones could be seen.

It has been said that dukes could travel all the way from Arundel Castle to their estates in Norfolk over land that they owned, which in 1840 included over 40 per cent of the parish of Newdigate and all of what is now Holmwood Common.

In the early 1840s, the Tithe Map and first detailed census give us a fairly clear picture of what Newdigate was like at the time.

When the Village Hall was built in 1901, a straggling row of tiny squatters' cottages along the edge of the Brocus were demolished to make way for the new building. So little is known about them that it is not even clear how many there were. The Tithe Redemption Map seems to show five, and by 1871 there were probably nine or ten families living there, although there is nothing to say whether each family was in a separate cottage or if there were two or three families crammed into a tiny building. Two of the cottages are supposed to have been almshouses, built only 20 years before under the will of William Farnell-Watson senr; they vanished with the rest.

Lucy's Cottage was a squatters' cottage, but brick-built and more substantial than many, so it survived for many years close to the Village Hall. Lucy Gadd was born in the cottage in the 1890s and lived there for around 80 years, while her brother Luke, a shoe repairer, had his workshop in the garden. All the cottages along that edge of the Brocus were built between the edge of the road and a stream, and although this is now culverted, it must have been a very wet site; certainly in the 1960s floods inundated the ground floor of Lucy's Cottage and other houses.

The original cottage was demolished after Lucy's death, and another of the same name built nearby.

Squatters' cottages, built with whatever materials were at hand on any available scrap of land, must often have been short-lived. Buckhurst Cottage was on West Buckhurst field, now the top corner of the Brocus, near the cricket pavilion; gooseberry bushes which must be survivors from its garden are still growing in the hedge. It was apparently built in the 1840s, but had disappeared by 1871. We can only speculate on the flimsy construction of a cottage that lasted less than 30 years. Such was the shortage of housing that one census records a former soldier who had apparently set up home in an old limekiln in Parkgate.

A little more is known about some cottages. In the mid-nineteenth century, Tulley's House stood on the corner of Blanks and Partridge Lanes. It had half an acre of garden and orchard, and is described as a house and not a cottage, so it was a substantial building. In a deed of 1756 it had 14 acres of land and was called Baldock; a conveyance of 1845 refers to Baldocks Farm having four fields, two called Tilleys Mead, and a house, buildings, orchard and garden. At some stage the name changed to Tulley's House, but by 1861, it is called a cottage, suggesting that it was in a poor condition. Once the roof of a timber-framed building had leaked for a few years, structural timbers would rot; eventually a crucial component of the roof or wall gave way and part of the house would literally collapse. By 1871, Tulley's House was uninhabited.

Old Joe's was an isolated cottage reached by footpaths from Broad Lane or Blanks Lane, and was abandoned some time after the 1881 census. By 1891 the last occupants, a 78-year-old agricultural labourer and his wife (who had also been the last occupiers of Tulley's House) had moved to a cottage on Partridge Lane, although Old Joe's Barn, or at least its name, still existed in the 1930s.

On Village Street, the Tithe Map shows a building divided into three dwellings which has since disappeared. This once belonged to the parish and was used as a poorhouse, providing rent-free accommodation for some of the poorest families, until the late 1830s when a change in the system forced them into the Dorking Union Workhouse. The building was sold in 1840, but continued to be inhabited until about 1872, when William Farnell-Watson bought most of the houses on Village Street. He did not demolish the old houses wholesale, but the old workhouses must have been dilapidated, because he replaced them with the pair of semi-detached cottages now called Myrtle Villa and The Laurels.

The building next door, known as Johnson's or Collinson's Cottage from two families who lived there in the late-nineteenth century, survived until 1959. A four-roomed house with an attached cart-shed, it then belonged to a local builder, Archie

*Little Cherryhurst shortly before its demolition in 1965.*

*Oak Tree Cottages.*

Above: *Dukes Cottages, early 1900s, with a well conveniently outside the door.*

Right: *Rakemaker's Cottage in 1939.*

Morris, who replaced the house and garden with several new houses.

The Clerk's House (see p.90) stood in the village on the corner of Church Lane. The Parish Clerk, Stephen Tidy, lived there for many years, hence its name, but censuses show that in the mid-nineteenth century it usually housed at least two families and possibly more. Another house just around the corner, on the site of the modern Tamarinda, is shown on the Tithe Map, but not even its name is known with certainty. It may have vanished around the time of the Tithe Survey, or it may be indistinguishable from the Clerk's House in the censuses, which often describe each household as 'village cottage'. The Clerk's House was demolished in the early 1860s, and replaced by the terrace of four cottages which were originally called Clerk's Cottages but are now Church Cottages; they are said to contain reused timbers from the old house.

Loampits stood on the corner of Church and Cudworth Lanes, where Oakfield House now stands. It is mentioned in 1731, and was the home of the schoolmaster John Chart and his family from 1841 until the 1880s. By 1891 Loampits housed a matron, an assistant matron, and six girls aged 12 to 15 from central London who were listed as training to be domestic servants. An interview with an old Newdigate resident records that these were in fact 'girls who had stepped aside' – in other words, young unmarried mothers-to-be. Presumably each stayed for a few months, training as a servant until her baby had been born and taken for adoption, when she could be found a suitable post and her lapse conveniently forgotten. The 'training home' was probably still there in 1905, but the building was replaced a few years later by the present house, originally called Fairholme.

Little Cherryhurst was also known as Cherry End or simply Little Cottage, and usually referred to in censuses as 'cottage on Combers Lane' (i.e. on the road to Combers Farm). It stood on Partridge Lane, on the site of the modern house of the same name. A tiny cottage, it had just one room measuring 12 feet by 10 feet downstairs, and a ladder stair leading to a single bedroom set half in the roof space. The downstairs floor was sunken to give more headroom. It was probably built in the early-seventeenth century, and was reputed to have been a drover's cottage, erected on a corner of waste ground at the edge of the road for the use of the men who drove cattle and other animals from one place to another. It was occupied until the 1960s, when it was considered too small for modern use and replaced.

Broad Lane was developed piecemeal in the nineteenth century, and by the start of the twentieth there was a scatter of little cottages along the wide verges; only a few survive. Two cottages shown on the Tithe Map, on the site of the present Willow Cottage and End Gables, were demolished by a flying bomb during the Second World War. Oak Tree Cottages were semi-detached, very close to the road and weatherboarded but fairly substantial, with brick foundations and a brick party wall. Each had two storeys and a further attic room, with the kitchen in an 'outshot' at the back. They were replaced during the late-twentieth century by two semi-detached bungalows, one of them also called Oak Tree Cottage; the original oak tree, though right against the road, still survives.

Duke's Cottages were on Parkgate Road, very close to the junction with Broad Lane. Built by the Duke of Norfolk for his employees in the mid-nineteenth century, they were a pair of plain brick cottages, and no doubt regarded as excellent labourers' houses when they were built. A map of 1769 shows a pair of cottages on virtually the same site and described by Pevsner as a 'Wealden Farmhouse', which must have been replaced at some time by Duke's Cottages. Both the earlier cottages and their replacements were generally occupied by woodmen working in the coppices of Parkgate, and when these were neglected, Duke's Cottages fell vacant. By 1965 they had lain empty for several years and were beyond repair. The site is now part of a garden.

The Rakemaker's Cottage was just outside the parish boundary, roughly opposite Broomells on the road to Beare Green and Capel. It was occupied for many years by Joe Edwards, who made wooden rakes for use on the local farms, as well as walking sticks and perhaps other wooden articles. A weatherboarded cottage which stood close to the road, it was owned by the brickworks, who had it demolished in about 1960.

Other lost buildings are mentioned elsewhere in this book, including Newdigate Place (Chapter 2), the original Red House (Chapter 5), Morphew's Mission (Chapter 8), and the 'homes fit for heroes'(Chapter 6).

# Aircraft Incident in Newdigate

Villagers are used to seeing aircraft flying in to and out of Gatwick Airport, but on 17 February 1959 there was a most serious incident when an airliner carrying the Turkish Prime Minister, Mr Menderes, crashed into Jordan's Wood. A newspaper article reported that 60-year-old Adnan Menderes climbed out of the blazing wreckage of a Viscount airliner and was found staggering through a wood near Gatwick Airport. Unfortunately 14 of the 24 people on board died. The plane, bringing Turkish leaders to London from Ankara for top-level talks on the Cyprus settlement, was diverted to Gatwick because of fog at London Heathrow. Another plane diverted at the same time, bringing Mr Constantine Karamanlis, the Greek Premier, from Athens, landed safely 15 minutes later.

Mrs Margaret Bailey was in her sixteenth-century farmhouse (Oaklands Park Farm Cottage) three miles

Above: *The wrecked Viscount airliner.*

Above right: *Tony and Margaret Bailey welcoming Turkish premier Adnan Menderes and Dr Ronald Knight a week after the crash.*

Right: *The crash site at Jordan's Wood, 17 February 1959.*

Below: *Adnan Menderes awaiting execution having fallen foul of the Turkish authorities.*

from the end of the runway when her husband Anthony rushed in from the fields, where he had seen the Viscount loom out of the fog and crash. They drove to the scene through the narrow Surrey lanes. Mrs Bailey said:

*I saw three figures stumbling towards me out of the wreckage of the plane. They looked dreadful as they came out of the fog. I did not know who they were but I piled them into the car, and a man I later found to be Mr Menderes' equerry told me that one of them was the Turkish Premier. I drove back to the farmhouse and my husband stayed on to see if he could be of help. Mr Menderes could not speak; he was obviously badly shocked.*

He was later taken to hospital.

First on the scene were gardeners Peter Weller and Peter Heather who had been working at Jordan's, and Jack Marshall from Rusper. They went into the blazing plane on three occasions and pulled out six injured passengers. The Viscount was a ball of wreckage; it cut a swathe through the woods and the tail came off. A Gatwick Airport official who went to the scene said he found the dead 'strewn everywhere'.

A week after the crash Mr Menderes returned to visit Mr and Mrs Bailey. He also met Dr Ronald Knight of Crawley who had given medical assistance. The Premier and his private secretary stayed for half an hour chatting with them over a glass of sherry.

Some time after the incident Mr Menderes fell foul of the Turkish establishment. It was alleged that he had been trying to stage a coup d'etat and appoint himself dictator of the country. He was arrested, put on trial and condemned to death for treason. He was taken to an island off the Turkish coast, where he was hanged.

# St Peter's 800th Anniversary (c.1175–1975)

On the 30 June 1975 the rector, the Revd Dennis Parker, received a telegram from Buckingham Palace:

*Please convey the sincere thanks of the Queen to the churchwardens and members of the parish of St Peter for their kind message of loyal greetings sent on the occasion of the 800th anniversary of the church. Her Majesty much appreciates this message and sends her best wishes to all concerned on this notable occasion.*

Many events had been planned throughout the year but the climax came with a week of activities starting on Saturday, 28 June.

A Festival of Flowers in the church was organised by Mrs Dorothy Fear and portrayed aspects of the life, teaching and experiences of Peter, the fisherman, disciple and apostle of the Lord. Special church services and organ recitals were held and John Alexander Smith conducted the St Peter's Festival Choir in Handel's 'Messiah'.

Alan Banks organised an exhibition of pictures depicting Newdigate through the ages and Vic Cloke narrated 'The Village Story', a history of the village in sound, pictures and light.

The climax came on the following Saturday – Village Day. There was a parade of the Surrey and North Sussex Beagles, a tug-of-war, maypole and morris dancing, a pram race, archery, go-carting and a cricket match with the players bewhiskered and top-hatted. The village's bell-ringers, Pony Club, Brownies, Guides and Scouts, Choral Society, Football Club, Friendship Group, Horticultural Society, School and PTA, Parish Council, Parochial Church Council, Play Group, St Peter's Youth, Tennis Club, Royal British Legion, Village Club and Women's Institute all joined in the activities.

The festivities continued into the evening, with a dance and cabaret, barbecue, camp-fire and a giant fireworks display supplied by Schermuly Ltd which finished, according to the *County Post*:

*... with a 100-foot-long sparkler proclaiming 'Newdigate 800th Celebrations' in a thunder of fire and smoke to the crowd of open-mouthed, gog-eyed spectators.*

It was estimated that some 2,000 people attended the day.

A selection of commemorative tankards, plates, tiles and notelets, all drawn by Eric Faunch, were available, 120 church kneelers were worked by 100 people and 593 parishioners wrote their names in the 800th Anniversary Bible. Following a proposal from Alan Posner it was decided that as a small surplus had been made, £150 should be put towards a new Communion table, which was constructed by David Crump.

Other activities had been organised during the year and none of these would have been possible without the work of a dedicated committee which consisted of: John Alexander Smith (chairman), Dreda Boyd (secretary), Gerry Mitchell (treasurer), Roger Sawtell (publicity), Al Boyd (souvenirs), Bill MacKay (events manager), Roy MacIntosh (Village Day co-ordinator), Hazel Wheeler (catering), Jack Carter (invitations), Alan Posner (anniversary Bible) and a standing committee of Kathy Bettesworth, Gladys Caporn, Mollie Posner, and Frank Mottershead.

Further responsibilities included: the rector (services), Dorothy Fear (flower festival), Hugh Eller (drama), Charles Thompson (concerts), Eric Faunch (artwork), and Simon Lankester (insurance).

The school and representatives from all the village societies together with the numerous patrons contributed substantially as well.

## The Millennium

Newdigate, in common with the rest of the world, celebrated the dawning of a new millennium in style. On 31 December 1999 the cricket club played its last game of the century and next morning a few hardy souls played the first of the new century. Private parties were enjoyed throughout the village and a candelit service was held in the church at midnight followed by an impromptu singing of 'Auld Lang Syne' between the church and the Six Bells Public House by about 200 villagers.

*Surrey Village of the Year, 2000.*

Diana Salisbury oversaw the design and completion of the Newdigate Millennium Embroidery which was worked by 44 villagers. It depicts the wildlife, houses, shops, church, pubs, clubs and history of the village. It is made up of 228,150 stitches, took approximately 2,281 hours to complete, and now hangs in the Village Hall.

The Newdigate Society produced a 'Millennium Snapshot' in which villagers wrote a short history of themselves, describing life in the village at the close of the twentieth century.

In 2000 Newdigate was the overall winner of the Surrey Village of the Year, and winner of the category for older people, with a 'highly commended' in the category for community life. In 2001 the category for 'young people' was won. The village is judged during June and July when questions are asked about planning, events, the environment and organisations. The judges then tour the village.

Newdigate moved into the twenty-first century with many people reflecting upon the enormous changes that the previous 100 years had brought while anticipating the challenges of the future.

## Challenge & Change

For many years the residents of Newdigate sought change and improvement in their village. At the start of the twenty-first century, however, the opposite is largely true. Events, both natural and man-made, may threaten the character of the village and are often therefore resisted.

### The Great Gales & Other Weather

Autumn 1987 was very wet and the trees had not lost their leaves when at midnight on 16 October temperatures soared to 17/18°C and a tremendous storm broke across the south of England with gusts of 104mph being recorded at Gatwick. Many people in the village were unable to sleep, but it was so dark that they could only guess at what was happening outside. Dawn revealed utter devastation. Great numbers of trees were uprooted or torn asunder. Several oaks on the north side of the Brocus were uprooted and Village Street, Broad Lane, Partridge Lane and Rusper Road were all impassable. Hatchetts was completely isolated. A 'blitz' spirit enveloped the village. Those with electricity shared their homes, telephones and freezers with those without power. Everywhere was covered with a white salt and it was estimated that 15 million trees in the south of England fell that night.

It did not seem possible that history would repeat itself but during daylight on 25 January 1990 another wild gale blew up causing much structural damage and again Newdigate was without electricity. The large conifer on the south-east corner of the Brocus crashed down, taking the village sign with it.

Throughout these gales the great 'Jackson' Oak on the Brocus survived practically unscathed and became a symbol to the village of the continuity of life and the power of nature.

Extreme weather has occurred before in Newdigate. The effects of the great storm of 1703 are not known, but the parish magazines at the end of the nineteenth century recorded temperatures of 87°–90°F in August and September of that year, while

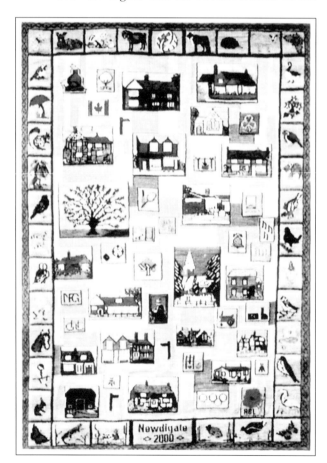

*The Millennium Embroidery.*

in January 1881 the roads were blocked by 4 feet of snow and the cold lingered into March. This caused great distress because men could not work in the fields and received no pay.

In March 1842 the *Sussex Agricultural Express* reported that the torrents of rain and hail that fell, and the loud peals of thunder combined with the vividness of the lightning, were enough to awe the most courageous. A large oak tree at Parkgate, the property of the Duke of Norfolk, was riven into splinters and some of the bark was blown from it upwards of 20 feet. A rooster and two hens had got underneath the tree for shelter, and not surprisingly after the fury of the tempest was over, were discovered dead.

Floods were also a problem, as is illustrated by this report from 1899:

*The horseman of a local farmer named Thomas Webb was bringing a wagon load of chalk from Dorking, and the floods at Cudworth by the Manor House were so high over the road and bridge that when the horseman tried to drive through he went off the roadway. One horse was drowned and the wagon wrecked, and he was saved by clutching an overhead branch of an oak tree. Two men heard him shouting at the top of his voice and when they arrived on the scene he was so unnerved by his tragic experience, that all he could do was to call out, 'Our Father which art in Heaven, Our Father which art in Heaven!!'*

Peter Monk recalled a similar flood at the same place some 70 years later and further problems occurred during 2001.

*The hurricane on 16 October 1987 resulted in storm damage on the Brocus.*

## The Leisure Plot Rumpus

In June 1974 a headline in the *Dorking Advertiser* read 'Newdigate Land Deal – Mystery Man in the Middle'. A mystery buyer negotiated the purchase of five acres of green-belt land and before the deal was sealed a London development company sold the land in 20 individual building plots. That sale raised a storm of protest when local planning officials said the plots had no chance of getting planning permission. An investigative journalist on the *Dorking Advertiser* tried to unravel a tangled skein of companies involved and found there were 13 in all.

The news of these happenings faded until banner headlines in the *Dorking Advertiser* of 22 August 1975 proclaimed 'Leisure Land Deals – Rumpus Breaks'. It appeared that the two men behind the previous land deals were back in Newdigate, this time trying to sell 106 plots of land in Parkgate Road for 'leisure'. They had divided up a 15-acre field and were selling small plots for 'vegetable, flower, fruit growing, grazing and investment'. It was believed that they paid between £300 and £1,000 per acre and were selling plots for £195 to £795.

There was a storm of protest from local residents and confrontation in Parkgate Road. Placard-waving villagers picketed the entrance to the field in a bid to warn prospective buyers of the problems of buying the land. It was feared that the site would deteriorate into a 'shanty town' or 'gypsy camp' as picnicking Londoners flocked down to the plots at weekends.

The householders handed out leaflets to the customers warning them, 'Before you buy, take legal advice' and 'This is agricultural land and its use is restricted by law'.

Mole Valley District Council then got involved in the affair and slapped an Article Four directive on the land which ensured that nothing could be done to it without council permission. The dust settled, and Parkgate Road returned to its former tranquillity – although occasionally residents are still asked the whereabouts of the Parkgate Road estate by someone who has inherited what looks, from the deeds, like a valuable development site!

## The Brickyard Saga

After the Second World War, Fred Corroyer sold the brickworks. It was taken over first by Hall & Co. and then by the Ready Mixed Concrete Company. The firm prospered until 1974 when there was a fall in demand for bricks and the site was abandoned, the buildings boarded up and nature allowed to take over. It became a haven for wildlife and the deep lakes in the excavated areas were a favourite haunt of fishermen.

In March 1980 a subsidiary of RMC, Hales Containers Ltd, submitted an application for:

*... the refilling of site by controlled tipping of industrial, domestic and commercial wastes within a total area of approximately 50.58 acres, Newdigate Brick Works, New Barn Lane, Newdigate.*

At the Annual Parish Meeting on 17 March a large number of people gathered and formed a protest group called The Anti-Tipping Action Committee, henceforth known as ATAC. E.J. Webber was chairman, with Mrs N. Webber as secretary, Mrs H. Lucas as treasurer, and A.G. Boyd, D. Brearley, D. Dovey, D.W. Harrington, A.E. Posner, and G.H. Yeoman.

The village was up in arms and headlines announced, 'Angry villagers launch protest – Fight to stop rubbish tip.' With the prospect of 50 lorries a day rumbling along narrow country lanes it was hardly surprising that feelings ran high. The ATAC group were professionally highly qualified to put up a stiff resistance and on the day of the planning committee meeting in March 1982, 60 villagers travelled to County Hall and packed the public gallery. The application was refused on the basis of an inadequate approach road.

Hales Containers subsequently lodged an appeal, by which time ATAC had been dissolved and John Webber had left the area. The cudgels were taken up by the Parish Council under its chairman, Roger Sawtell, and at the last minute Hales Containers withdrew their appeal.

The menace continued to hang over the village with the threat from Hales Containers that it would be back. In 1989 there were two tragic drownings in the lakes and calls for RMC to fill them in; and in 1999 reopening as a working brickpit was proposed, with the prospect of huge modern lorries passing through the village. In 2001 building started on the site which is being turned into a landscaped housing estate, The Mulberries, and a nature reserve.

### The Oak Trees in Village Street

In 2001 a large branch fell from one of the two oak trees in the garden of Glebe Cottages and the owners, the church commissioners, consulted a leading tree expert who said that the trees should be felled. A number of villagers led by Nina Ziegler, Peter Gibbs of Marelands along with Chris and Louise Jones from Hatchetts felt that as the trees were such important

*Newdigate Rights of Way Group, 14 April 1988.
Diana Salisbury receives an award of £250 from
Pat Lucas of Shell UK.* Watching, left to right:
*Ann Baldwin, Jean Sherman and Janet Hogg.*

landmarks further advice should be sought. An independent expert gave a different opinion and said that the trees could be saved if they were properly managed.

However, the church commissioners would not alter their stance, so early on Monday, 22 October 2001, the day scheduled for the felling, many villagers turned up in force to protest and to obstruct the tree surgeons. Vans were parked under the trees and a tea and coffee table was set up in anticipation of a long stay. Lorna Doubtfire, of Badger Park in Parkgate Road, a veteran CND and Ban-the-Bomb campaigner, brought a chair and sat on the footpath – 'I will not be moved'.

The police arrived in an attempt to allow the contractors to do their 'legal work', but news came through that the church commissioners had agreed to a compromise. The trees were to be considerably reduced but not felled, and the protest ended.

### Agriculture in the Twenty-First Century

Paul Bailey farmed at Oaklands Park. His father Gordon was brought up there by Captain and Mrs Palmer and farmed at Oaklands Park from the Second World War until his death in 1973. He was a great stamp collector and after he sold his collection he bought Ivy House Farm with the proceeds. He was never able to accept the dramatic changes made by Gatwick Airport and resented the intrusion caused by aircraft noise until the day he died. Paul now paints a dismal picture of modern-day farming in Surrey and is unable to see a light at the end of the tunnel. Following the opening of the golf course on farmland between Newdigate and Rusper the area does not need a second golf course so there are, he believes, only two alternatives: to open farmland for pleasure activities such as riding, clay-pigeon shooting and paint-ball games, or to plant fast-growing trees for fuel.

On 3 September 2003, the Crutcher family will have farmed New House Farm for 100 years. Tony Crutcher describes his life:

*I grow oats and make hay as a cash crop. I have tried linseed, flax and hemp as politically introduced industrial crops and I apply for the subsidies available to underwrite the growing costs.*

*My wife's support, and her input as a horticulturalist growing bedding plants and hanging baskets, and her ability to manage the farm books, are a substantial contribution to the farm.*

*The farm buildings no longer house livestock. I have a cabinet-maker in the cowshed, a scaffolder in the silage pit, a sail-maker in the old dairy, a storage unit in the Granary Meadow, a model-aeroplane-flying club uses Kemp's Meadow, and an equestrian toll rides around the headland of the fields. I am a rent collector on the first of the month, which allows me to play on my tractor and enjoy the farm.*

*What will happen in the future and will my children carry on with the farm? I don't know! My ego is fuelled by the thought that maybe my family will continue to live and farm at New House Farm. I feel I have a duty and a desire to pass on the land to the next keeper in better heart than when I began.*

*The hunt meets at the Six Bells.*

*Bill Kear, with his hounds, outside the Six Bells in 1995.*

*The late Jim Crutcher at New House Farm.*

*Charlie Frost's steam-traction engine in 1987. Joy Smith and son Mike are at the controls.*

Charlie Frost farms at Dean House Farm and although his diverse business is generally successful he is confronted with two major problems – people and bureaucracy:

*I find golf and cricket balls on the field adjoining Parkgate Road which can be lethal to animals eating grass or silage. Every Saturday people come to the farm to train their dogs to do tracking, but other dog walkers do not stick to the footpaths, and this spoils the dog trainers' enjoyment. Also dogs running loose not only scare the livestock but in the months from April to June they destroy the breeding cycle of country animals. I appeal for people to give more thought to the consequences of their actions.*

*It is becoming increasingly difficult to have a land use that is profitable, and beef, dairy, sheep and cereals are not viable. The only crop that has shown a profit has been the Christmas trees. Form filling and office work are not farmers' favourite pastimes, and I would rather be in the fields working on crops or animals, even though it's at a loss. Perhaps with the diversity of interests within my business the profits of one will offset the losses of another and I can enjoy and remain at Dean House Farm.*

## 60 Years of Agriculture
### By Pearl and Alec Bourhill of Horsielands Farm

*In 1942 big dairy herds, housed in cow stalls, were milked by machine but 'finished' by hand, although many smaller herds were still milked by hand. Milk was strained through muslin, then run over a corrugated water-cooler into churns. The machines and churns were sterilised in a steam chest or just scrubbed out. The average cow gave two gallons of milk.*

*A lot of labour was needed to make hay into stacks or cocks; corn had long stalks of straw, harvested with a binder into stooks which were stood up against one another in groups by hand (and were often full of* thistles). *They were then made into corn ricks and thatched until threshed in the autumn by a threshing machine worked by a tractor or steam engine. Tractors were replacing horses. Silage (grass stacked in concrete towers) was for winter feed and mangolds were chopped by a hand-turned crusher, as were sheets of compressed linseed to make gruel for calves.*

*After the war, food was in such short supply that great strides were made to build bigger tractors and, with the combine harvester, fields needed to be larger. With research for heavier corn crops, straw became shorter and sprays were introduced to combat weeds and pests. In the 1960s artificial insemination did much to improve milk yields and the use of antibiotics improved the animals' health; pigs were able to have more litters a year and chickens could be kept in cages. Electric fencing controlled the cows' grazing, so a good living could be had from a small acreage.*

*The small farmers' scheme started by the Government in the late 1960s helped many farmers to build milking parlours, enabling one man to milk more cows. The milk was pumped into a refridgerated tank for cooling and was collected by tanker. Buildings were constructed for loose housing beef, or cubicles for cows to lay down on straw beds or foam mattresses. Winter feed was given by tractor into troughs and as cows were eating the silage, less hay was being made. Later silage would be stored in large plastic-covered round bales.*

*In the 1970s and '80s, with the media promoting dieting, less fat was needed so Channel Island cattle (high in butter fat) were replaced with Fresians and our native beef breeds crossed wth continental breeds.*

*Nowadays people are more interested in where their food has come from and how it is produced. Some farmers are going organic, but with low world prices and the stranglehold of supermarkets, farmers are diversifying; turning farm buildings into offices or craft centres, setting up play areas, selling local produce, etc. The big farms are having to expand. The computer is now essential in the milking parlour to regulate feed, and in the office, to enable farmers to keep up with increasing requirements to record everything from pedigrees to costings.*

*Although help is given to hill farmers and there are subsidies for some crops, the small farm is no longer viable. Farms will need to cooperate to survive as I think subsidies will go. Farming is no longer 'a way of life', but a business.*

The problems of the modern-day farmer would be familiar to Thomas Duncomb over 200 years ago.

## The Capel Incinerator

An early-twenty-first-century proposal to build a large incinerator at the Clock House Works, Capel has met with huge opposition from all the surrounding villages. The plan is to dispose of enormous quantities of waste, largely generated in the north of the county, and transported by about 70 lorries per day through the county and down the A24. The County Council refused two other incinerators, but approved that at Capel, despite the 'proximity principle' that waste should be disposed of as close as possible to where it is generated. The plans were referred to Westminster, but regarded as a local issue and returned.

## The Proposed Second Runway at Gatwick

Perhaps the biggest worry for villagers is the possibility of a second runway at Gatwick Airport. The plans proposed in 1993 saw the end of the runway pointing at the parish like the barrel of a shotgun, with aircraft taking off and landing close to the parish border at Cudworth.

Private flying started at Hunts Farm in Tinsley Green in 1930, and in 1936 the site was opened as Gatwick Airport. It was enlarged during the Second World War but still had grass runways when the Government announced in 1952 that 'it had decided to develop Gatwick as a southern alternative to London Airport... ' (*Hansard*, 30 July 1952). Building demolished over 60 homes including the village of Lowfield Heath. The airport was opened in June 1958.

If a second runway to the north of the existing one were to be built this would result in Charlwood, including the Norman church of St Nicholas and a wealth of historic buildings, being sandwiched between the existing airport and the new runway. A huge cutting through Stan Hill would dwarf that which was driven through Twyford Down in Hampshire. Brendon Sewill from the Gatwick Area Conservation Campaign (GACC) explained that a northern runway would result in aircraft flying over Newdigate every 70 seconds at a height of 1,000 feet.

Under an existing legal agreement a new runway cannot be built until August 2019 and the latest consultation document issued by the Government in July 2002 does not include Gatwick for further expansion, but the story is far from over.

*Protests against second runway, 1992.*

*Protest in Newdigate against the expansion at Gatwick Airport, 1980.*

*Charles Thompson receiving the Best Kept Village Award in 1985.*

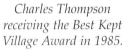

*A different kind of challenge. On New Year's Day 1999 a few hardy souls swam around the moat at Cudworth Manor. Left to right: Nick Rogers, Dai Fraser, ?, ?, Tony Ivey, David Callcut, Paul Hartt, ?.*

**Right and far right:** *The wall painting of St Christopher that dated from about 1470 was destroyed when the north aisle was added in 1876/7.*

Above: *St Peter's Church prior to restoration, c.1870.*

*The west end showing the gallery rail which is now stored in the base of the tower. Painting by J. Hassell in 1828.*

Above: *St Peter's Church, c.1910.*

Right: *The church interior in the 1930s.*

Chapter 8

# INSTITUTIONS & ORGANISATIONS

## St Peter's Church
### By Joyce Banks

### The Fabric

Although there is probably a small core of twelfth-century work hidden in the walls, the earliest dateable features of the church are from c.1200 when it consisted of a chancel, nave and south aisle. The triplet of lancets in the east window of the chancel and the two single lancets to the north and south of it are from this date. The two-light window and the 'Priest's Door' in the chancel wall were installed about 50 years later. All these were heavily restored in 1876–7 together with the upper parts of the east and south chancel walls, although reuse of original materials was insisted upon.

Building stone is rare in the clay soil of the Weald so it had to be transported from outside the area. There is 'paludina' limestone which was probably quarried at Stanhill, Tilgate sandstone from a small quarry about a mile north-east of the church, Bargate stone which outcrops near Halesbridge, and some fragments of iron pan from the plateau gravel at Henfold. Some Reigate stone also appears, and even puddingstone, a dark-coloured conglomerate.

In the early-fourteenth century the south aisle was extended to form the Cudworth Chapel whose two-light window and piscina are also of this date. The south pier of the chancel was pierced and a jamb of the 'Priests Door' cut away to make a squint, giving a view of the high altar. The south aisle is narrow and therefore early, and the massive pier opposite the south door has diagonal tooling. This, and its shape and size, indicate that it was built no later than the east end of the chancel. The pier is therefore a survival from before the arcade was remodelled in the

*The interior prior to the addition of the chancel screen, c.1900. Note the hanging brass lamps.*

fifteenth century; its octagonal capital was added then. On the side facing the door, its surface has been flattened, perhaps to hold the holy-water stoup mentioned in the inventories of 1547–53. There are also deep holes where a chained bible was attached, and a collection of incised crosses. Before the north aisle was added in 1876–7 there was a painting of St Christopher on the north wall, probably dating from about 1470 when there was a cult of this saint in England. However, this was later whitewashed, and only rediscovered in 1859. The north side of the chancel, which was not rebuilt in 1876–7, showed signs of an earlier disturbance and patching prior to the building of the vestry, so perhaps it was connected with the removal of St Margaret's Chapel, mentioned in the wills of the Newdigate family and described in 1521 as 'in the churchyard of Newdigate'. However, George Horley (church-warden 1923–74) maintained that foundations, possibly of the chapel, were found when the flagstaff was erected in 1947. The chancel roof was constructed of trussed rafters until 1876, when it was replaced by the present one, which differs only slightly in form. The early-medieval nave roof remains, with three tie-beams, one supporting a post under a collar, and was left exposed after the Victorian restoration.

The great oak tower was probably built at the end of the fourteenth century or the beginning of the fifteenth. This is the church's most distinctive feature and only one other in Surrey (Burstow) has a similar plan and is wholly built of timber. Its total height is 60 feet. The tower has three square storeys surmounted by an octagonal spire, its main weight being carried by four great oak timbers, 16 to 17 inches square and 11 feet apart, each standing on a massive slab of wood. The aisle which runs outside them also serves as a buttress, and between the main

103

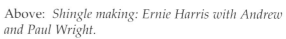

Above: *Shingle making: Ernie Harris with Andrew and Paul Wright.*

Left: *St Peter's Church and the new war memorial, 1921.*

Below left: *St Peter's Church in the 1990s.*

Below: *Re-shingling in 1981.*

posts is an elaborate system of cross-bracing. Smaller upright timbers surround the ground floor and are set only 6 to 7 inches apart. This lowest section is covered externally with weatherboarding, the sloping part above with oak shingles. Above these are the weatherboarded belfry and shingled spire. The number of bells was increased from five to six in 1805 and the clock commemorates Queen Victoria's diamond jubilee in 1897. The belfry has served at different times as a temporary vestry, robing place for clergy, Sunday school, and a resting place for the parish chest and the carved front of the former gallery.

The church was often described as being dank and dilapidated and in 1857 the curate, the Revd Samuel Mayhew, said it was colour-washed an unseemly red. The population of the village was increasing, and in 1873 an architect, T.E.C. Streatfeild, submitted plans for renovations and the addition of a north aisle. The work was carried out in 1876–7 at a cost of £2,100. The north arcade was built to correspond with the south one, the original north windows copied, and some of their glass reset. This meant the destruction of the wall painting, already 'much obliterated'. The gallery was removed, and the chest and its records moved to the 'Cudworth Pew'.

The south porch and brick vestry were demolished and the present porch built. A new vestry was added north of the chancel with an entrance from the new north aisle, and the old door on the south of the chancel closed. The two dormer windows (1627) and the pulpit of 1626 (which stood in the north-east angle of the nave) were removed, as were all the old pews which were 'much decayed'. The older parts of the church were re-covered with Horsham stone in 1876–7.

Mrs Ellen Janson donated the present pulpit and chancel screen in 1906 and her carving class presented the church with the pew ends and other items, including the communion table in the Cudworth Chapel in memory of the former headmaster Henry Hackwood, who died in 1915. Also in 1906, the organ, by W. Hill & Sons, was presented in memory of Sir Henry Tyler MP of High Trees.

In September 1876 the stone slab marking the burial place of William de Newdigate was taken up, and is now set in the floor of the tower in the south side.

The kneelers were worked by local people, in memory of George Horley and to celebrate the 800th anniversary of the church in 1975. Shortly afterwards David Crump, a local craftsman, made the plain communion table from a single piece of 4-inch-thick oak, together with the cross and the candlesticks.

In 1989 an extension to the vestry, including kitchen and toilet facilities, was built. A stone fragment from Cologne Cathedral, presented by a male-voice choir from Vogelsang who regularly exchanged visits with the Beare Green and Newdigate Choral Society, has been incorporated into the extension.

## Memorials

Many churches boast a fine selection of marble tablets dating from the eighteenth and early-nineteenth century, but Newdigate during that period was wretchedly poor and there are very few memorials of any description.

Just behind the font is a lead plaque engraved in Latin to the effect that:

*Here lieth Margaret, daughter of Edward Gage (of Firle, Sussex) wife of Henry Darell of Scotney (Kent), owner of the ironworks at Ewood from 1553. She lived always in the Holy Catholic church and died, aged 58, 22nd August 1616.*

On the south wall of the chancel is a brass plate which says:

*Here lieth ye body of Joane, daughter of Thomas Smallpiece and late ye wife of George Steere, Parson of the parish. She died Dec. 7 An. Dom. 1634 and expecteth a blessed resurrection.*

Elizabeth, the wife of a later rector, has a marble tablet on the north wall of the chancel. The reference in the inscription, 'Transported from her native soil...' is to the fact that she was the daughter of a merchant of Königsberg. She married William Bickerton, rector 1725–40, and in 1734 was 'buried in the chancel within the rails about the middle' according to the register.

On the south wall of the Cudworth Chapel is a tablet to Richard Morton who lived at Ewood from about 1733, and his wife Mary (née Ede of Cudworth).

More modern memorials include a bronze plaque to Henry Caporn (d.1951) on the north side of the chancel, a brass plate commemorating Lancelot Studdert Kennedy, rector 1869–99, and a memorial to the members of the Herron family killed in action. The ashes of John William Ward, rector 1927–37, were interred in the sanctuary in the year following his death and a tablet in the chancel floor commemorates him.

## Font

This dates from 1877 when it replaced a plain stone one which stood in front of the tower. The present font was formerly nearer the south door.

## Chest

This has been hollowed out of an oak log. Such 'dug out' chests are difficult to date, because although typical ones date from before the thirteenth century when the art of joinery developed, they continued to be made as late as the fifteenth century. It was originally used for the safe keeping of the parish records and treasury and it has the traditional three locks –

The late Gladys Caporn opening the rectory fête in 1980. She had attended every fête since 1946. She is accompanied by Tony Watts and Dorothy Parker.

Newdigate rectory, demolished in 1880.

Dancing the 'Spider's Web' on the rectory lawn.

Newdigate rectory in 1828 from a painting by J. Hassell.

Harvest Procession in 1990.

one key was held by the rector and one each by the churchwardens.

## Silver

A paten and a silver bell-shaped cup on a short thick stem were made by Anthony Nelme of Ave Maria Lane in London in 1699–1700. Both have a contemporary engraved design of the cross, nails and IHS within a star, and the cup has an early-nineteenth-century inscription, 'Newdigate Rectory', on the other side of the bowl. A silver-plated flagon and paten were given in memory of Elizabeth Pocock in 1886 and a solid-silver chalice and paten by William Farnell Watson in 1893. The unusual seventeenth-century 'alms bason' was probably originally used for eating or drinking. The bowl is round with a slight lip and stands on a flat base – it could be of German or Swedish manufacture. In 1848 the rural dean reported the presence of 'a silver bowl for alms not produced in 1829'. A silver ciborium and a travelling three-piece communion set have been given in memory of former parishioners. The church plate is now in the vaults of Lloyds TSB Bank.

## Bells

The will of Alice Newdigate of 1489 mentions five bells and the inventory of church goods from 1553 lists 'four bells and a sacring bell'. There remained five bells until 1803 when Thomas Mears cast six new ones. These were recast by the Whitechapel Bell Foundry in 1969 and new bell ropes were made in 1985.

## Glass

When the church was being refurbished in 1876–7 the architect followed the trend to make the church more suitable for sacramental worship. Thus the clear windows were replaced with stained-glass windows, all made by the same firm, James Powell & Sons of Whitefriars. The company made its own high-quality coloured glass and a number of windows in the church can be attributed to Henry Holiday.

## The Churchyard

Until at least the beginning of the nineteenth century, Newdigate shared the Wealden tradition that owners of land were liable for the upkeep of the church fence in proportion to the size of their properties. By 1883 the system had broken down.

In 1883 A. Ridley Bax made a collection of epitaphs from Surrey churches and in 1978–9 Jean Shelley and friends transcribed all the monumental inscriptions. Memorials to the Farnell-Watsons, the Goldbergs and Mrs Janson can be found, together with graves of well-known Newdigate families such as Weller, King, Butcher, Burberry, Lucas and Hopkins.

To the east of the path leading to the church is a memorial to Amos Morley of Dean House Farm:

*All you that pass this way along*
*Think how suddenly I was gone.*
*God does not all a warning give*
*Therefore be careful how you live.*

Two gravestones record misfortunes: Eliza Privett, killed in 1870 'by the discharge of a gun', and the brothers William and Spencer Lucas, killed when sinking a well at Boothlands in 1876.

The gates in the lych-gate were made by David Crump, and the flagstaff was given in 1947 by Col French in memory of his wife. The war memorial was made from Portland Stone in 1920 by Messrs Gilliam of Dorking to a design by J. Hatchard Smith. The kerb was added in 1927 and the memorial rededicated in November 1948 when the brass plates of those fallen in both wars replaced the earlier First World War inscriptions.

The grass in the churchyard is kept neatly trimmed by Mick Hogg and his band of grass cutters and the flower-bed around the memorial is maintained by Dennis Buckle.

## The Shingles Project
### By Roger Sawtell

Following the hot summer of 1976 many of the oak shingles on the tower were curling and splitting, and it was decided that they must be replaced. The National Trust said that oak shingles were virtually unobtainable as the manufacturing skill had been lost, so advertisements were placed nationally seeking assistance.

A shingles-maker from Leicestershire was tracked down and he demonstrated his craft in early 1979. A total of £8,000 was raised in the parish, and help obtained from charitable trusts and the Department of the Environment. One of Dr Bill Wheeler's oak trees was felled and cut into logs, and local craftsmen Paul and Andrew Wright made some shingles. This crude feasibility study gave them the confidence to encourage the shingle-maker to come down from Leicestershire with his wife for a week in May 1979. Ernie Harris taught the Wright brothers his skills and gave them some of his tools and equipment.

The art of cleaving shingles from oak is that the cleaver follows the grain of the wood and does not cut across the fibres as with a saw. Following the grain gives the shingles a stable and waterproof quality. With oak that means splitting on the radius. The tree must have at least a 2-metre girth and a straight, branch-free stem. Logs the length of the shingle (30 centimeters) are split into eight cheese-like wedges, and the centre point and curved sapwood cleaved off. The remaining block is only roughly square but the cleaver is able to divide it, always splitting in the middle to equalise the pressure. The shingle, about a centimetre thick and 11 centimetres wide, is finished off with a draw-knife.

The Wright brothers needed to maintain their

*Newdigate rectory, c.1900.*

*John Buckner LLD, rector of Newdigate 1789–98.*

*Revd Hugh Nelson-Ward, rector 1899–1906.*

*St Peter's Church Choir in 1993.* Left to right, back row: *Mollie Posner, Anne Tyrrell, Vera Monk, Brian Hounsfield, Hugh Eller, Charles Manchester (rector), Alan Posner, Peter Monk, Jane Steel, Clyde Wallace, Diana Salisbury, Roy Mackintosh, Anne Stephens;* front: *Tina Callcut, Kathy Bettesworth, Janet Brearley, Gill Mackintosh, Colina Livingstone (organist), Rosemary Thompson, Olive Cloke, Barbara Peake and Helen Sloane.*

*Revd J.W. Ward, rector 1927–37, with Mrs French in March 1937.*

*Revd Dennis Parker, rector 1970–87.*

bread-and-butter activities, so shingles had to take second place. Creditably they maintained their enthusiasm, and completed 12,000–16,000 shingles in six years using 12 oak trees.

The Newdigate Shingles Project provoked much sympathetic interest and support, notably from Alec Clifton-Taylor, whose BBC television series was then being shown. *The Sunday Times* supplement featured the project and Bob Danvers-Walker recorded a BBC programme. This publicity helped with the fund-raising and the generosity of past and present residents, a City Livery Company, two charitable trusts concerned with the preservation of buildings of historical interest and a top-up from the Department of the Environment ensured that the necessary funds were raised.

The steeplejack who mounted all the shingles, Peter Harknett, remarked that it must be unique in the twentieth century for a church spire to be clad in shingles made in the village by village craftsmen from village oak trees.

## The Rectory

A Tudor rectory was probably built during the incumbency of Matthew Belle (1507–38). In 1829 the rural dean reported that 'The Glebe House is in bad condition' and a candidate for the living in 1855 refused it 'in consequence of the badness of the Glebe House'. The Revd L. Studdert-Kennedy replaced this 'almost ruinous house' in 1880 by the building now known as the 'Old Rectory', which has been used as a residential home for elderly people and has been converted into apartments called Medlars Court. A tithe barn once stood in its front garden, which much later was the setting for an annual fête with maypole dancing by the schoolchildren. The present rectory was built in 1975.

## Records

The earliest Parish Register contains baptisms 1560–1705, marriages 1565–1705 and burials 1559–1705. A note among the baptisms in 1627–8 records the erection of the gallery and other work on the church. At the end of the second volume is a list of briefs (1686–91) containing details of collections made to relieve distress caused by fire and misfortune, including such distant places as Thirsk and Morpeth; there is one for the relief of French Protestants in 1686 and another for Irish Protestants in 1691. Much later an entry details a contribution towards the relief of suffering following the Indian Mutiny of 1857.

## Changing Times within the Church

There were great religious changes during the Tudor period and the Dissolution of the Monasteries affected Newdigate in that the living passed to the Crown where it has remained. The injunction of 1547 condemned pictures and most lights in church, a copy of the Great Bible had to be placed in churches and the

Gospel and Epistle had to be read in English. The 1549 Proclamations abolished images and the Act of Uniformity enforced the use of the new Prayer Book in English. The wall-painting of St Christopher was probably whitewashed at this time. John Morgan was dispossessed of the living during the reign of Mary Tudor when Roman rites were reintroduced, but he returned in 1558. Not everyone accepted the reformed church; the Darrels of Ewood ironworks, among others, were fined for recusancy, and one branch of the Newdigate family remained Roman Catholics.

The incumbency of George Steere (1610–60) covered the whole of the Civil War and Cromwellian Commonwealth; the wars left Newdigate virtually untouched. Steere was a Puritan by inclination but John Bonwicke who succeeded him had fought for the Royalist cause. He noted in the register: 'King Charles II was crowned at Westminster on St George's Day, who God grant long to reign.'

The eighteenth century was a time of poverty among the population, with absentee rectors and ill-paid curates, and this situation continued into the early part of the nineteenth century.

With the increasing population the church was enlarged and renovated. The Revd Lancelot Studdert-Kennedy, who held the living from 1869–99 and was the uncle of 'Woodbine Willy' of First World War fame, supervised the changes.

The 'newcomers' who came to live in the village before and after 1900 included a number of benefactors to the church, and pews and heating were renovated. The 1930s saw an increase in the congregation and the Revd J.W. Ward was particularly remembered for his stirring sermons. By the 1950s the Revd Bruce-Walker was much concerned about falling church attendance, but as the century progressed so people returned.

In 1977, a group of 60 volunteers repainted the church using a traditional limewash, the recipe for which is pasted in the back of the churchwardens' log-book.

The Friends of St Peter's (St Peter's Trust) which ensures that finances are available to maintain the fabric of the church was first registered as a charity (278650) on 17 September 1979. The first formal meeting was attended by Roger Sawtell (chairman), Charles Thompson (treasurer), David Newbery (secretary), Eddie Atkinson and Alan Posner, with apologies for absence from Derek Brearley. The stated objects of the trust are:

*... promoting the permanent preservation of the church of St Peter's, Newdigate as a place of religious worship and of its fixtures, fittings, furnishings, ornaments and churchyard and in furtherance thereof, but not otherwise, repairing, maintaining, lighting, heating, insuring, restoring, replacing, improving, extending, fitting, equipping and furnishing the same respectively when and so often as may be required.*

The value of the Trust Fund and Income Fund combined is £95,000 and the trust receives support from covenants, bequests and donations, which should enable both funds to grow steadily. The current trustees are Derek Brearley (chairman), John Humphreys (treasurer), Gerry Mitchell (church-warden), David Newbery (churchwarden), Michael Young (secretary) and Jeffrey Risk.

In 2002, a wide range of services suits all tastes and the children's services and associated worship groups are well attended. Church-related activities flourish. A Newcomers' Party is organised and a successful and enjoyable fête is held in the school. The Mothers' Union remains extremely active and work with the young continues with Explorers, Youth House Groups and a Youth Club developed from an organisation started by George Green in the 1950s. The Steere and Booth Foundation has continued its support of the school, including for example the Literacy Scheme, and has offered small grants to needy students. The choir sings at weddings, funerals and regular services and the Luncheon Club, for over-60s who live alone, thrives. The church is deeply involved in the life of the community, not only in Newdigate but, through Dorking Deanery Synod and Churches Together in Dorking, in surrounding parishes and Dorking itself. Following the departure of Christopher Blissard-Barnes in 2001 the Benefice of Newdigate was suspended and plans put in hand to establish a Team Ministry covering Capel, Holmwood and Newdigate. The Revd Andrew Coe has been appointed Priest in Charge/Team Rector Designate.

The church's mission:

*St Peter's Church aims to be a welcoming and caring community, growing in the knowledge and love of God and sharing his love with others in Newdigate and beyond, trusting in the authority of Scripture, the guidance of the Holy Spirit, and the power of prayer.*

*Revd Henry G. Bird MA, rector 1913–21, arriving with his chauffeur, Bob Saggars, at a Scout Jambouree in 1912. Did these include Newdigate Scouts? Unfortunately records do not go back that far.*

## Rectors of Newdigate

Ranulf (or Ralph) de Brok c.1271–c.1285
Matthew Bell mentioned 1291 and 131–?
Nicholas de Oxonia 1313
Thomas Salmon 1464
Hugh ? 1465–88
William Goldesmyth 1488–1506
Matthew Belle 1507–38
John Bavande 1538–42
Philip Mesmer 1542–47
John Morgan 1547–54 & 1558–76
Henry George 1554–58
William Lawe 1567–93
Gerard Williamson MA 1593–1610
George Steere MA 1610–60
John Bonwicke 1660–98
Andrew Cranston 1699–1709
Samuel Billingsley 1709–25
William Bickerton 1725–40
David Campbell LLD 1740–76
George Allen 1776–87
Henry Jackson Close 1787–89

John Buckner LLD 1789–98
Henry Woodcock 1798–99
William Langford 1799–1814
Henry John Ridley 1814–25
Charles V.H. Sumner 1825–34
John Young LLD 1834–52
Henry A. Sugden MA 1852–68
L. Studdert-Kennedy MA 1869–99
Hugh H.E. Nelson Ward 1899–1906
William Noble MA 1906–09
F.O. Sutton MA, LLB 1909–13
Henry G. Bird MA 1913–21
J.M. La F. McAnally 1921–27
J.W. Ward 1927–37
Albert Stone 1937–45
Donald Bruce-Walker 1945–61
John Cunningham 1962–70
Dennis Parker 1970–87
Charles Manchester 1988–93
Christopher Blissard-Barnes MA 1994–2001
Andrew Coe 2002–

# Other Places of Worship

### The Congregational Chapel

The Risbridger family were Nonconformists and in the early 1800s Joseph Risbridger, whose brother John built the chapel at nearby Gadbrook, became the tenant at Gaterounds. His son, another Joseph, held evening services in the house. In about 1876 Charles Shearman, assisted by several other young men from the Dorking Congregational Church, held open-air services at Parkgate during the summer.

In 1880 a sympathetic resident invited the workers to hold their meetings at Sot's Hole (now Partridge Cottage). As more space became necessary, a larger room was taken under the granary at High Trees Farm. Here there were numerous conversions and the work grew apace. Then opposition began to appear, the room had to be closed, and the work for a short time discontinued.

Soon one of the converts threw open his cottage in Broad Lane and the work was resumed with renewed vigour, and much success. Frequently the parlour, kitchen and staircase were crowded, and 'the power of the Lord was present to heal'.

After much prayer, land was procured in Broad Lane and, largely through the kindness and energy of Mr J. Todman of Dorking, an iron mission hall with vestry attached was purchased from a catalogue in kit form and erected. The opening services were held on 2 June 1885. The first sermon was preached by the Revd Newman Hall LLB and in the evening a large and enthusiastic meeting, presided over by General Sir Arthur Cotton, was addressed by the Revds J.S. Bright, G.J. Adeney and others. Evangelists were appointed and one of them, Gabriel Woodward, remained active for 13 years from 1888–1901. The Manse was built for his occupancy.

In addition to the Sunday services, other forms of worship were offered, including Sunday school, weekly meetings, prayer meetings and Bible classes. Later, numbers diminished and the chapel, also known as the Jubilee Hall and colloquially as the 'Tin Tabernacle', was closed in the early 1960s. It remains empty in 2002.

### Morphew's Mission

Mr and Mrs Morphew were Nonconformist missionaries in China, and moved to Ockley Lodge in the 1930s. They are said to have taken a mission building with them wherever they went, and in Newdigate it was erected in the field opposite the Forge Garage, which became known as Chapel Field. It was apparently removed in the 1940s when they left the district.

# Newdigate Schools

The school was endowed in 1660 by the Revd George Steere when he had completed 50 years as rector of Newdigate and was 82 years old. In his will, written a year later, he states:

*I leave the Parish of Newdigate forever, a School house, which be built upon part of the land called 'Clarke' for the teaching of young persons at and in the said School house, and not for a place of habitation for any person or*

*Left:  Morphew's Mission in Rusper Road in the 1930s.*

*Below:  The manse and the Congregational Chapel in Broad Lane, c.1905.*

Above and right:  *Early school records.*

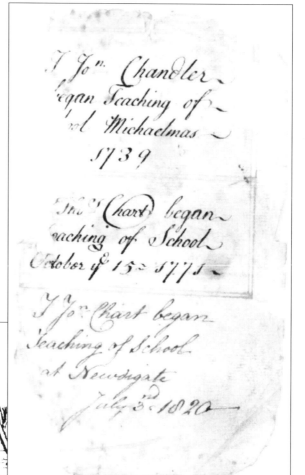

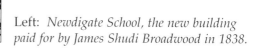

*Left:  Newdigate School, the new building paid for by James Shudi Broadwood in 1838.*

*persons, and to be maintained by the parish for such use, and I charge my other lands with an annual payment of £6.13s.4d. for the catechizing, teaching and instruction in reading, writing and other good learning forever of four young persons, born in the parish, sons of goodly parents.*

The number of children was increased to seven in 1681 when George Booth left £100 'for and towards the schooling, educating and teaching of three poor children in the parish of Newdigate in the School house'. After improvements in the management of the endowment the income was increased, and the schoolmaster Thomas Chart agreed to teach nine children in 1771. By 1794 there were 18 pupils. (The good works of Steere and Booth are continued today through the Steere and Booth Foundation which supports the school and its pupils.)

John Chandler was headmaster from 1739 until he died in 1771. Over the following 139 years to 1910, except for five years, the headmastership of the school was held by only three men, all related. Thomas Chart held the position for 49 years until 1820, and the following examples of problems set in school in 1817 are from his book:

*If a Footman travell 250 miles in 9 Dayes, when the day is 9 hours long, I demand how many days he may travel 830 miles when ye Dayes are 14 hours long.*

*4 Gills make 1 pint; 8 pints make 1 Gallon; 63 Gallons make 1 Hogshead; 2 Hogsheads make 1 Butt or Pipe; and 4 Hogsheads make 1 Sun. How many Gills in 97 Suns, 2 Hogsheads, 62 Gallons and 7 Pints?*

Thomas Chart ends his book thus:

*I Could have been more Large on each Rule, and proceeded to the rule of Loss and Gain, Discount and Rebate, Alligations of both natures. The Doctrine of Vulgar Fractions, and Decimals. The Mensuration of Surfaces and Solids; also Geometry and Trigonometry; Algebra and Merchants Accompts; but my time and paper will not permitt.*

This must have come as something of a relief to his pupils!

He was followed by his grandson, John Chart, who remained at the school for 47 years until 1867 when he became a trustee of the new governing body. His family lived at a house called Loampits on the site now occupied by Oakfield House.

In 1830 there were 18 pupils in the school whose education was provided for by the endowment. The first admission register was set up before any grants were given; two of the trustees were Mr Isaac Hayler and Mr John Burberry, and the names of the children were:

| For One Year | For Two Years | For Three Years |
|---|---|---|
| William Weller | Ellen Gad | Mary Tugwell |
| Alexander Tidy | Maria Gad | Louisa Lucas |
| Edward Gad | Peter Smith | John Weller-Hill |
| Adah Kempshall | Fred Weller | Mary Weller |
| Harriott Elliott | Peter Hopkins | William Banks |
| Tamah Weller | Austin Tidy | Peter Taylor |

Out of a total of 159 days' possible attendances Tamah Weller made 153 days but Austin Tidy only put in 22 days, as did William Banks. The children paid no fee and only stayed at school for three years.

The original school had fallen into decay and in 1838 a new school was erected thanks to the generosity of James Shudi Broadwood of Lyne. There were still 18 free places but from 1839 the headmaster also took in children who paid and this continued until 1872. By 1846 there was also a National School and two Dame Schools.

John Chart died in 1878 at the age of 79; a window in the south aisle of the church is in his memory.

Christopher Search was appointed headmaster in 1867 at a salary of £35 per year, and in 1870 the First Education Act was passed, giving local school boards the power to compel all children between the ages of five and ten years to attend school.

In 1872 the old schoolhouse, on the site of the present George Horley Place, was demolished and a new school built in its place. The Charity Commissioners stated that the new building cost £1,100; the Steere and Booth charity provided £800, and the sale of a school building, now the Old Post Office, £200. During this period the children had their lessons in the downstairs rooms of the Old Post Office whilst the scholars of the Dame School continued with their studies upstairs. According to the 1871 census Melina Rudd, a widow, was described as 'governess of the girls' school' and later that year she married Christopher Search. In 1873 all the children from both schools moved to the new building, which became known as Newdigate Endowed Church of England School.

In December 1872, Henry Ferdinand Hackwood, who was born in Portobello near Wolverhampton, was appointed headmaster at a commencing salary of £75 per annum. He was assisted by a sewing mistress, Miss K. Chart, a pupil teacher, Miss Blanche Chart, and a monitor. The syllabus was reading, writing, arithmetic, religious instruction and sewing. The free places were abolished and all children had to pay 3d. per week, except where there were three in one family when the fees were 3d., 2d. and 1d.

The first register of the new school showed that 63 children came from the old school and 35 from the Dame School, so 98 children were taught by Mr Hackwood and his assistants! An annual inspection took place – an occasion of great trepidation.

Children had to help on the land, and as this was a poor agricultural community all hands were

*Schoolchildren in 1875.*

*The Schoolhouse (1872–1965) with headmaster, Henry Hackwood, by the entrance.*

*Charles Brackley with the pupils at Newdigate Place lakes in the 1920s.*

*Henry Ferdinand Hackwood, headmaster 1873–1910. He used a quill pen and wrote s in the old-fashioned way as f.*

*The School and Dean House Farm Cottages, c.1930. Violet Buckman, later Higgs, is leaning against the fence.*

needed to gather the harvest on which everyone's livelihood depended. The children's small wages added to each family's income and this was more important than education. Thus each June and July Mr Hackwood recorded such items as 'several away haying'. The harvest was during September but sometimes in October children were absent to go 'acorn picking' to feed the family pig.

Sickness among the children was a continuing problem. Each year there was the usual incidence of colds and 'flu, often affecting many at a time. Most cottages were cold, damp and insanitary, and children walked to school in all weathers in inadequate clothing. More serious were the epidemics of all the usual children's diseases – whooping cough, measles, German measles, chicken pox, mumps and diphtheria. These were treated with caution and sometimes the school was closed for a period.

*Newdigate School in 1894.*

Many of the children had to walk long distances to school and there are accounts of low attendances due to 'snow being 3 feet deep', 'several great floods in the Parish', 'roads all flooded, school closed'. In 1891 all school fees were abolished under the Free Education Act and in 1898 the three-term system was instigated and the curriculum emphasis changed towards English and Geography.

In 1895 gypsies were a common sight in Newdigate and sometimes 30 caravans gathered near Cider Mill. The boys would rush from school along the Cudworth Lane to see them and listen to their wonderful stories. One day there was a fight outside the Surrey Oaks Inn between two gypsies, Manny Gobi and Doc Brazil. It lasted for three hours and quite a crowd gathered to watch. Numbers of tramps used to come along the road from Horsham to Dorking and the local boys often hid behind hedges and greeted them with fusilades of stones. Some of these tramps became well known and had such names as 'Happy Jack', 'Soldier Dick', and 'Willy Wicks'.

When the children were 11 years old they could leave school if they passed a special leavers' examination. If they failed, they had to stay for another year. Some qualified to go to Dorking High School, but that meant walking a long way.

Before 1900 it was the habit of the farmers to dress girls in red flannel underclothes and give the boys long soft-leather leggings which came right up to the waist.

By the end of 1904 the roll was 113 and the staff reduced to just two, Henry Hackwood and E.E.M.

Rusbridge. A report stated, 'The Master has a large and difficult class and needs help.'

Mr Hackwood retired in 1910, shortly after the new infants' room was completed. Apart from his life as headmaster he had been a churchwarden since 1876, and a member of the church choir and assistant organist for many years; he possessed a splendid resonant baritone voice. He was chairman and treasurer to the Henry Smith Charity, collector of tithes and taxes, founder and secretary of the rifle club, secretary of the village institute and parliamentary chairman to all committees at general elections. He was always most courteous to those of his friends who were in opposition to him in politics. Meetings where he presided ended with the exhortation, 'Be straight, fear God, honour the King.' One of his great hobbies was woodcarving and after his death the members of the woodcarving club made the communion table in the Cudworth Chapel of St Peter's Church in his memory.

Mr John Steeds, a keen sportsman from Cranleigh, took up his duties as schoolmaster in 1910 at a salary of £104 per annum. He was assisted by three other members of staff and in 1911 instruction in woodworking, gardening and cookery was given for the first time.

On 14 January 1915 a biplane descended in the large grass field at the rear of the school and the whole school were allowed to go out to see it. The plane had run out of fuel and as soon as it was refilled it took off again. Following heavy snow in December 1916 attendances were very bad and parents were urged to get their children to school as they would be 'the men and women of the next generation'.

Mr Steeds spent part of the First World War in the Services, when the school was administered by a headmistress, and on his return in 1919 he resigned to take up a position in Ash.

The entry in the log on Charles Brackley's first day as headmaster in 1919 read, 'I took over duties today, but did not reach school until 2.30p.m. owing to the Railway Strike.' There were 103 children on the roll and the other members of staff were Miss Lawrence, Miss Archer and Miss Dynes.

Mr Brackley was a keen walker and in 1924 he took part in the traditional 'Beating of the Bounds', together with the rector and William Dean, but the distance of 18½ miles proved too much for the participants. The circuit was not completed, and it has not been attempted again.

Empire Day celebrations were always a highlight of the school's year and in 1920 the programme was:

*Unfurling the flag*
*Saluting*
*Song: 'Ye Mariners of England'*
*Address by Col Nicholls*
*Hymn*
*Vote of thanks to Col Nicholls and Capt. Evelyn*
*    Broadwood MC*
*The National Anthem*

Charles Brackley was interested in football and cricket, and his enthusiasm helped the school football team win the local Schools' League in 1920 and 1921. He took the children swimming in one of Mrs Janson's lakes, and in the summer gave some of them a fortnight's holiday on his houseboat on the Thames.

Mrs Minnie Elliott Palmer of Oaklands Park paid for a hot meal from November to March for all the schoolchildren who lived too far away to walk home for lunch. She built a kitchen behind the school and provided the boiler and utensils. Harriett Burberry was the cook. On Monday and Tuesday the children were given the choice of two different soups, Wednesday was 'meat pudding day', and Thursday and Friday were back to soup. Captain and Mrs Elliot Palmer were great benefactors to the village and the underprivileged in general. She was an eminent opera singer from America and her family were connected with Standard Oil and Pullman whose name was given to the luxury rail carriages. They gave generously to the Hoxton Market Mission in London and provided the schoolchildren with mackintoshes and sou'westers. When Mrs Palmer suffered a stroke, her husband bought a bath chair with a shaft together with a Shetland pony called Brownie that had been retired from a circus. This enabled her to continue seeing the grounds of Oaklands Park. She died on Derby Day in 1934, two years after her husband.

Picture opposite above: *Newdigate School Football Team, 1920–1.* Left to right, back row: *Jessie Burrows, ?, Charlie Burrows, Charles Brackley (headmaster), Harry Lucas, Fred Collinson;* centre: *John Tullett, Bob Carpenter, Dick Fowler, Charlie Spooner, Alf Tullett;* front: *Toby Spiller, Francis Potter, Bill Spooner, Chris Lucas.*

Opposite below: *School class, c.1921.* Left to right, back row: *Charles Brackley (headmaster), Elsie Tyler, Fred Collinson, Bob Carpenter;* fourth row: *Lily Bradshaw, Maggie Sparks, Bill Lucas, Dick Fowler;* third row: *Annie Richardson, Elsie Trow, Charlie Burrows, George Sparks;* second row: *Dolly Voice, Eunice Edwards, Bill Spooner, Alf Tullett;* front row: *Amy Edwards, Sophie Cheesman, Jack Tullett, Toby Spiller.*

On 29 October 1930 the log-book states: 'On this date, the village assembled to present to Mr C.H. Brackley, a beautiful mahogany upright piano as a parting gift.'

Miss de Voil and her assistants Miss Archer and Miss Ethel Dynes inherited a school of just 76 pupils.

The formal ceremony of the 'Crowning the May Queen' started at the school in 1931 thanks to the enthusiasm of Miss de Voil, although maypole dancing itself began in the village in 1910. Miss Broughton, the church organist, spent many evenings training the maypole dancers and the parish magazine reported, 'our own children had been beautifully drilled in the 'Plume Dance', which they executed with much grace.' John Ruskin, who believed in 'cherishing and developing the noblest type of manhood and womenhood, alike in beauty, intelligence, and in character', championed the art of maypole dancing and wrote:

*The girl chosen should have a strong character, strong to approve of what is right and to denounce wrong. She should be modest, unselfish and straightforward. If, with these attributes, she was pretty and graceful, so much the better, but character should be the test.*

Electric light was installed in the school in 1932. A year later the soup kitchen closed down, having served 4,758 dinners since 1924.

Miss de Voil resigned in 1934 and Mr C.F. Paine became headmaster. He tried to give the children a real interest in matters of the countryside, and soon the children started weaving. On 25 February 1939 Marion Milne, Brenda Beadle and Olive Pescud, all aged 13, went to the BBC and gave a broadcast describing their activities.

Boys still left school at the earliest opportunity and a contemporary report stated:

*The Admission Register shows that for some years now, there has been a considerable fluctuation in the school population. Since January 1934, 101 children have been admitted or readmitted. Of the 46 children who have left, five only have reached the legal age.*

In 1939 Mr Paine was appointed headmaster of Lingfield and Mr Gurr took over. An entry in the log-book records:

*Fraulein Elsa Hess and Fraulein Elsa Gebhardt, two young girls of the German Youth Movement, spent the last half hour this morning with Class 1, dancing and singing German folk music.*

This was on 27 July 1939, only a few weeks before the outbreak of war.

Once the Second World War began, many children were evacuated to Newdigate and the school roll increased to 150 children. Miss Dynes resigned in

117

*Oaklands Park. Left to right: Leon Steadman, Mr Steadman, Capt. Palmer, Mrs Palmer, Miss Helen Palmer and Nurse Vanner.*

*Oaklands Park in the 1930s.*

*Right: The first cook, Harriett Burberry, handing out suet puddings to Dora Platt.*

*Above: Crowning of the May Queen, 1951. Daphne Goodall is with her attendants Pat Blanks and Alan Wheeler.*

*Right: School spinning and weaving class. Left to right: Roma Halsey, Brenda Dennis, Pearl Jones, and Ailsa Pescud in the 1930s.*

*In the school garden, 1937.*

Above: *School class in 1947.* Left to right, back row: *Robbie Trower, Roy Simmons, Arthur Minns, Alan Wheeler, Mrs Booker (née Leadbetter), David Still, Bob Bettesworth, Gary Beedle, Michael Welfare;* centre: *Joy Couling, Andrea Halsey, Sheila Lines, Barbara Spiller, Beryl Tucker, Valerie Stevens, Philip Beedle, Peggy Hayman;* front: *John Underhill, Marion Pratt, Sheila Collinson, Pat Wilby, Christine Goddard, Pat Blanks, Frankie Lucas.*

Right: *Dedication of the new school.* Left to right: *Revd D. Bruce-Walker (rector 1945–59), the Bishop of Guildford, George Reindorp and the lay reader, Geoffrey Underwood.*

*Building the school.* Left to right: *Archie Morris, Cyril Goodall, Bob Gadd, Vic Cloke, ?.*

*The new school on completion in 1965.*

Right: *Barbara Norman and George Green at a garden party at Buckingham Palace in July 1973.*

Below: *The school float, Village Day, 1986.*

Above right: *Dorothy May Peake, who lived at Normans Cottage from 1919–79, died aged 100 in 1986.*

Above: *Continuing the tradition: Madeleine Tomlinson of Broad Lane is the May Queen, her escort is Charlie White and her attendants are Igraine Spiers and Jack Rogers. The ceremony together with maypole dancing was held on the Brocus as part of Queen Elizabeth II's golden jubilee celebrations on 15 June 2002.*

Below: *Newdigate Play Group: Nativity Play, Christmas 1984.*

*Crowning the May Queen, 1987. Zoe White with her escort William Parkhouse.*

*Newdigate School in 1990.*

1943 after serving for 22 years and Mr Gurr, who was suffering from ill health, had to contend with staff shortages and overcrowding. In December 1945 he resigned and with the opening of the new Secondary Modern School at Beare Green, the school became a mixed junior and infant school.

Miss Elwood became headmistress and with her staff of Miss Archer and Miss Brooker taught 73 children. Woodworking, gardening and cookery were removed from the curriculum and the gardens were turned into lawns for physical training and country-dancing lessons. The Parent Teacher Association was formed.

In July 1948 Miss Archer resigned after 27 years and Miss Elwood accepted another appointment at Kingsnympton. In 1952 Mr W.H. Chouler became headmaster. He wrote *A Village School – Its Birth and Growth, 1660–1955*, and much of this text is extracted from that book. The roll was 130 children under the age of 12, and he was assisted by Mr A.G. Groom, Miss S.D. Hunt and Mrs E. Rogers. The board of managers comprised the rector, the Revd D. Bruce-Walker as chairman, Mrs Trouncer, Miss Bowden, Capt. E. Broadwood, MC, Mr G. Horley, and Mr R. Rickard; the correspondent to the managers was Mr Maskrey. The governors of the Endowment Trust were the Revd D. Bruce-Walker, Mrs D. Geake (who later gave a generous 'anonymous' donation to the school), Mrs Thompson and Mr Lapworth.

John Alexander Smith became headmaster in 1958 and was followed by Miss Barbara Norman in January 1965. On 28 June 1965 the present school was opened on what had been the Glebe Field (also called Rectory Meadow) and dedicated by the Bishop of Guildford. The old school was demolished to make way for George Horley Place and the doctors' surgery. A group of fathers and helpers excavated the swimming pool which was used for the first time on 21 July 1967.

Two years later it became necessary to have a temporary classroom, and the annexe was built in April 1969. For several years the school had five classes and up to 161 children on the roll.

Newdigate now had a First School, taking ages five to eight, in 1976, so the numbers reduced and there were only three classes. May 1981 marked the golden jubilee of the crowning of the May Queen and in that year Miss Norman retired and was succeeded by her deputy, Mrs Janet Brearley.

With 67 children on the roll Mrs Brearley introduced new strategies for the teaching of reading and writing and oversaw the first National Curriculum in the school. She was seconded to the London Education Authority in 1987 and Mrs Linda Green led the school in her absence.

Mrs Christine Hayler became head teacher in January 1989 and in September 1994 the school became an Infants' School, teaching children aged five to seven, and numbers were further reduced to

57. However, in 1996 Newdigate Pre-School began to meet in a classroom in the school instead of in the Village Hall, leading to a rise in numbers for both schools and strengthening ties between them.

In April 1996 Mrs Hayler left and Mrs Christine Cullen became the latest in a very long line of head-teachers. Within five months the school had its first OFSTED inspection, the report of which was complimentary. The number of children rose to 96 in 2000.

The millennium was marked by the building of an office extension incorporating a new staff room, opened by the Bishop of Guildford, the planting of an oak sapling on the school field in association with the parish tree warden and Newdigate Horticultural Society, and the gift of a commemoration mug to each child by the Parochial Church Council.

Newdigate Endowed Church of England Infant School now has over 100 pupils aged four to seven years in four classes, and the Pre-School has 55 children aged two to four. Liaison between them is close; they share assemblies, meet for lunch, use the swimming pool and join for special events such as the Easter Hat Parade.

The school follows the DfES curriculum guidelines rigorously. Computers are accessible to all children from age four. By age seven they are competent in basic word processing, can print their work, send an e-mail, download information from the internet and 'talk IT'. In March 2002 OFSTED Inspectors commented on the children's very good social and interpersonal skills and on the Christian ethic underpinning the school's activities.

The school has been served by able and dedicated teachers and support staff. Links with the community are strong, with support from St Peter's Church, the PTA, Henry Smith's Charity, the Steere and Booth Trust, the Horticultural Society and a host of volunteers.

## Newdigate Pre-School

In September 1969, Sylvia Cunningham, the rector's wife, called a meeting to discuss the formation of a playgroup for three-year-old children. Amongst those involved in the early days were Mollie Posner, Ann Watson, Mary Watts, Janet Brearley, Nina Warman, Heather Mackay, Pat Jenner and Ann Sloane.

The group started in January 1970 in the Village Hall with 21 children and they met on Tuesday and Thursday mornings. The cost was 4s. (20p) per session. Shortly after, Trish Morbey started helping on Mondays, and from this early beginning a lifetime of devotion evolved. In 2002 Mrs Morbey is still the supervisor. Over the years there has been a very stable group of helpers and assistants including Pat Jenner, Marianne Tartari, Ann Moss, Diane Nowland, Pauline Austin, Sue Martin and Linda Strudwick. Decisions, however, have always been committee based.

In 1998 the group moved to the school and the excellent relationship with the school and its staff became even closer. The group is now available to children that are two-and-a-half years of age and has nine sessions a week with 60 children on the register.

Another group for even younger children was started in 1977 by Celia Newbury, meeting in the rear room of the Six Bells. Today the group, which is called Baby Bells, meets in the Village Hall once a week on Fridays.

## Newdigate Surgery

At the beginning of the twentieth century Newdigate had no doctor of its own. The parish was served by Dr Wakefield of Norwood Hill who in 1897 had one of the first motor cars, and Dr Ward-Clarke of Capel who was still making house calls by horse and cart in the 1920s.

Dr Hopkins opened the first surgery at Simons in 1934. Later Dr Gordon Fear had a surgery at Brooklag Farm and then at Grove House in Parkgate Road.

When George Horley Place was built, Dr Allison and Dr Russell started their practice in the purpose-built surgery.

The present practice covers an area of approximately 100 square miles, with the surgery at the side of George Horley Place, served by doctors from the main surgery at Brockham. Demand for GP services is outgrowing the existing premises, but at the time of writing attempts to find another site have been unsuccessful. The practice doctors in 2002 are: Dr Peter H. Kober, Dr Graeme J. Jenner, Dr Jonathan D. Richards and Dr Lucy E. Rawson.

*Dr Wakefield's car outside the Six Bells.*
*Tom Voice is in the foreground.*

## Shops & Shopping

One of the earliest records of a shop in Newdigate is in the transcripts of the *Surrey Quarter Sessions* of 1661:

*Matthew Day, of Dorking, yeoman, 1 April 1661 forcibly erected a building called 'a shoppe' on the common waste from Dorking to Newdigate to the great nuisance and detriment of the inhabitants, an evil example – and against the peace.*

Later it was recorded:

*Whereas Nathaniel Ward of Newdigate, victualler, has lately kept a very disorderly house by suffering company to continue drinking and tippling on the Lord's Day and*

*otherwise, which has now been proved in Court on Oath, it is ordered he is to be suppressed from keeping his victualling or tippling house and from selling beer or ale there.*

There are two old Newdigate wills referring to tradesmen, although no details are given – William Bull, a shopkeeper, 1767, and Jn Sayers, butcher, 1752.

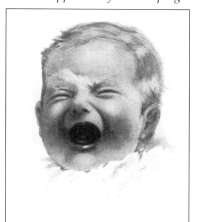

**Open all night at Newdigate**

Furthermore, in 1817 Thomas Burberry of Sot's Hole Shop was held responsible for the upkeep of 5 feet of the church fence.

It is not until the 1840s that census returns and the *Post Office Directory* begin to give us a clearer picture of the Newdigate shops. In 1841 James Humphrey, aged 75, was listed as a grocer in the building which is now Ziegler's but was for many years the village shop. Thomas Baker was a butcher in what is believed to be the front room of Wirmwood; the extra-wide front door that accommodated the sides of meat and butcher's hooks under the porch still survive. Meat was probably served through a sliding window in the front of the house.

At Parkgate there was another shop run by Robert Upton in what is now Saplings but was at one time called Upton House. Robert Upton was variously described as 'grocer' and 'beerhouse keeper and hawker'.

By 1871 James Farindon junr was described as grocer, draper, provision merchant and postmaster in the village shop. In the mid 1890s, with an increased population, a veritable shopping centre developed in the middle of the village. Alfred Dean took over the village stores, the Old Post Office became a shop, and at the turn of the century Foresters Villas and what is now the Old Bakery were built and opened as shops.

### Ziegler's

James Farindon retired to Kingsland and on 28 December 1901 he was buried at St Peter's, having been the postmaster for over 40 years; his daughter

*Fred Dean and Mark Weller outside the shop.*

*Dean Bros. in 1921.*

**WHY?** Go to Dorking, London, or elsewhere for

Grocery, Drapery, Clothing (*Ready-made or to measure*), Hats, Boots, Ironmongery, Earthenware, Garden Tools, etc., etc.

When you can obtain them on best terms at

**ALFRED DEAN'S**

GENERAL • SUPPLY • STORES,

NEWDIGATE.

ANY ARTICLE NOT IN STOCK PROCURED ON SHORT NOTICE.

**ALFRED DEAN,**

GROCER, DRAPER, BAKER, AND PROVISION MERCHANT,

GENERAL SUPPLY STORES,

NEWDIGATE.

MEN'S & BOY'S CLOTHING Ready-made and to Measure.

SHIRTS, PANTS, &c.     BOOTS AND SHOES
in great variety.

Ironmongery, Earthenware and Tin Goods

Allinsons' Wholemeal Bread.     Schweppes' Mineral Waters.

had already taken over as postmistress at what is believed to be No. 2 Kingsland. His successor was Alfred Dean, who ran the business as a general store, advertising it as a 'local store with London prices'. The bacon and large cheeses were kept in what is now the front room of Wirmwood and carried through the front door and round to the shop when required. There was sawdust on the floor, and sugar, currants and flour were weighed individually and coffee was ground upstairs. After Alfred retired his nephews William Luther (Billy) and Fred Dean continued the business.

Until the 1930s bread was baked in a building to the south of the stores by Walter Carpenter. This building and a small cobbler's shop, both in a dilapidated state, were dismantled in the summer of 1988 and removed for eventual re-erection at the Weald and Downland Museum at Singleton.

In 1930 Dean Brothers took over the Post Office and in 1933 they opened another shop in Leigh. The telephone exchange was situated in the present living-room of Wirmwood. In 1939 William Luther Dean sublet the premises to Arthur James Stanford and in 1943 Harry Victor Whiting took over the running of the shop.

The shop and house were part of the Farnell-Watson estate, and in 1945 were sold at auction to Mr Stanford, who appointed Mr and Mrs Jennings as managers. In 1955 Douglas and Hilda Hayward bought the premises for £5,500; they built the kitchen and bedroom extension to the north and transformed the interior of the house and shop to its present appearance.

In July 1981 they retired to Pulborough and sold the premises to John, Tina and Wally Callcut who continued to run the shop as a general store and Post Office whilst opening the first floor as a coffee and gift shop. At 2.45a.m. on 3 July 1986 the store was deliberately rammed by a lorry in an attempt to burgle the property, demolishing the whole left-hand front of the shop. This was later repaired by skilled carpenters in the identical style to the original.

In December 1988 the shop and house were divided and the shop sold to Stephen Obank, who employed a manager. By this time, most people did their bulk shopping in town, and for a period the shop closed down. However, in 1994 it was refurbished and opened as a bakery and delicatessen by Lisa Fidler, with a coffee shop which became very popular with villagers and cyclists, but long hours and relatively small returns meant that the shop finally closed as a food store in 1998. It is currently owned by Nina Ziegler who sells statuary and garden ornaments.

### Bettesworth's

The double-fronted premises called Foresters Villas were built by the Ancient Order of Foresters. In 1909, J. Rusbridge, one of the church sidesmen, had the

*Left:* The Coffee Shop on the first floor of the Village Stores.

*Below:* Dismantling the derelict bakery at the Village Stores prior to removal to the Weald and Downland Museum at Singleton in 1988. Heather Champion from the museum is on the roof.

butcher's shop in the left-hand side and William Greenfield ran a saddlery in the other half. After the First World War the butcher's shop was taken over by George Peters and in 1930 Roy Peters took over the family business. William Luther Dean took on the saddlery business in 1930 and in 1932, during the proprietorship of A.E. Wyatt, a serious fire occurred. Within ten minutes of the discovery of the blaze, the shop was an inferno and the roof on that side collapsed. The fire was eventually controlled by the Dorking and District Fire Brigade but Mrs Greenfield, who was living upstairs, was not insured and lost all her possessions including her clothes. After repairs, the shop was converted into a private home.

The butcher's shop closed during the Second World War and was used to house some of those whose homes in Broad Lane were struck by a doodlebug V1 rocket. After the war Maurice Kensett reopened the butcher's shop and it changed hands again in 1973 when Bryan Thompson took over the business. In January 1987, Travers & Bawden from Woking took over, then the Kensett family, and finally Phillip Bradley, who was forced to close down in August 1997. Apart from a period during and after the Second World War the shop had been continuously in use as a butcher's since 1909.

In 1954, Charles Bettesworth opened a newsagent's shop in the former saddlery, and today his son Bob occupies the whole premises and runs it as a newsagent, Post Office and general store. It is affectionately known simply as 'Bob's shop' and is a focal point for much village gossip.

## The Old Bakery

This building was originally two separate shops; A. Crowder ran a butcher's shop until about 1915 and Henry T. Whittington was a family baker, pastry cook and confectioner. It is hard to imagine, but at this time the village boasted two butchers and two bakers. A Mr Connor ran a fishmongering business from Crowder's old shop during the 1930s but then Mr Whittington took over the entire premises and ran it as a general store and bakery in direct competition with Dean's Stores.

He retired and lived at Marena (now called Oakside) in Village Street, and the shop became known as Forrest Stores. Several managers ran the business but it finally closed in the early 1970s when the premises were converted into a private home.

## The Old Post Office

This property was used as a Dame School until 1873, and then sold by the Charity Commissioners to William Farnell-Watson for £200.

In the early part of the twentieth century it became a drapery and was run by Henry Rowland, the Parish Clerk and sexton. During the First World War it became a stationery store and Post Office run by Michael Dean with help from his assistant Daisy Clark-Jones. He published many postcards of Newdigate, wrote a history of the Village Institute, and had the prestigious telephone number of Newdigate 1. In 1930 he ceased trading and the Post Office became the business of his son, William Luther Dean.

*J. Rusbridge the butcher and W. Greenfield the saddler at Foresters Villas, c.1910.*

Left: *The fire pump after attending the fire at Foresters Villas.*

Below: *Foresters Villas after the fire.*

*Foresters Villas, c.1950.*

Newdigate butchers in 1986. Left to right: *Philip Bradley, Bryan Thompson and Bill.*

Below: *Forrest Stores for sale in 1974. The village could no longer support two general stores so the shop was converted to a private dwelling and is now called the Old Bakery.*

Below left: *Village shops, in 1905. A. Crowder was a butcher and Henry Whittingham ran a general stores. Thus the village was able to support two butcher's shops and two general stores and there were also two bakeries.*

Above: *Bob Bettesworth outside his shop in 2002.*

*The Stationery Stores and Post Office, now the Old Post Office, with Michael Dean in the doorway.*

### THE STATIONERY STORES.

### LOCAL VIEW CARDS.

BIRTHDAY & CHRISTMAS CARDS.

Account Books : Memos : Games
Playing Cards : Jam Covers : Jam
Labels : Pocket Books &c., &c., &c.

DISH PAPERS and OTHER TABLE STATIONERY.

Estimates for Printing and Stationery.

### POST OFFICE, NEWDIGATE.

The shop later became a hairdresser's and was run by Beattie Fowler whose family had the Duke's Head in Beare Green. By the start of the Second World War the property was owned by Arthur James Stanford and was used as a warden's post.

From 1951 until 1959 the shop was called The Needlework Box and was run by George and Louie Green selling wools, patterns, etc. For a short period it then became a café called the Copper Kettle but in 1960 it was converted into a private house now called The Old Post Office.

### HENRY HORLEY, WOOD MERCHANT.

Oak Logs, Cordwood, Faggots, Stakes, etc.

### NEWDIGATE.

## The Ali Raj

Henry Horley was a wood merchant from Parkgate. In 1899 he owned several adjacent properties there: a smithy roughly where the telephone box is now, the building believed to be the Forge (now the Ali Raj), Little Trees (now Innstead), and Saplings. His wife ran a grocery shop, first from Saplings and then from the Forge, but this was closed when she died in 1924.

William Luther Dean took the shop over and opened occasionally for the use of the people of Parkgate, who had to pay a premium of one halfpenny to cover carriage from his main store in Newdigate. In 1935, A. Rose was running a shoeing and general smith business from the smithy.

After the Second World War the shop was reopened when Joe Batchelor's wife ran it as a café, said to have been much used by workers at Schermulys. In the early 1970s it became known as the Forge Restaurant and was successfully run by an Austrian couple. After they left the restaurant was briefly known as Gamages before becoming the popular Indian restaurant called the Ali Raj.

*Henry Horley with Emily Susan Horley and Albert Henry Horley (seated).*

### A. ROSE,
Shoeing and General Smith, Hot Water Fitting,
### THE FORGE, NEWDIGATE.

*The Forge for sale in 1924.*

Bottom left: *The Skinner family at Kingsland in 1918. John Henry is driving and Herbert is seated next to him. In the rear are Leonard, Violet and Emily.*

Below: *Brewing at Parkgate.*

Above: *The Ali Raj in 2002. Now a popular Indian restaurant, the building was formerly called the Forge Café and Restaurant.*

## Other Businesses

It is unclear how long the Post Office was situated at No. 2 Kingsland in the early-twentieth century. Many people remember the Victorian postbox which was hidden in the front hedge and only removed in the last part of the twentieth century; inside the cottage the floorboards are heavily worn near where the counter used to be.

Next door, W. Fuller sold corn, meal, eggs, poultry and rabbits. He hired out a pony and trap, and later progressed to hiring motor vans as well as open and closed cars.

J. Broughton made and sold cycles from his home in Kingsland and A. Monk was a coal and coke merchant. The Monk family also ran the brewery at Kingsland and another brewery was operating at Parkgate.

The King family were the local blacksmiths for many years working at their forge in Rusper Road. With the advent of cars, S. Barrow opened the Forge Garage as a motor and general engineer advertising 'landaulette car for hire' and 'Pratts' Golden Petrol Pump'. Over the ensuing years F.S. Grinsted, Jack Nagle and Ivor Lowndes all ran the Forge Garage, providing petrol and car repairs for the village. It is now owned by Mike Harrison and specialises in bodywork repairs, tyres and general car maintenance.

There was a laundry at Brooklag Farm, which employed local girls at the end of the nineteenth century and beginning of the twentieth. It probably started as a private laundry for Henfold House and later became a public one. Washing was hard work and all the water had to be drawn from the well at the back, but there were compensations for the laundry maids as dances were held in the large room and these apparently were 'jolly affairs'. Laundry Hill and Laundry Hill Cottage take their names from this businsess.

Granny Roffey, who was over 100 years of age when she died, used to sell sweets from her cottage at Sot's Hole. She did not understand weights, so her lodger, Jack Knight, used to weigh them for her – a farthing usually bought 4 ounces of aniseed balls. She was frequently followed about the cottage by pigs who were made at home. The sty was about 20 yards from the door of the cottage. Farmers often gave away the small pigs of a farrow, called 'daudling' pigs.

In the centre of the village, on the site of Inglenook Yard, T.W. Jackson and later Jim Nagle ran their coal merchant's business for many years. In the 1970s William Way, the builder's merchants, built a shop, offices and a yard on the site. The area became very busy and it was not unusual to see two or three large trucks blocking Village Street offloading sand, ballast and all types of building material. Eakins later took over and subsequently sold the site for a

*The Old Brewery, Kingsland, c.1910. Pictured are the Monk family. Lavinia is on the left and Albert to the right. Helen is the smallest girl and Albert's mother, Mary, is in the centre.*

*The Forge Garage, Rusper Road in 1990.*

*Laundry maids were paid 2d. per hour.*

*Traffic congestion outside William Way's yard in 1988 – just a memory, following its closure and the building of Inglenook Yard.*

Left: *Sot's Hole, now Partridge Cottage.* Left to right: *Ada Roffey on her 100th birthday talking to Misses Maud and Lizzie Goldberg of the Red House.*

*Bill Tanner and Jim Nagle at the coal yard.*

*Alfred Dean, treasurer of the Newdigate Club, 1904–25.*

small housing development which has been called Inglenook Yard.

At an earlier date, on the site of the first houses on the left in Underhill Road, Henry Whittingham had a small second-hand business. His nephew, Archie Morris, built many houses in Newdigate and used the premises as a builder's yard. Allan Trower later took over and he too ran a building business.

The Lucas family had long connections with Newdigate going back to the eighteenth century and they too ran a building business from a yard on the site of Brocus House in Parkgate Road.

Outbuildings at Dean House Farm, New House Farm and Sturtwood Farm have now been converted into business units and a glance through advertisements in the parish magazine shows that small businesses in Newdigate are alive and well.

## Newdigate Village Club & Hall

At the beginning of the twentieth century, the rector, the Revd Hugh Nelson-Ward, a great-grandson of Horatio Nelson, noted that there was:

*... a lack of recreation and an absence of healthy amusements and occupations for the mind in dull seasons – a colony of pessimists had been bred who had nowhere to go – but out, and nowhere to stay – but in.*

*The Village Club as originally built in 1901.*

He approached Mrs Farnell-Watson, whose husband had died in 1897, and she agreed to have a Village Club built in his memory on the site of some squatters' cottages and two almshouses on the edge of Buckhurst Meadow (now the Brocus).

The memorial stone was laid on 27 April 1901 by Mrs Farnell-Watson herself, inscribed:

*Erected in 1901, in Memory of William Farnell-Watson, Esq., of Henfold, and presented by his widow to the Parish of Newdigate, is under the management of Trustees Alfred Dean, Hon. Treasurer; Henry Whittingham, Hon. Secretary.*

A large number of parishioners assembled, and the choir, robed and led by Mr Warner, the organist, attended. Col H.H. Graves of Hatchetts presented Mrs Farnell-Watson with a silver trowel, subscribed for by over 120 men of Newdigate, and Mr Hackwood read an illuminated address, thanking her for her kindness in giving so valuable a gift to the parish.

A large bottle, containing papers announcing Queen Victoria's recent death, together with a copy of *The Times* for the day, the current issue of the parish magazine and some coins of the realm bearing the latest date, were then enclosed in a tin box and laid in place beneath the stone.

The Foresters' Friendly Society held a meeting of 'Court Farnell-Watson' to end an eventful day. Michael Dean, of the Post Office, was moved to write:

*The opening of the Club in 1901 coincided with the establishment of a telegraph office in Newdigate – quite a sign of determined progress!*

The first caretaker was Sgt Bowtell, who had served in the Boer War and was wounded in Bethlehem by a Mauser bullet, necessitating the amputation of a leg. After ten years' service he resigned and Mr and Mrs E. Vine filled the vacancy. Alfred Dean was appointed treasurer in 1904 and held the position for 20 years.

A billiard table was installed and contests in whist, draughts, cribbage and other games were arranged amongst the members and with other parishes and institutes. The local Miniature Rifle Club was formed and the hall was used by the Choral Society, the Adult School, and the Nursing Association, as well as for concerts, dances, cookery and woodworking classes, etc.

In 1924 it was decided to extend the hall and install central heating at a cost of £589. The current Village Club was added in 1935 and was licensed to sell alcohol. Mrs Farnell-Watson was opposed to drink, although the family fortune came from brewing, and tradition says that she ordered the memorial stone and presumably its contents to be removed. In 1989 a further extension was added which included the committee room and shower facilities.

In March 1987 a group of nine people from the Village Club were enjoying a visit to Europe. They were booked to return on the night of 6 March from Zeebrugge – their ferry was the *Herald of Free Enterprise*. One mile from the Belgian port the ferry capsized and rolled over into the bitterly cold waters and next morning villagers woke to see the terrible pictures of the stricken ferry. The personal involvement within the village was rapidly realised. Becky Ede did not know whether her parents, Ann and John, had survived and more and more people gravitated to the shop, which became an information

Below: *The Village Club showing the hall extension in the 1920s. The words 'Newdigate Village Club' are still inscribed in the brick arch over the entrance, but 'Club' has been painted over with the word 'Hall'.*

Above: *The Village Club after completion in 1935.*

Right: *The Village Pond, c.1920.*

Left: *Lesley Heard editing the parish magazine in 2002.*

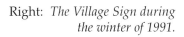

Right: *The Village Sign during the winter of 1991.*

centre. Gradually survivors called home until all nine were thankfully accounted for – their personal traumas, however, had only just begun.

Today the hall is constantly in use for private functions and by village organisations. The club is well attended, running teams in the local snooker, pool and darts leagues. Margaret Read and Doug Hopkins look after the whole building, which is under the control of the trustees of the Newdigate Community Centre.

## The Parish Magazine

The earliest surviving parish magazine dates from January 1884 and covered the parishes of Capel, Ockley and Newdigate. It was priced at 1d. and distributed with a copy of *The Dawn of Day*, a beautifully produced magazine with fine prints, stories, scriptures and religious history. The locally produced four-page supplement gave news about the church, the village and the school together with births, deaths and marriages.

At the end of 1899 Mr J. Lee Jardine, who edited the magazine and organised the distribution, retired. Capel and Ockley decided to have their own publications, and for the first two months of 1900 Newdigate was without a magazine. Then the rector, the Revd Hugh Nelson-Ward, produced a four-page newsletter which was stapled inside *Goodwill Magazine*, a publication similar in content to *The Dawn of Day* but with photographs. Gradually the newsletter increased in size and by 1904 more than 50 per cent of the six pages was devoted to advertisements.

Due to wartime pressures the magazine ceased in early 1918 and was not revived again until 1924 when the Revd J. McAnally was rector. It became the *Newdigate Church Magazine* and the publication *Home Words* was also included. December 1940 saw the end of production but after the Second World War the publication reappeared as the *St Peter's Review* and was priced at 3d. A new typewritten format was introduced in January 1958, presumably to keep costs down, and this continued until April 1965 when the *St Peter's Newdigate Newsletter* was printed in an A4 format, folded to give four pages of text. There were no advertisements and the magazine was distributed free of charge. In 1972, for the first time since 1899, the name of the then editor was revealed, namely Barbara Norman, the school's headmistress.

After 168 issues the format changed again in April 1979 and the 32-page magazine was introduced in its current form in January 1990.

The parish magazine contains information about forthcoming activities, and publicises various schemes within the village, including tree warden activities, village 'litter picks' and the Infant Welfare Clinic, as well as Newdigate Surgery opening times. Although public transport is virtually non-existent in the village; the problem is ameliorated by 'Dial-a-Ride' and 'Good Neighbours' Transport Schemes, which both feature in the magazine.

The present title is *St Peter's Newdigate Magazine* and the editor, Lesley Heard, retired in the summer of 2002 after nine years. George Brind took over the reins, assisted by Diana Salisbury (distribution), Gina Mitchell (collation), Donald Thwaites (advertising) and Alma Brookman (diary editor). Some 740 copies are produced each month and distributed free throughout the parish.

## The Parish Council

The Parish Council meets every month in the Village Hall and, under James Turnbull (Chairman) and Bob Warner (Parish Clerk), members discuss all the matters which affect the village. Planning applications are high on the agenda as are such concerns as litter, the state of the roads, transport and footpaths. Perennial problems include speeding commuter traffic, parking in the village centre and general wear and tear exacerbated by heavy vehicles using roads originally built for horse and cart. The village is also proving attractive to increasing numbers of leisure and racing cyclists. There are problems at times on the narrow, busy roads where motor vehicles, cyclists, horses and pedestrians do not always see eye to eye.

Villagers are kept informed of all parish matters through a monthly report which is published in the parish magazine and people are welcome to attend, particularly when such topics as the incinerator and developments at Gatwick are discussed.

## The Village Pond

The pond in Church Road is a cart pond, originally used to swell the wooden wheels of farm carts so the iron rims fitted securely. During dry, hot summers this would probably have been done quite frequently.

The pond does not have any through-flow but simply takes drainage water from the adjacent fields and road.

It was cleaned out in 1973 by British Trust for Nature Conservation volunteers, when George Green, a member of the Parish Council, arranged for the work to be done. In 1984 another group of volunteers with help from the Surrey Trust for Nature Conservation did a similar job; this time the pond was drained and the sludge cleared right down to the chalk bottom.

Since then the pond has been regularly cleared by groups of volunteers led by Diana Salisbury.

## The Village Sign

Mrs Janson was inspired by a competition in the *Daily Mail* to design and erect a village sign. She incorporated the coat of arms of the Newdigate

family, granted to Sir John Newdigate by Edward III for his services in the war in France, and added the words Foyal Loyal. The present sign was made by Mr Wilson in the 1950s.

# Henry Smith's Charity

Henry Smith's Charity (Newdigate) is administered by eight trustees, four appointed by the Parish Council and four co-opted. They disburse the monies received from the main Henry Smith Charity in London for the benefit of the poor and distressed in the parish. In 1963 the Newdigate branch of the Charity received £63 from London but by the end of the century this had risen to over £5,000.

Henry Smith was an extremely wealthy London merchant, born in 1548, who was a member of the Worshipful Company of Salters and an Alderman of the City. He took a keen interest in the plight of the poor and needy (including, for example, seamen captured and then released by Turkish pirates and clergy adversely affected by the Dissolution of the Monastries). He died in 1627 and, after caring for his family, left money for the purchase of land, the income from which was to be used for the relief of the poor in Surrey and elsewhere.

Almost every parish in Surrey benefits from Henry Smith's Charity. It is believed by some that the amount each parish receives reflects the treatment given by the parish to Henry Smith when he travelled the country disguised as a vagrant. This is a pleasant belief, but sadly not founded in fact. The story almost certainly arises from confusion with another Smith – 'Dog' Smith or 'Beggar' Smith, otherwise known as the Lambeth Pedlar – who did indeed travel as a vagrant in South London.

At first the trustees were severely restricted in how they could spend their monies. Their income was, and remains, primarily for the poor but it could not be given to those who had lived in the parish for fewer than five years, or were swearers, irregular church attenders, saucy to their masters or, being able to work, chose not to do so. These restrictions have been eased but the prime aim remains the relief of the individual.

In Newdigate there is one exception to this: the Old Folks' Christmas Lunch in the Village Hall, which is enjoyed by over 100 people and has become a major annual event. Each diner is presented with a paper napkin bearing the names of all those attending.

In 2001 Dr Bill Wheeler and his wife Hazel retired as trustees after giving a combined total of 58 years' service. In 2002, Donald Thwaites is chairman.

*Left: Lunch to commemorate the retirement of Dr Bill Wheeler and his wife Hazel in 2001, after giving a combined total of 58 years' service as trustees of the Henry Smith's Charity. Trustees, left to right: Bob Bettesworth, Mary Crutcher, Hazel Wheeler, Kathy Bettesworth, Diana Salisbury, Donald Thwaites, Ann Hanson, George Brind; seated: Dr Bill Wheeler. Missing from the picture is John Callcut who took the photograph.*

*Right: Making Christmas puddings for Henry Smith's Charity Lunch, 1990. Left to right: Diana Salisbury, Hazel Wheeler, Barbara Norman and Mary Crutcher.*

*Opposite above: Old Folks' Dinner in the Village Hall in 1939. The rector is Albert Stone and George Horley is standing next to him at the rear.*

*Opposite below: Henry Smith's Charity Lunch in the Village Hall, 11 January 1992.*

*Placing the wreath on the war memorial in 1938.*

*11th Dorking (Newdigate) troop, Whit Saturday 1941.*

*Newdigate Cubs in 1978. Left to right: Spencer Morbey, Anthony James, Martin Jenner, N. Stock and Mark Randall.*

Above: *Newdigate Brownies outside the lych-gate, c.1947. Left to right: Pam Beedle, Daphne Goodall, Barbara Spiller, Sue Pearce, ?.*

**The Church Parade, 14 October 1956.**

Left: *Len Taylor at the first weekend camp in 1966.*

*Remembrance Day Parade with leaders Trish Morbey and Marianne Mortlock in 1984.*

*12th Dorking (Newdigate) Scouts in 1990. Left to right, back row: Daniel Procter, Tina Callcut, James Penfold, Richard Brown; front: Alwyn Kear, David Callcut, Edward Brown, Sam McGill, Ben Trotter, Adam Trotter, Simon Hayward and Robert McSorley.*

# Chapter 9

# VILLAGE ACTIVITIES

## Brownies & Guides

The first mention of the Brownies was in the 1930s. They were active during the 1940s when Elsie Hale was Brown Owl and Louie Green was Tawny Owl. Over the following years Eileen Tuppen, Marion Dare and Carol Cobb have all been Brown Owls. The group still meets in the Village Hall and the current leader is Trish Morbey.

Vere Wallis started a Girl Guide company on 3 December 1927. It was known as the 1st Newdigate Company and the headquarters was at the rectory. A year later they moved to the Village Hall, or Club as it was then known, and Nancy French was Lieutenant, Mrs Haig was Tawny Owl and Miss Davis was Brown Owl. The company moved to Reffolds in January 1931.

Today, the Guides are no longer in existence, but hopefully when a suitable leader can be found the tradition will continue. Vere Wallis was faced with a similar situation in 1935 when she closed the Rangers down due to a lack of headquarters, very few members and general slackness. She started the group again in November 1938 in a room behind the Six Bells, then called the Buffaloes room, and the group continued until the late 1990s or early 2000.

## Cubs & Scouts

Though no records survive, it appears scouting reached Newdigate just before the Second World War, when Miss Blanche Darbyshire founded what is thought to have been the 11th Dorking Scout Group. Cecil Boorman was the first Newdigate Scout Leader, but the troop folded (possibly when he was called up). Cecil died in 1944 and his grave in Newdigate churchyard bears the words 'I have gone home', which is the phrase used by Scouts when they finish laying a trail.

A 12-year-old Patrol Leader in the group of 1939 was young Len Taylor. In 1964, by then married to June Taylor and with a son of his own, he became Scout Leader of the newly-formed 12th Dorking Group, with Assistant Scout Leader Dick Abbott. June ran the Cubs and, supported by a committee including Louie Green as treasurer, and chairman Peter Higgs

(who, it is believed, may have been a Scout Leader under Miss Darbyshire), the group flourished.

Meetings were held initially in the old school building, but soon plans were afoot for a Scout Hut. Funds were raised by a team of parents, and a post-war London prefab was dismantled and transported to the Brocus field to be re-erected there in 1968. With extension and refurbishment at its silver jubilee in 1993, it has done sterling service for the group ever since.

Bernard Howes and Charlie Gibbs subsequently took over the Scout Troop. When, in 1977 after 13 years, June Taylor retired as Cub Leader, a replacement was sought. A friend of Bernard's happened to notice a car belonging to a young neighbour, newly arrived in the village, sporting a Scouts sticker. A deputation arrived on the doorstep of Barbara Roger, of 2 Halesbridge Cottages, who at that time was still running a Cub Pack in Camberwell. Duly recruited, she ran Newdigate Cubs for the next 16 years until 1993, moving on to become District Commissioner (a post from which she only retired in 2002).

By 1979, Bernard was seeking a replacement to look after the Scouts, and with Joe Bradley (a committee member for many years) led a further deputation to the doorstep of another newly arrived local, Richard Brown of Holly Tree Cottage, since it was rumoured that he too had Scouting connections. A new Scout Leader was born, who held the post for the next ten years. In 1989 his wife Penny was one of the first leaders of the newly formed Beaver Colony for six-to-eight year olds, and then moved on to help run the Cubs. As a couple, the Browns remained actively involved with Scouting in Newdigate until 1996. Another founding Beaver leader was Diana Foreman, whose son Andrew had been a Cub and Scout with the group and went on to help with the Beavers until Diana retired after nine years in 1998.

Steve Martin took over the Scouts in 1995, and Sue Hayward has been the Cub leader since 1996. Tina Callcut has been involved since the late 1980s as helper, committee member, Scout Leader and now Group Scout Leader. Among these stalwarts, many other enthusiastic leaders and committee members have assured the uninterrupted continuation of Scouting in Newdigate, with all three sections – Beavers, Cub Scouts and Scouts – to the present day.

*Beare Green and Newdigate Choral Society in 2002.* Left to right, back row: *Carole Brough, Mary Huggins, Alfreda Sparks, Anthea Smallwood (Accompanist), Ian Lawrence, Ian Macro, Ian Peterson, Geoff Collins, Liz Wadlow, Ann Peterson, Pam Keeble, Maureen Jones;* third row: *Val Collins, Bertie Gallagher, Shona Hoad, Mollie Posner, Tim Reynoldson, Peter Lilley, Gerald Thorpe, David Booth, Lesley Heard, Rosemary Revell, Jackie Westerman, Mary Olive, Janet Brearley;* second row: *Yvonne Chapman, Maureen Figg, John Mears, Bill MacKay, Jamie Cordell (Conductor), Alan Posner, Jeff Moss, Rosemary Thompson, Barbara Peake;* front: *Prue Young, Tina Callcut, Jenny Clark, Diana Pledge, Anne Delnevo, Jane Reeves.*

*Newdigate Bowls Club in June 2000.* Left to right, back row: *Michael Head, George Cumpstey, Jim Fulbrook, George Stevens, Alan Lomas, Ivan Atkinson (captain), John Hanson, Andrew Simmons, Mick Gull, Ken Smith, John Charman, Martin Morris, Tony Frost, John Claridge, Eric Humphries, Terry Richardson, Ernie Winnett, Michael Frith, Tony Venn, David Pickering;* front: *Grace Fulbrook, Pam Venn, Ruth Channing, H. Smith, Jan O'Reilly, Barbara Stevens, Pat Smith, Pat Claridge, Patricia Frith, Brenda Humphries, Lesley Head, Stella Walton, Jenny Sweetland, Ronnie Pickering, Judy Morris, Mary Gull, Marion Lomas.*

# Beare Green & Newdigate Choral Society

In 1910 the rector, the Revd F.O. Sutton, noticed that many neighbouring villages had flourishing choral societies and suggested that one could perhaps be formed in Newdigate. A meeting was held in the school on 18 May, after which the Choral Society was formed under the direction of Mr E. Withers of Dorking Parish Church and Dorking Glee and Madrigal Society.

The Leith Hill Musical Festival was founded by the Vaughan Williams and Farrer families in 1905 with the aim of encouraging choral singing in the villages around Leith Hill. The very first festival conductor was the composer Ralph Vaughan Williams and in 1914 Newdigate's Choral Society participated. The parish magazine reported:

*Under the able conductorship of the rector, the Revd Bird, the Society boldly stood their ground and faced the audience, and held their own admirably from beginning to end. At the close of the competition they stood an easy fifth from the top, and in one piece lost the banner by only two points.*

To many in the Society it was the first time they had taken part in a competition of this sort, and for many, if not all, it was one of the happiest days of their lives.

The First World War meant that the men's voices were lost; the choir was discontinued and did not participate in the festival again until 1937/38 when it was re-formed and conducted by Mr H.M. Trouncer of Henfold. The choir colours were then pale blue and pink.

The choir celebrated its 60th birthday in 1997 with a visit from the German Male Voice Choir, an association which started in 1974. In 1999, under the baton of conductor Jamie Cordell, the choir was the overall winner at the Leith Hill Musical Festival, and in October 2000 a visit to Saratoga Springs in the United States was accomplished. The choir's colours are now black and white.

# Newdigate Bowls Club

For many years Bernard Howes and Eric Humphries ran the Village Day, so with their penchant for getting things done it is no surprise that when they decided that the village needed a bowling green, that is exactly what happened. Eric takes up the story:

*The idea of a bowls club was first mooted in the mid to late 1940s and after a certain amount of ground work was carried out on a half-size green, the project seemed to collapse for a variety of reasons.*

*In 1976, Bernard Howes and I, together with our wives Betty and Brenda, decided to resurrect the project,*

*but as there was little interest in the village we made virtually no progress. However, I had not taken into account the determination and drive of Bernard and 12 years later a club was formed with around 26 members.*

*We set ourselves a target of raising £3,000 (a professionally built green would have cost around £45,000 in those days) and this was achieved by knocking on doors and our wives selling home-made cakes from a table by the lych-gate.*

*All construction work was carried out by members, particularly Bill Homewood and the late John Hoare of Hammonds Farm, together with a huge amount of assistance from our President, Bill Kear.*

*The year 1989 saw the first matches being played on the green and since then the membership has grown to over 60. The green is in marvellous condition thanks to the green keeper, John Hanson.*

*On the playing front, one member has won the London and Southern Counties Singles Title and the club has won the Surrey Top Four on two occasions. Bob Harrow was the first member to win the Surrey County Badge and is now qualified to play for the county.*

*The ultimate ambition has been achieved with the construction of a very fine club house and car park which was made possible by the efforts of the club members and a 10 per cent grant from Mole Valley District Council.*

*What started as a fun village project has now evolved into a widely known and successful club which still retains the friendliness of a real village organisation.*

# Newdigate Cricket Club

The first recorded cricket match by a team from Newdigate was against Beare Green and was played away on Easter Monday in 1886. Regular matches were played until 1939 on the field opposite the Surrey Oaks, and the club was known as the Parkgate and Newdigate Cricket Club.

Before 1914 the rector's son Wilfred Bird, who kept wicket for Middlesex CCC and the MCC, regularly brought teams to play against Newdigate. He lost his life in the First World War.

After the Second World War the village purchased

*The cricket team at Parkgate in 1908.*

*Derek Underwood (Kent CCC and England) formally opened the nets at the cricket club, assisted by the colts, on 12 July 1994.*

Above: *Newdigate Cricket Club entertains the Surrey County Cricket Club, 23 September 1997. Amongst the Surrey stars are Alec Stewart* (far right), *Martin and Darren Bicknell, Alex Tudor, Joey Benjamin, Jonathan Batty and Jason Ratcliffe.*

Right: *Newdigate Football Club, 24 February 2001. Left to right, back row: James Bettesworth, John Morris, Shaun Trower, Lee Nash, Mark Trower, Graham ?, Mick Whiffen; front: Butch Robinson, Paul ?, Martin O'Donnell, Matt Gibbs, Anthony Roberts.*

the Brocus and the club has been playing there ever since. In 1975 the club played against the England Women's team as part of the 800th anniversary celebrations of St Peter's Church, and in both 1997 and 1999 Surrey County Cricket Club brought a team to play against the village.

The club runs two sides on Saturday and two on Sunday, as well as a Wednesday evening team and a junior section with over 60 youngsters. In 2001 the 1st XI were runners-up in the Surrey Downs League. The players regularly have a tour to Somerset and in 2000 and 2002 they took a team to Menorca.

# Newdigate Football Club

Newdigate played its first recorded friendly football match on 9 November 1924 at Charlwood, and their first home match against Leigh in February 1925 when they won 3–2. Also in 1925 the club affiliated to the Surrey County FA and played in the Redhill and District League. Their strip was scarlet shirts and white shorts; the present colours are green-and-white hoops with green shorts and green-and-white socks.

The club originally played at Hatchetts but after the war they moved to the Brocus. After a spell in the Dorking and District League the club moved back to Redhill before transferring in 1986 to the West Sussex League where they currently have two teams.

# Friendship Group

The group was formed in 1957 for young wives and mothers with the purpose of meeting and widening their outlook by means of talks and discussions on everyday affairs.

The group is a non-denominational organisation but is true to the ideals of Christianity and supports a different charity each year. Between 20 and 30 ladies meet fortnightly on a Monday evening in the Village Hall and speakers are frequently invited.

# The Good Companions

The club for retired over-60s who live in Newdigate was founded in 1982 at the request of several friends of Barbara Norman, a former headmistress of

*The Good Companions in 2000. Left to right, back row: E. Hardy, R. Powell, G. Stevens, B. Stevens, B. Wood, S. Nias; fourth row: C. Powell, J. Beer, Y. Ranson, S. Roberts, E. Warren; third row: R. Luff, P. Bourhill, P. Durant, T. Wyatt, G. Wyatt, E. Puttock, E. Funnell, S. Lyon, H. Francis, C. Smith; second row: J. Hoare, B. Nias, L. Mansbridge, B. Cutler, J. Wood, C. Durant, B. Tanner, L. Carpenter, D. Tanner, L. Kimber, P. Dunne, H. Jones, W. Chisnall; front: E. Tribe, L. Beedle, C. Puttock, O. Cloke, R. Thompson, B. Norman, C. Wheeler, P. Higgs, M. Whiffen. Absent members: Mrs S. Wates (president), E. Swain, J. Smith, N. Crutcher, A. Luke, L. Luke, B. Humphries, F. Bailey, J. Bailey, D. Tidbury and C. White.*

Below: *For many years Colin and Marion Hales have orchestrated the poppy appeal in Newdigate and have been instrumental in raising thousands of pounds for the Royal British Legion. They are pictured here in October 1999.*

*Newdigate Netball Club, 2002.* Left to right, back row: *Beth Jessop, Stephanie Dillnutt, Sue Greenhalgh, Paula Paddison, Julia Smith, Theri Bailey, Celia Weller, Clare Laker, Vivien Turnbull, Siobhan Smith, Alcia Loach, Fiona Addison, Shona Hoad, Jacqui Hiscocks, Liz Wiles, Amaris Wiles, Chris Pearce, Davida Hall, Sue Chiverton, Susan Brind, Gill Bouch, Melanie Doyle;* front: *Sophie Scowen, Laura Hall, Rianna Lucas, Stephanie Briscoe, Louisa Watts, Toni-Ann Trower, Emma Bouch, Teresa Trower (coach), Sophie Hall, Alice Turnbull, Imogen Moore, Rosanna Pearce, Natasha Dillnutt, Frankie Paul.*

Above: *The Royal British Legion stall at Village Day in 1994. Left to right: John Day, Dot Carpenter, ?, Peter Smith, Gerry Mitchell, Bert Mills and John Bunton.*

Right: *Women's Institute 75th Anniversary, 11 September 1990. Maudie Hopkins and Mary Crutcher cut the cake with Eileen Funnell behind.*

Newdigate school. Age Concern gave the club a grant to help them over the first six months and since then it has been self-funding.

The club has enlarged to allow members who have moved from Newdigate to join in the meetings, which are held every first and third Wednesday afternoon of the month. Talks, slide shows, socials and a week's summer coach holiday are among the many activities.

# Newdigate Horticultural Society

The Society was co-founded with Capel and Ockley in 1893 and expanded to include other villages, so that in 1926 it became known as the Capel and District Horticultural Society. Newdigate had its own show in 1940 and continued independently throughout the Second World War.

In 1993 it was decided to hold two shows each year. Craft, cookery, photography, children's classes and early crops are exhibited in June, and fruit, flowers and vegetables in September, when cups are awarded. Membership is around 120.

# Newdigate Netball Club

Following the installation of a new hard court on the Brocus in 2002 by the Community Centre, the decision was taken to form a netball club. The idea proved very popular and within two months the club had 30 members.

The club is very fortunate to have an excellent coach in Teresa Trower, and it received financial support from the Community Centre and Henry Smith's Charity. It is hoped eventually to install flood lighting for evening play in the winter months and to enter one or two teams in different leagues.

Barbara Norman has donated a cup to be given annually to the most improved player.

# The Royal British Legion, Newdigate Branch

The Branch was formed in 1931 and currently has just over 60 members. Many activities are enjoyed including the annual garden party, barbecue, barn dance, dinner and wine-and-cheese party, as well as trips to places of interest.

The branch used to meet in what is now the storeroom in the Village Sports and Social Club but in 1971 they were allocated a dedicated Legion Room.

Colin and Marion Hales have for many years organised the Poppy Appeal throughout the village to support the Legion's benevolent work and have raised a substantial amount of money through house-to-house and static collections.

The Women's Section was inaugurated on 22 May 1966 and closed 30 years later on 18 October 1993. After closure many of the former members joined the RBL Newdigate Branch as associate members.

# Tennis Club

Tennis was mostly played in the large houses, but there used to be a grass court opposite the Village Hall which was destroyed when Winfield Grove was built. After the Second World War the public court was constructed on the Brocus and tennis is now enjoyed there by about 40 club members.

# Women's Institute

The Newdigate membership is about 50 and the group takes part in many voluntary projects such as the St Catherine's Hospice workshop, village transport scheme, hospital car service, litter picks and meals on wheels.

There are outings and regular meetings with guest speakers and a play-reading group and craft group supplement the mainstream WI activities.

# Newdigate Bell-Ringers

Henry Burstow was a Horsham bell-ringer and song man who became dissatisfied with the performance of his local ringers. One Saturday afternoon he decided to visit Newdigate, where the change-ringers enjoyed the reputation of champions. He walked there and met Tom Gadd, the head ringer, made a good impression and was given an open invitation.

Henry wrote:

*The company of the ringers, too, I found very enjoyable, and they always seemed pleased to see me come. Alec Gadd lent me their ringing book to copy out; this I did, committing the changes to memory... Every Saturday evening I walked there – eight miles – arriving about seven o'clock. We rang up to ten o'clock, and then all of us ringers and friends used to adjourn to the Six Bells Public House for a jollification, drinking and smoking and song singing in turn. I was just in my element; I knew so many songs at this time that I sang them a fresh lot every time I went: they knew but a few, and these I quickly learnt and added to my stock. We invariably kept the merriment going up to twelve o'clock, after which I used to walk home, usually arriving between two and three o'clock in the morning.*

Thomas Anscombe Gadd was conductor of the Newdigate bell-ringers in the 1840s. In the belfry at St Peter's Church are boards commemorating two special events. On 22 December 1841 Thomas Gadd led his band in ringing 5,040 changes in seven different methods, which lasted two hours and 52 minutes. Then on 29 January 1845 they rang 12,960 changes in the Oxford Treble and Oxford Single Bob methods (or tunes) in seven hours and 21 minutes. Ringing for over seven hours without a mistake must have required both skill and endurance and the six bell-ringers must have been extremely fit young men. No wonder that Henry Burstow called them champions.

Bell-ringing in Newdigate has remained popular. George Horley was one of the longest-serving members – having started ringing in 1897 he finally retired in 1954. On 23 December 1943 the *Daily Herald* carried an article about Ted Vine, the care-taker of the Village Hall, who celebrated his 50th anniversary as a bell-ringer on Christmas Day. Tony Wales, the author of *Ballads, Bands and Bell-Ringers*, wrote, 'Once a ringer, always a ringer.'

In 1991 a band of touring bell-ringers from Cambridge University came to St Peter's to ring Newdigate's own tune (known as a 'method') called 'Poynton' or 'Newdigate Delight'. Traditionally methods are named by the band that first rings them in a full peal, about three hours ringing, consisting of over 5,000 changes. It is impossible to state when this was first rung in Newdigate, but it was probably around 1880 or 1890 when there was great local enthusiasm for bell-ringing.

Newdigate belongs to the Leatherhead District of the Guildford Guild and the Southern District of the Surrey Association. In 2002 the captain is Jenny Clark.

## Mothers' Union

The Mothers' Union was founded by Mary Sumner in Old Aylesford in 1876 and the Newdigate branch first met in 1891 although records date only from the 1930s.

The Mothers' Union has certain basic principles:

*To uphold Christian marriage.*
*To encourage parents to bring up their children in the faith and life of the church.*
*To maintain a worldwide fellowship of Christians, united in prayer, worship and service.*
*To promote conditions in society favourable to stable family life and the protection of children.*
*To help disadvantaged families.*

*Bell-ringers in 2001. Left to right: John Chaplin, Ian Macro, Neil Carter, David Finch, Jenny Clark and Jane Maden.*

*Members of the Mothers' Union having received their certificate for over 40 years' service from the President of the Guildford Diocesan of the Mothers' Union, Ann Fraser. Left to right, back row: Marion Hales, Mollie Posner, Jenny Booth, Bella Nias, Eileen Funnell; front: Lillian Carpenter, Ann Fraser and Olive Cloke.*

Meetings are held once a month in the Village Hall when there is a time for prayer followed by a speaker on a theme which follows the chosen pattern for the year. On the first Wednesday of each month there is a special activity and Bible storytelling for the under fours known as 'Wheels and Squeals'.

Members provide a crèche for the youngest children at the morning services at St Peter's, and there are regular prison visits to look after children whose mothers are visiting their fathers.

## The Newdigate Society

The Society was founded in 1984 following an initiative from Charles Thompson and George Green: its purpose is to preserve objects of local interest, to record past and current events, and to take action where appropriate to preserve and protect Newdigate's heritage.

A large collection of photographs has been gathered, many of which appear in this publication, and artefacts and archives of general interest have been preserved.

The Newdigate Society magazine is published two or three times a year with talks and outings arranged.

*Chapter 10*

# COUNTRY FOLK

Due to the remoteness of the village it was not uncommon in the past for families to stay for many generations. Times have changed, and the high cost of housing now forces young people to move away. There have been a number of attempts to provide 'affordable' homes but these are always beyond the budgets of first-time buyers. Here are a few of the families who made their homes in Newdigate and stayed for many years.

## *Burberry*
### *By Wendy Stott*

Surrey has been home to the Burberry family since the marriage of William Burberry and Eleanor Shoe in Horley in 1658. One of their sons, John, married Sarah Gatford in 1697 and they moved to Newdigate soon after this.

The first documented evidence of Burberrys living in Newdigate is in the Parish Register of St Peter's Church where it states, 'Mary daughter of John Burberry baptised 17 April 1706.' Soon after, her burial is also recorded: 'Mary, daughter of John Burberry buried 3 November 1706'; a sad reflection of the high infant-mortality rate at those times.

John and Sarah were farmers at Newdigate Place. They had six children. Their son Thomas, born in 1707, married Elizabeth and they had ten children. At Thomas' death in 1776 the rector recorded that he was 'a very honest and capital farmer'.

Thomas' surviving children all had large families and most continued to live in the village, although one son married and raised his family in Horley, and another at Ifield in Sussex. Three of Thomas' sons held positions of great responsibility as churchwardens and trustees of the village school, while others were constables, land-tax collectors, headbarroughs (deputy constables) and surveyors of highways. A glance through more than 100 years of Surrey Poor Law Index entries shows the Burberry name listed over and over again as son followed father in observing their civic responsibilities.

One of Thomas' sons, William, married Jane Burstow and their eldest son Thomas was also baptised in the parish in 1774. This Thomas Burberry first married Rebecca Wonham in 1794 and had four children, but unfortunately by 1820 Rebecca and all their children had died. In the Newdigate Parish Register entry for Rebecca's burial her husband, Thomas, was styled 'Steward to the Duke of Norfolk'. He was married a second time in 1832 to Elizabeth Flint, this time in Betchworth, and the subsequent history of this branch of the Burberry family takes place away from Newdigate. However, this is probably the most famous branch of the family as Thomas and Elizabeth's eldest son Thomas went on to found the Burberry clothing empire.

Burberry's of London began as an outfitters shop in Basingstoke. As a result of an innovative new rainproof fabric designed by Thomas Burberry the company expanded rapidly and actually supplied raincoats and warm-weather clothing to the Army and intrepid Victorian explorers. Although not owned by the Burberry family today, the company has become a favourite clothing manufacturer in the fashion industry and the famous Burberry plaid is an internationally recognised trademark.

During the later 1700s and into the 1800s Newdigate village was inhabited by many Burberry families, all descended from John and Sarah. Many of the farms and cottages which exist today have been occupied and farmed by them at some time: Newdigate Place, Tanhouse, Halesbridge, Ockley House Farm, Harlings, Reffolds, Nightingales, Little Paddock (now Lance's Cottage), Kingsland, Greens Farm, Blanks Farm (which Stephen Burberry left to his daughter Sarah, wife of John Humphrey, in his will proved in 1856), Givons Cottage, Brook Cottages, lands at Curls, Parson Land, Hales and Brooks in Parkgate and Woods Hill Cottage which was the home of Sidney and Harriet Burberry in the early-twentieth century. It was from here that Sidney John Burberry left to join the Army, only to be killed in 1914 aged just 19 years.

## *Elliott*
### *By James Elliott*

The Elliott family lived in Newdigate for over 200 years; the earliest record is the marriage of James Elliott to Ann Tyler in 1777. There has been a James in every generation since.

Their son James, an agricultural labourer, married Sarah Killick in 1810. Their children attended

Above: *Woodshill Cottage, the home of the Burberry family.*

Above: *Lucy Elizabeth Gadd (1895–1971) who gave her name to Lucy's Cottage.*

Sidney John Burberry, aged 90, in 1955.

Left: *Frederick George Elliott (1871–1950), c.1902.*

*Westley John and Robert Luke Gad (Bob) under the Village Sign. In the background can be seen the fire-damaged Foresters Villas and the builder's yard beyond, c.1932.*

*George William Burrows ('Dawsey'). This photograph was taken by Dr F.G. Chandler in the 1930s.*

Newdigate School and by 1841 they were living in a cottage in Broad Lane.

James (3) married Charlotte Jenkins in 1846 and they had seven children. The census records show that the family moved frequently; they were living in Sot's Hole in 1851, Beambrook Lane Cottage in 1861, Newdigate Lane, Capel in 1871 and The Knowle in 1891. Charlotte died in 1898 and James in 1901 and they are both buried in the churchyard.

James (4) married Elizabeth Burrows in 1867 and they had six children: Edward who was killed on the railways, Frederick George, William who worked for Courages at Tower Bridge, Mark who died from croup at the age of seven, John who lived at Henfold Cottages and was a gamekeeper, and James who lived at Dean Cottage in Blanks Lane. In 1871 the family were living in Broad Lane and their address in 1881 is shown as Broad Lane Farm (Hammonds). By 1891 they were living at Stockrydons in Henfold Lane.

James (5) was a gamekeeper, together with his brother and father, for William Farnell-Watson, who in his will of 1880 left, 'To my keepers James Elliott senior and James Elliott junior £10 each and George Elliott £5.' James' claim to fame was that he was pictured with his two dogs on the front cover of *The Gamekeeper* magazine. In 1918 he was living at Clairbrook Cottage in Parkgate Road and had a horse stabled in Hogspudding Lane. One morning he went to feed it and failed to return. He was found dead in the stable and was buried at St Peter's Church.

His brother Frederick married Elizabeth Butcher in 1902 when he was a gamekeeper for Sir Jeremiah Colman at Gatton Park, Redhill. He then worked for the Earl of Darnley at Cobham Hall in Kent and later for General Pitt-Rivers at Cranborne Chase in Wiltshire. They had two children, Lillian and Frederick. They then returned to Newdigate to live in the cottage at Ewood Farm where Frederick was a farm bailiff for Frederick Lewis Crowe of Shellwood Manor Farm and had three more children, Winifred, Dorothy and Ernest. They later moved to Brook Lodge Farm.

Frederick (2) recalled as a boy seeing the young men in 1914 mustering outside the Surrey Oaks before going off to war, and in 1917 cutting grass for fodder for the war horses in Henfold Park with German prisoners of war. He married in 1929 and had three daughters and James Elliot, the author of this piece. He was born in Reigate and has lived there ever since.

## Evershed
### From an article by Peter Evershed

Thomas Eversede of Newdigate was buried in Rusper churchyard on 17 October 1603 and was a member of the Ockley family. It seems certain that he lived at Chaffolds, which is described as Evershed's Farm on some old maps.

His son Richard, who had married Mary Gardener in 1598, probably took over Chaffolds in 1603 upon the death of his father. Their children were all baptised in Newdigate. In about 1631 he acquired the freehold messuage in Charlwood called Moores and in his will of 1639 he left his property to his son Thomas (1606–70).

Thomas married Susan Kempsell at Rusper in 1631, and after her death married Catherine Pledge, a widow, at Newdigate in 1643. They had a large family who were all baptised at Newdigate, and he was buried there in 1670.

Thomas' son Thomas (1633–84) married twice, first to Susanna Collins at Rusper in 1663 and second to Joanne Tovest of Newdigate at Wotton in 1678. He made his will in 1684 and left property to his infant sons.

John, baptised in 1678, and Thomas, baptised in 1680, were the fifth and last generation of Eversheds in Newdigate. They are later to be found as farmers at Rudgwick and Slinfold in Sussex.

## Gadd
### By Christine Gallivan

The Gad or Gadd name has been recorded in Parish Registers throughout Surrey and Sussex since the early 1600s, but in Newdigate only since around 1700. The family was generally poor, hard working and living from hand to mouth on the wages of an agricultural labourer or carter.

They generally appear to have been law abiding although in 1832 John Gadd was imprisoned for two months for an assault on Isaac Hayler.

Thomas Anscombe Gadd and his brother George were members of the Newdigate Bell-ringers and their names are recorded on special boards in the belfry.

Luke Gadd was a member of Mrs Janson's wood-carving class and carved two of the pew ends in the church. He was apprenticed to Greenfields the saddler, but became a boot and shoe repairer and had a workshop in the garden of Lucy's Cottage. His son Bob recalled how he would be given 3s.6d. for a repair and would then cycle to Redhill to buy leather to do the next repair. Lucy, Luke's sister, was a dressmaker and looked after the well-known village character, George William Burrows ('Dawsey'), her half brother. He became an eccentric after being bitten in the calf by a boar whilst working at High Trees Farm. After the accident he took up hedging and ditching for Mr Spiller at Laundry Hill (Brooklag Farm) but after work he did not change but went straight to bed in the clothes he had been wearing. When he acquired a new hat, he cut a hole in the crown, put it on top of the others and pulled his hair through. On his death he was found to have several hats on his head entangled with hair.

Over the years the family has married into other Newdigate families such as Charman, Weller,

*James Frederick Hopkins (1875–1953).*

*Below: Four generations of the Hopkins family in 1928. Left to right: William (1862–1931), William Robert (1895–1957) holding Harold, and William (1841–1934).*

Above: *Diplomat Alan Banks greeting Field Marshal Viscount Montgomery at Zagreb in 1947.*

Above right: *George Horley on his post round in 1932.*

Left: *George Richard Horley (1886–1974).*

*Old Brewery Cottage, c.1905.*

Burrows and Flint, but now the Gadd name has vanished from the village. Every year, however, Bob Gadd and his wife Joan travel up from the South Coast to take part in the Remembrance Day Service at St Peter's Church.

# Hopkins
### By Harold Hopkins

William Hopkins (1841–1934) was known as 'Red' from the colour of his hair, and always wore a cap – an outdoor cap, an indoor cap and a cap for bedtime.

He worked at Gaterounds Farm. When the farm was given up it caused dissent between the three brothers which was never resolved. The farm was given over to Daniel, who started a smallholding for his children Maudie and Edgar next to the farm. After Edgar's death Maudie continued living at Homelea before moving to the Old Rectory where she died in the late 1990s.

William's son, another William, was born in 1862 and was a woodsman. He married Ann Tew who was a maid to Mrs Farnell-Watson.

James Frederick Hopkins (1878–1953), the son of William (b.1841), was known as Fred and was the local slaughterman of pigs; many homes had large gardens and it was common practice to keep a pig and chickens. After doing a job refreshment was required, so he went into the Six Bells. He called these occasions 'The Pig Stickers' Ball'. His pony and trap would wait outside to get him home, but Fred was tipped into the pond at Gaterounds to sober up!

When he lived at Sot's Hole he used to do his washing in a galvanised bath by treading the clothes with his feet.

In the latter part of his life he would walk to Reigate to cut the grass in an orchard or garden and then walk all the way back home. A tall man, with a stoop in later years, he had a ruddy complexion, a long grey beard and a wicked twinkle in his eye.

William Robert Henry Hopkins (1895–1957), the son of William (b.1862), grew up in Newdigate, and enlisted during the First World War. In 1916 he found himself at the Battle of the Somme talking to a cameraman who was filming the soldiers waiting to go over the top. After the war he actually saw the film of himself climbing out of his trench.

Later, a dum-dum bullet blew his leg to pieces; he was shipped back to England and nursed in Wigan Infirmary. However, gangrene set in and his leg was amputated, but thanks to the skill of a young South African doctor, Dr Whaddle, who gave him a pint of his own blood, his life was saved.

After the war Will and the family moved to Our Cott in Parkgate Road which was one of the many 'homes fit for heroes'. Will later worked at the Thermega factory at Ashtead making electric blankets and airmen's suits and the family moved to the ex-services estate nearby.

Eva, one of Will's sisters, continued living at Kingsland. She worked first at Cudworth Manor, during the war years at Schermuly's, and afterwards at Dr French's factory. The front garden at Kingsland was always planted with flowers and bulbs and in the summer it was a riot of colour with bedding plants. They vied with their neighbours, the Broughtons, for the title 'cottage garden of the village'.

# Horley
### From an article by the late Alan Banks

The Horley family in Newdigate can be traced back to 1690 but we will concentrate on George Richard Horley whose name is commemorated by the building in Church Road named George Horley Place, which contains flats for the elderly. There could be no more fitting memorial to a man who devoted his life to the well-being of the people of Newdigate. He died in 1974 and his ashes are interred in the churchyard of St Peter's where he gave such dedicated service throughout his lifetime. He had a great sense of history and what went on in the village was of great importance to him – he knew every inch, and his knowledge of people and places was encyclopaedic.

George was born on 18 December 1886 and was the youngest son of seven children of Henry Horley, tenant farmer and wood merchant, who farmed at High Trees Farm. From the age of eight, each child had to milk three cows before leaving for school. Wages at that time were not very high – his father employed ten men and their wages together came to only £5 per week – so George joined the Post Office at the age of 13 as one of the two part-time postmen for Newdigate. By July 1906 he had become Newdigate's first full-time postman, a position he retained until the age of 60 when he received the Imperial Service Medal for over 47 years' service.

He began work for 16s. a week, starting at 6.50a.m. and finishing at 6.15p.m. having covered 23½ miles each day on foot. The mail was brought to Newdigate each day by Richard Fogden, a part-time postman who, it was said in the parish magazine of November 1904, had walked 226,908 miles in the course of his duties since he started in 1862. George Horley's daily round took him past Brooklag Farm, Henfold, Hogspudding Lane, Parkgate, Broad Lane, Park House and Dowces, Red House, Beam Brook, Blanks Farm and Halesbridge. After five years' service he was given a gold bar to wear on his uniform and a rise of 1s.

He was a fine sportsman, and captain of both Newdigate cricket and football teams and the Miniature Rifle Club. He served in the Territorial Army and was in the Army Service Corps during the First World War.

He was a bell-ringer and a churchwarden for over 50 years and it was appropriate that his home opposite the church should be called The Chimes. He was chairman of the Parish Council and a governor of a number of the local schools. In all he held 32 public service positions.

In September 1962, George and his wife Louisa (née Hills) celebrated their golden wedding anniversary with a party in the Village Hall, and ten years later the Queen and the Bishop of Guildford were among those who sent messages of congratulations on the occasion of their diamond wedding.

# Kempshall
### From an article by Alan John Frost

The family is first mentioned in Newdigate in 1605 when Richard Kempsell and his wife Susan moved from Chipstead and baptised their first five children at St Peter's Church. The family moved to Rusper, and when Richard died in 1637 an inventory of his goods included cows, horses, sheep, pigs, poultry, 13 acres of wheat, unspecified acreages of oats and peas, and implements of husbandry. His household goods included 16 pairs of sheets, six tablecloths and two dozen table napkins. The list even includes a stool of bees. His estate was valued at £214.12s.8d.

Richard's son, another Richard, is listed in the Hearth Tax Returns of 1664 as having four hearths, the greatest number for any property in Rusper. He had a son, who was described in 1699 as the late occupier of Rusper Manor, and a daughter, Susan, who married Thomas Evershed from Newdigate. During the seventeenth century the family were mostly Quakers.

The Kempshalls (note the modern spelling) lived in the Newdigate/Rusper area for the next 100 years but during the latter part of the eighteenth century the fortunes of the family declined. There are many entries in the Newdigate Poor Books:

*1784: Paid 12s. to John Kempshall towards rent.*
*1793: Paid 2s.6d. to Dame Taylor for laying of John Kempshall's wife (Ann, née Lucas, on the birth of Susanna).*
*1800: Paid 10s.6d. to Abraham Kitchen – a present for curing Phoebe Kempshall's fits.*

Between 1791 and 1801 John (the younger) and his brother William were mentioned no less than 27 times in the distribution of Henry Smith's Charity. The Newdigate Pauper Children's Book has a number of entries such as:

*23 March 1803: Stephen Burberry to have Sarah Kempshall till Lady Day 1804 at 1s. a week and the parish to clothe her. (Daughter of John and Ann, aged 12.)*

Thomas Kempshall was baptised at St Peter's Church on 21 April 1811, and in 1854 he emigrated together with his family to the United States of America. Three of his sons fought in the American Civil War for the Confederates.

The census returns show Kempshalls living at various places in the village. John Kempshall, son of Henry and Alice from North Barn, was killed in the First World War.

Laura Kempshall, the daughter of James and Maria, married William Thomas Eade, a labourer from Dowces Farm in Newdigate in 1910. After the war they moved to Chipstead where she died in 1940 and was buried amongst her wealthy ancestors. Thus the story had turned full circle.

# Monk
### From an article by the late Charles Thompson

William and Mary Monk moved to Newdigate in the 1860s, living at Ewood Farm and later Kingsland Brewery and Kingsland Farm. They had eight children and by 1883 William was described as a dealer in horses; he also ran the brewery as an off-licence, bringing in beer from the Rock Brewery in Brighton and storing it in a large tank in the upper part of the building. The beer was dispensed at a little window on the ground floor and often drunk on the premises from pewter mugs.

One of their sons, George, married Kate Weller in 1883 and moved to Wellbury in Hertfordshire. After the death of his wife, he and his four children moved back to Newdigate; one of his sons, Corporal Arthur Henry Monk, died in the First World War. The rector described him as 'one who was revered and respected by all – one of the straightest and nicest young men in the village.'

Another son was Albert William, who also went to work in Wellbury. When he left his employment he was presented with a horse. He had to ride all the way back to Newdigate to join his wife, Lavinia, and his parents at the brewery, and arrived so stiff that he could hardly dismount. Albert began dairy farming at Kingsland Farm, renting 30 acres from the Broadwood estate, and for 30 years he retailed milk around the village. By 1925 he was able to purchase the freehold of the farmhouse and yard. The responsibility for running the farm was taken over by Albert's two sons, William Fowler, who lived at The Orchard, and Francis Drury, who shared the farmhouse with his sister Helen. Francis died in 1957 when he was struck by a motorcyclist as he walked back after an evening in the Village Club. William died suddenly in 1962.

The youngest of William and Mary's sons, Ernest Frederick, became a coachman for the Goldbergs at the Red House, and later for the Nestle family at Mill House on Holmwood Common. He then became estate manager and gardener for Dr French at Cudworth Manor where he planted many fruit trees and bushes and eventually managed 300 acres. He and his wife Harriett had three sons, one of whom was born just two weeks after Corporal Monk's death, and was named after him. He is known as Peter and at the time of writing still lives in the village with his wife Vera at Highlands.

# Tidy
### From an article by Marian Medhurst

Apart from an isolated burial in the year 1636, the Tidy family first appears in the Parish Registers when three marriages took place between November 1663 and October 1664, shortly after the Restoration of Charles II.

The first was a wedding between John Tydie, yeoman, and Elizabeth Browne; his house was taxed on three hearths in 1664.

The second was the wedding of David Tydie, yeoman, to Joane Poulsden of Newdigate. He had recently inherited Waterlands Farm in Abinger, which had been in the Tydie family for at least three generations, together with other properties. The rector at Newdigate, the Revd John Bonwick, was a Royalist, and David's father was a leader of the organisation of the 'Free and Voluntary Present to Charles II' and appeared before a committee considering cases of 'plundered ministers', while his father-in-law, William Poulsden, contributed 20s. to the Free and Voluntary Present, which was the largest independent payment made in Newdigate.

The third wedding was that of William Tydie and Eleanor (Ellen) Butcher, and it was this wedding which gave rise to the Tidy family which remained in Newdigate until 1929.

One of their children, Joseph, secured the lease of New House Farm (thought to be Nyes Place) in 1691

and married Jane Nayland at St Peter's Church in the following year. By 1736 he was assessed to pay Land Tax of £13 on Clarks Farm (Dean House Farm). Joseph and Jane had ten children, but the children of their eldest surviving son Joseph, who married Ann Avelyn in 1724, all died within two weeks of their birth.

The family line only survived thanks to Joseph and Jane's youngest son, Thomas. He married twice and both unions were fruitful, but in common with many Newdigate families of this period, there was a downhill slide into poverty, and all but one son moved away to seek their fortunes elsewhere. This was yet another Joseph, who married Elizabeth Tayler in Capel in 1872. By the time his children were baptised he was described as a labourer, and after he died in 1788, aged 28, the responsibility for maintaining his young family fell to the parish.

Stephen Tidy was Parish Clerk from 1820–61 and had three sons, Austin Frederic, Alexander and Herbert. Austin and Alexander both attended the Free School in the village, but out of a possible attendance of 159 days Austin was only registered on 22 days and Alexander on 47. It may seem strange that the children of the Parish Clerk should be called upon to work instead of attending school, but in 1830 times were very hard and even small hands could earn something.

Stephen also worked as a bricklayer and two sons, Alexander and Herbert, worked with their father and learned the trade. Alexander was a bell-ringer and continued until at least 1887 when he was approaching the age of 70; perhaps all the hod carrying built up the stamina and arm muscles needed for his outstanding bell-ringing feats.

The shadow of the workhouse fell across the family only once in this generation, in 1844, when

*The Monk family at the Old Brewery, Kingsland in 1894.*
Left to right: *Ernest Frederick (1873–1954), Mary, née Coppard (1837–1911), Herbert John (1870–1945), Lavinia, née Fowler (1870–1942), Ethel Maud (1894–1957) and Albert William (1864–1941).*

*Vera and Peter Monk in 1991.*

Stephen's second wife, Eleanor Batchelor, was in the Dorking Union Workhouse when her daughter Jane was born. Perhaps there had been complications with the pregnancy and birth since Jane was baptised in Dorking when she was only six days old. Both mother and daughter returned to Newdigate where Jane was baptised for a second time at St Peter's Church. Jane never married but lived out her long life in Newdigate, attending her last Old Folk's Dinner in December 1927, and died, aged 85, early in 1929.

## Weller

*By Jeffrey Herbert*

In 1851 Newdigate was home to 43 Wellers, who married other well-known Newdigate families such as Taylor, Gadd and Horley. The men were mostly agricultural workers living in and around Workhouse Green. They often had large families. For example, Emily Sarah, great-grandmother to Jeffrey Herbert, the author of this piece, was the fourth of 11 children born to

*The Charman family in 1908. Left to right: Emily Sarah, née Weller, and Charles Charman with ten of their 12 children.*

Charles Weller (b.1841) and his wife Elizabeth, née Brooker. Emily (b.1869) married Charles Henry Charman, a carter, and they had 12 children. They moved to Mitcham where a number of Wellers were involved in the mustard and cress trade at St Marks Road Farm. One was credited with inventing a small basket for the mustard and cress together with a production machine.

Many Wellers continue to live at Mitcham and the name can still be found in Newdigate.

## Wonham

*From an article by the late Charles Thompson*

The first recorded Wonham in Newdigate was William, whose daughter Jane was baptised at St Peter's Church on 8 January 1578. But the forebear of all the other Wonhams in Newdigate was Thomas. He married Mabell Wheler at Betchworth and then settled in Newdigate where his name can be found in the Lay Subsidy return of 1593/4. He was one of only 14 Newdigate residents who had sufficient wealth to be assessed to the Lay Subsidy and his assessment was in goods not lands. By 1634 the family had acquired sufficient wealth to obtain the freehold of Sturtwood Farm which was inherited in

turn by his son John (b.1598) and his grandson Christopher (b.1630). Christopher married Anne Smallpeece who was the niece of the Revd George Steere and they had seven children, one of whom, Thomas (b.1660), also inherited Sturtwood.

Through the next two generations the family fortunes declined and in 1782, Thomas (b.1730) took out a mortgage for £750 using Sturtwood as security. Large families and poor farming conditions probably contributed to their problems but when he died in 1805 he left Sturtwood with only 80 acres to his son Thomas, Cheesmans (now Blanks Farm) with 35 acres to another son Christopher and several other small legacies.

Thomas junr died six years after his father in 1811, leaving Sturtwood in trust to his wife, daughter Mary and son Thomas.

A dispute between the family and the trustees must have arisen because in 1824, when Thomas was aged 23 and should have inherited, two actions were held in the Court of Chancery. Sturtwood was ordered to be sold and Thomas lived alone in Deanhurst Cottage and finally died unmarried in the Dorking Union Workhouse in 1869. So ended the Wonham connection with Newdigate.

## Notable Villagers

We have looked at just a few of the many families who lived and worked for generations in Newdigate without ever hitting the headlines, but in recent times a few Newdigate residents have become well known.

Comedian Frankie Howerd lived at Sot's Hole for a while and it is said that it was he who renamed it Partridge Cottage. John Bird, well known as a regular contributor with John Fortune on the Rory Bremner show, lives at Ewood.

The late George Owen, the landlord of the Six Bells, liked to tell the story of how Paul McCartney and his then girlfriend Jane Asher would visit the pub in the 1960s when they stayed at a house in Dukes Road to avoid the fans. They were very nice, he said, 'but that John Lennon was a little strange'. Another pop star, Hurricane Smith, used to live at Sturtwood.

Jill Parker, formerly Hammersley, lived at Tanglewood in Broad Lane and became the Women's

European Champion table tennis player in 1977. She could often be seen running around the lanes as part of her fitness programme.

When Rough Quest won the Grand National at Aintree, he and his owner Andrew Wates received a warm welcome upon their return to the stables at Henfold House.

Two young people from Newdigate have recently made the headlines in totally different ways. Esther Watts was born in 1972 and lived with her parents and brother at Hunters Moon in Hogspudding Lane. She attended Newdigate School and has always been a member of the Church but in 1999, whilst working for an Aid and Development Organisation called Concern, she was posted to Bangladesh. She requested placement on the Rapid Deployment Unit, a section which responded to emergencies. She was soon asked to travel to Afghanistan to assist in the emergency response following the terrorist attack on New York on 11 September 2001, but due to visa problems was sent to Quetta to do camp management for the expected influx of Afghan refugees crossing the border into Pakistan. The person responsible for site planning and preparation had to leave so Esther, the lass who, in her own words, finds it difficult to change a light bulb, was left with the responsibility. She said that there were times when she thought that she would lose her mind from the stress and responsibility but as the fences and tents were erected she felt a great sense of achievement. By the time she left there were about 4,000 refugees in one camp and 3,000 in the staging camp.

*Having returned from her travels, Esther Watts is back with her parents, Tony and Mary.*

Esther still continues her work with Concern, being prepared to travel anywhere in the world where humanitarian aid is required.

Simon Hiscocks and his family live at Cudworth Gate in Burnt Oak Lane and he too received his early education at Newdigate School. His family have always been keen on sailing and when he was 14 Simon bought a Mirror dinghy, funded from paper rounds at Bettesworth's, gardening at Gaterounds and cream making at Horsielands. Before long he was creating an impression and the officers at his sailing club recommended him for RYA training. He continued working in order to upgrade and replace equipment but soon realised that the prohibitive costs meant that he had to take up double-handed sailing, and he paired up with his friend Richard Tew.

Simon's skills were being widely recognised and he was asked to crew for others in a variety of boats when he was not sailing with Richard. This led to him being invited to crew a '49er', which was a new boat, in the RYA Olympic Squad, and as Richard was getting married he urged Simon to take the opportunity.

Simon paired up with Ian Barker. They sailed well together and competed on the international circuit, always coming within the top ten. They were selected for the Sydney Olympics following a nail-biting trial which they eventually won by one point!

They went to the Olympic Games in 2000 as 'medal outsiders' but it was their focussed attitude and consistency that won them the Silver Medal after a series of 14 races.

*Simon Hiscocks and Ian Barker crewing their 49er at Sydney.*

*Simon Hiscocks* (left) *and Ian Barker with their Silver Medals at the Sydney Olympics in 2000.*

Above: *A festive Eileen Funnell.*

Below: *Sarah Metcalf and her spit roasts.*

Above: Left to right: *Kathy Bettesworth, Arthur Hansford and Roger Sawtell.*

Below: *The 2002 golden jubilee party with Village Street closed to traffic.*

Below: *Peter Hall of Green Lane Farm built the barn at Gildings Farm and also found time to refurbish the caravan which he displayed on the Brocus on Jubilee Day.*

Above: Left to right: *Joanna Woodward, Elaine and Charlie Frost with grandson Tom, and Peter Hall.*

# Final Thought

This book has told the story of the development of Newdigate, its land, its houses and its people.  Most recently, the village's celebrations during June 2002 to commemorate Queen Elizabeth II's golden jubilee, organised by Sarah Metcalf, Steve Martin and Bill Mackay, proved that the community spirit within Newdigate is alive and well.  The crowning of the May Queen was celebrated for the first time on the Brocus and this was followed by a party in Village Street when about 600 villagers sat down for lunch and drinks.  Fun and games on the Brocus followed and dancing continued  into the night.

All villagers are trustees for the brief period of time that they live in Newdigate and it is the responsibility of each to cherish and preserve the village for future generations.  May they succeed.

*The End*

# SUBSCRIBERS

Mrs Pamela Ablitt, Horley, Surrey
J. Alexander, Horsham, Sussex
R.C. and I.J. Alexander, Newdigate, Surrey
John F.C. Andrews
Dennis and Val Archer, Barry, Vale of Glamorgan
Marian Atkinson, Crawley, West Sussex
Joyce B. Audric, Horsham, West Sussex
Neil and Pauline Austin, Newdigate, Surrey
Mr and Mrs John Aylwin, Newdigate, Surrey
Mrs Margaret Bailey, Newdigate, Surrey
Teresa and Paul Baker, Southwater
James and Kirsty Baker, Newdigate, Surrey
Henry and Marion Baker, Newdigate, Surrey
Joyce Banks, formerly of Newdigate, Surrey
Mrs Maureen Barker (née Cole), Great Bookham, Surrey
Mrs Daphne Barnes (née Dennis), Ferring, Sussex
Mrs Hazel Barrett (née Hopkins), Pyrford, Surrey
Verna M. Barty, Newdigate, Surrey
Winifred E. Beadle (née Horley), Hythe, Kent
Violet D. Beedle, Hooley, Surrey
Ivy Beedle, Newdigate, Surrey
Pam Beedle, Newdigate, Surrey
Ivy H. Beedle, Capel, Surrey
The Bennett family, Newdigate, Surrey
Marco and James Bernardis, Newdigate, Surrey
Urbano and Susan Bernardis, Newdigate, Surrey
Tom, Peter and John Birch
Peter C. Bonner, Capel, Surrey
Mr David Booth
Mr R. and Mrs A. Bothwell
Pearl and Alec Bourhill, Newdigate, Surrey
Bruce and Rebecca Boychuk, Newdigate, Surrey
Mr and Mrs G.M. Boyd, Saratoga Springs, New York
Yvonne Braham, Toronto, Canada
Derek and Janet Brearley, Newdigate, Surrey
John D. Bridle, Petersfield, Hampshire
George and Susan Brind, Newdigate, Surrey
Diana Brooker, Castle Cary, Somerset
John W. Brown, Local History Publications
Richard N. Brown, Newdigate, Surrey
Glennis R. Browne, Cleeve, Bristol
Dennis and Sally Buckle, Newdigate, Surrey
W.H. Callcut, Epsom, Surrey

Joan Campbell, Carrying Place, Ontario, Canada
Graham and Barbara Capel, Nyes Place, Newdigate, Surrey
J. Carter, Newdigate 1960–1984
Sir Geoffrey Chandler, Newdigate, Surrey
John Chaplin, Newdigate, Surrey
Mavis J. Chapman, Hythe, Kent
Christine Charles (née Wilson), Newdigate, Surrey
Michael and Jill Charnaud, Partridge Lane, Newdigate, Surrey
Amanda J. Chatt, Sussex
Mary Chouler, Irby, Wirral
Tony and Margaret Clapp, Newdigate, Surrey
Peter Clapp, Westcott, Surrey
Susan Clapp, Reigate, Surrey
Philip Clark, Horsham, West Sussex
Jenny Clark, Newdigate, Surrey
Mrs Audrey Clear (née Dennis), Dorking, Surrey
Kenneth Cloke, Holmwood, Surrey
Lynn and David Coates, Newdigate, Surrey
Dorothy and Malcolm Coates, Lathom, Lancashire
C. Cobb, Capel, Surrey
Revd Andrew Coe, Rector, St Peter's Church, Newdigate
Nell Cole, Newdigate, Surrey
Sheila Collinson, Newdigate, Surrey
Lillian H. Constable, Newdigate, Surrey
Mrs Hazel Coombes, Dorking
Nick and Ann Crawford, Newdigate, Surrey
Tony and Carrie Crutcher, New House Farm, Newdigate, Surrey
Mrs Nan Crutcher, Newdigate, Surrey
Mary D. Crutcher, Newdigate, Surrey
Marian and Chris Dare, Newdigate, Surrey
Rt Hon. Viscount Daventry, Arbury
John Day, Southsea
Mollie Dean, East Grinstead, Sussex
Ruth Derisley, Burnt Oak Lane, Newdigate, Surrey
Mr Michael W. Dickie, Newdigate, Surrey
Jean Dixon (née Kent), Beare Green, Surrey
Stephen F. and Angela M. Dorey, Newdigate, Surrey
Lorna Doubtfire, Newdigate, Surrey
Richard Ede, Horsham, West Sussex
John Edwarde
Kenneth C. Edwards, Newdigate, Surrey
James F. Elliott, Reigate, Surrey

Kathleen R. Ensten, Newdigate, Surrey
Iris Exell, Newdigate, Surrey
Stephen Exell, Beare Green
John Exell, Brockham
K. Farley, Maidstone, Kent
Valerie A. Faux (née Stevens), Surbiton, Surrey
David R. Finch, Horsham, West Sussex
Doreen P. Finch, Newdigate, Surrey
Dorothy L. Fisher, Scarborough
David A. Fisher, Scarborough, North Yorkshire
Janet Foreman, Capel
J.M. Frogley, Cudworth, Newdigate, Surrey
Eileen M. Funnell (née Weller), Newdigate, Surrey
Bob and Joan Gadd, Telescombe Cliffs, East
    Sussex
Christine Gallivan, Tunbridge Wells, Kent
Dr and Mrs Martin Gilpin, Newdigate, Surrey
Jim Good, Worcester Park, Surrey
Mr and Mrs R.J. Gray, Newdigate, Surrey
Colin and Marion Hales, Kingsland, Newdigate,
    Surrey
Doreen and Peter Hall
Guy P., Christine A. and Marian Hall, Newdigate,
    Surrey
Elizabeth J. Hall (née Arrowsmith-Holt), Dorking
Arthur and Sheila Hansford (née Nagle),
    Newdigate, Surrey
John and Ann Hanson, Newdigate, Surrey
Ann and Martin Hare, Newdigate, Surrey
Joy Harman, Capel, Surrey
Mike Harrison, Garage Proprietor and Resident
Val and Dave Harrison, Sutton, Surrey
Derek F. Hart, Newdigate, Surrey
Richard and Sue Hayward, Barings Field Farm,
    Newdigate, Surrey
Michael C. Head, Newdigate, Surrey
Linda Heggie (née Bourhill), Streetly, West
    Midlands
John Hertel, Reydon, Southwold, Suffolk
Beryl Higgins, Brockham, Surrey
Graham, Niamh and Cameron Hill, Newdigate,
    Surrey
Alison Hiscocks, Cudworth, Newdigate, Surrey
Sarah Hiscocks, Cudworth, Newdigate, Surrey
Simon Hiscocks, Cudworth, Newdigate, Surrey
Arthur Hoad and Sons, South Holmwood, Surrey
Mollie R. Hogan (Burtwell)
Alwyn and Beryl Holder, Newdigate, Surrey
Roger and Fiona Holland
Pamela and Terence Hopkins, Newdigate, Surrey
Harold Hopkins, Great Bookham, Surrey
Anne Horrell (née Harding), Plumpton, East
    Sussex
Bill and Judy Houghton, Dorking, Surrey
Mr M.J. Huffey, Lord of the Manor of Cudworth
Colin and Ricki Hughes, Olde Cottage,
    Newdigate, Surrey
Eric and Brenda Humphries
Lesley and Peter Hussey, Beare Green, Surrey

Jenny and David Irwin, Ashington, West Sussex
Reginald Thomas and Lucy Claire Ivey,
    Newdigate, Surrey
Anthony John Joseph Ivey, Newdigate, Surrey
Carol and Robin Jenkinson MBE and family,
    Newdigate, Surrey
Henry J. John, Newdigate, Surrey
P.J. Johnson, Brockham, Surrey
David and Gelhi Jones, Newdigate, Surrey
Chris and Louise Jones, Newdigate, Surrey
Maureen A. Joseph (née Boon), Oxford
Jonathan Roger Kearl, born Newdigate, Surrey
Barry John Kearl, Newdigate, Surrey
Charles Leonard Thomas Kearl, Newdigate,
    Surrey
Gregory John Kearl, Newdigate, Surrey
Mrs B.P. Kearl, Evergreen Farm, Newdigate,
    Surrey
Kenneth William Kearl, born Newdigate, Surrey
Kathryn F. Keeble, San Francisco, USA
Pam Keeble, Newdigate, Surrey
Mr and Mrs Keith Kenward, Farnham, Surrey
Sheila Kettel (née Horley), Beckenham, Kent
The Kilbrides, Newdigate, Surrey
Bryan and Carole King, Wirmwood, Newdigate,
    Surrey
Gerhard and Louise Klassens, Ontario, Canada
Annette L. Legg, Banham, Norfolk
Jane and Pete Lilley, Lance's Cottage, Newdigate,
    Surrey
Ivor and Chris Lowndes, Forge Cottage,
    Newdigate, Surrey
Dr Robin Lucas, Diss, Norfolk
Herbert J. Luck, Newdigate, Surrey
Mrs S.D. Lyon, Newdigate, Surrey
Roger and Bridget Mackinnon, Newdigate, Surrey
Berta Mallet (née Wilson), Newdigate, Surrey
Canon and Mrs Charles Manchester
Michael Manning, Newdigate, Surrey
Graham Martin, Henfold Lane, Beare Green,
    Surrey
The Martin family, Newdigate, Surrey
Francis and Mary McDonnell
Ian and Rosemarie Mills, Becket Wood,
    Newdigate, Surrey
Gerry and Gina Mitchell, Newdigate Road, Beare
    Green, Surrey
Anne and Peter Mitchell, Newdigate, Surrey
Dee and Gordon Monk, Newdigate, Surrey
Thelma Monk
Tony and Christine Monk, formerly of Newdigate
Peter and Vera Monk and family, Newdigate,
    Surrey
Mrs Pearl Moore (née Jones),
    Newdigate/Chichester
David and Marianne Mortlock, Newdigate, Surrey
Jeffrey N. Moss, Newdigate, Surrey
Mr Ramon Mott, Capel
Sue Brookshire Neudigate, Charleston, USA

William A. Neudigate, Florida, USA
David and Celia Newbery, Newdigate, Surrey
Mr Peter Nias, Horsham, West Sussex
Michelle A. Nudds, Sussex
Lindsey J. Oborne, Newdigate, Surrey
Mrs Brenda Oliver (née Dennis), Woking, Surrey
Miss K.E. Orme and Mr P.L. Claridge, Partridge
    Lane, Newdigate, Surrey
Andrew Osborn
Mike and Paula Paddison, Newdigate, Surrey
Alison and Jerry Parker, Hogspudding Cottage,
    Newdigate, Surrey
Caitlin Paul, Newdigate, Surrey
Dermot Pearce, Newdigate, Surrey
Ann Peterson, Newdigate, Surrey
Wendy Pike, Ongar, Essex
Diana Pledge
Keith Posner, S. Holmwood, Surrey
Mollie and Alan Posner, Beare Green, Surrey
Annette K. Poultney and David Stefanini,
    Newdigate, Surrey
Jon Pritchard, Newdigate, Surrey
Nick and Theresa Procter, Newdigate, Surrey
Dennis and Kathleen Race, Newdigate, Surrey
Mark, Jo and Ewan Railton Edwards, Newdigate,
    Surrey
Ben and Belinda Railton Edwards, Diss, Norfolk
Steven Reeves, Darragh House, Newdigate,
    Surrey
K.W. and S.A. Reynard
Michael J. and Denise M. Reynolds
Hugh and Wendy Richards, Ewood Old
    Farmhouse, Newdigate, Surrey
Ken and Margie Rock, Sturgeon Bay, USA
The Roger family, Newdigate, Surrey
Stuart J. Rumbold, Newdigate, Surrey
Patricia E. Rumbold, Newdigate, Surrey
Margaret and Russ Russell, Newdigate, Surrey
Jenifer Rutherford (née Bruce-Walker), Bickley,
    Kent
Peggy Sainsbury (née Tunmore), Holmwod,
    Surrey
Diana Salisbury, Newdigate, Surrey
Diane Scott, Newdigate, Surrey
Sonia Seagrave (née Gadd), Southwater, West
    Sussex
Cynthia and Gavin Sharpe
The Six Bells, Mr Martin and Mrs Jill Earp,
    Newdigate, Surrey
Sally Smith, Johannesburg, South Africa
Albert G. Smith, Wallis Wood, Surrey
Joy Smith, Newdigate, Surrey
Michael Smith, Charlwood
Bill L. Smith Esq., Newdigate, Surrey
The Smith family, Homelea, Newdigate, Surrey
Dr Julie Soranson, Hogspudding Lane,
    Newdigate, Surrey
Mr and Mrs Stuart Spiers, Newdigate, Surrey
Audrey Spinks, Tewkesbury, Glos.

Mr and Mrs A. Stamp, Newdigate, Surrey
Eileen F. Stanbridge, Dorking, Surrey
Carol Stewart, Dorking, Surrey
Simon N. Stock, Dorking, Surrey
George T. Stock, Newdigate, Surrey
Rosemary Stokoe (née Bruce-Walker), Somerset
Robert Strange, Basingstoke, Hampshire
Brendan and Anne Strijdom, Newdigate, Surrey
Tony, Joan and Mark Taylor, Newdigate, Surrey
June Taylor, Newdigate, Surrey
Technowaste Ltd, Newdigate, Surrey
Mr and Mrs M. Temple, Newdigate, Surrey
Mrs Rosemary Thompson, Coombers Farm,
    Newdigate, Surrey
Gerald Thorpe, Mill Cottage, Newdigate, Surrey
Donald Thwaites, Newdigate, Surrey
Gisela Thwaites, Newdigate, Surrey
Mrs Doreen S. Tidbury
Terence and Carol Tilbury
David and Val Troke, Fu-Chi Lodge, Newdigate,
    Surrey
Shaun P. Trower, Newdigate, Surrey
Viviane Turner, Marlborough, New Zealand
Colin F. Tyler, Rose Cottage, Newdigate, Surrey
Christopher A.A. Wallis, Effingham, Surrey
Jonathan and Philippa Wates, Cox Green
Richard and Melissa Wates, London
Simon Wates, London
Timothy and Annabel Wates, Slinfold
Andrew and Sarah Wates, Newdigate, Surrey
Anne Watson, Newdigate, Surrey
Stuart Watson and Carol Millard, Newdigate,
    Surrey
Esther Watts, Faizabad, Afghanistan
John Webber, The Cottage, Newdigate. 1966/82
Alan W. Wheeler, Horsham, West Sussex
Connie Wheeler, Hogspudding Lane, Newdigate,
    Surrey
Dr W.F. Wheeler, Newdigate, Surrey
Eben Whiffen, Newdigate, Surrey
Clive R. Whiffen, Horley, Surrey
Bryan K. Whiffen, Clapham, Sussex
John and Jane White, Newdigate, Surrey
Les and Shirley White, Beare Green, Dorking,
    Surrey
Sally, Mandy and Katie Wickes, Newdigate,
    Surrey
Alan and Jill Wickes, Newdigate, Surrey
Roger and Lindy Wiggs, Sanderstead
The Wisbey family, Newdigate, Surrey
Professor Joel Witz, Hogspudding Lane,
    Newdigate, Surrey
Andrew, Christina, Harriet and George Wood,
    Newdigate, Surrey
Mrs Kirstie Woodman (née Lucas), Horsham,
    West Sussex
Mr Ray Woods, Newdigate/Cheam, Surrey
Hazel C. Wright, Henfold Cottages, Newdigate,
    Surrey

## Titles from the Series

*The Book of Addiscombe* • Various
*The Book of Addiscombe, Vol. II* • Various
*The Book of Bampton* • Caroline Seward
*The Book of Barnstaple* • Avril Stone
*Book of Bickington* • Stuart Hands
*Blandford Forum: A Millennium Portrait* • Various
*The Book of Bridestowe* • R. Cann
*The Book of Brixham* • Frank Pearce
*The Book of Buckland Monachorum & Yelverton* • Hemery
*The Book of Carshalton* • Stella Wilks
*The Parish Book of Cerne Abbas* • Vale & Vale
*The Book of Chagford* • Ian Rice
*The Book of Chittlehamholt with Warkleigh & Satterleigh* • Richard Lethbridge
*The Book of Chittlehampton* • Various
*The Book of Colney Heath* • Bryan Lilley
*The Book of Constantine* • Moore & Trethowan
*The Book of Cornwood & Lutton* • Various
*The Book of Creech St Michael* • June Small
*The Book of Cullompton* • Various
*The Book of Dawlish* • Frank Pearce
*The Book of Dulverton, Brushford, Bury & Exebridge* • Various
*The Book of Dunster* • Hilary Binding
*The Ellacombe Book* • Sydney R. Langmead
*The Book of Exmouth* • W.H. Pascoe
*The Book of Grampound with Creed* • Bane & Oliver
*The Book of Hayling Island & Langstone* • Rogers
*The Book of Helston* • Jenkin with Carter
*The Book of Hemyock* • Clist & Dracott
*The Book of Hethersett* • Various
*The Book of High Bickington* • Avril Stone
*The Book of Ilsington* • Dick Wills
*The Book of Lamerton* • Ann Cole & Friends
*Lanner, A Cornish Mining Parish* • Scharron Schwartz & Roger Parker
*The Book of Leigh & Bransford* • Various
*The Book of Litcham with Lexham & Mileham* • Various
*The Book of Loddiswell* • Various
*The Book of Lulworth* • Rodney Legg
*The Book of Lustleigh* • Joe Crowdy
*The Book of Manaton* • Various
*The Book of Markyate* • Various
*The Book of Mawnan* • Various
*The Book of Meavy* • Pauline Hemery
*The Book of Minehead with Alcombe* • Binding & Stevens
*The Book of Morchard Bishop* • Jeff Kingaby
*The Book of Newdigate* • John Callcut
*The Book of Northlew with Ashbury* • Various
*The Book of North Newton* • Robins & Robins
*The Book of North Tawton* • Various
*The Book of Okehampton* • Radford & Radford
*The Book of Paignton* • Frank Pearce
*The Book of Penge, Anerley & Crystal Palace* • Various
*The Book of Peter Tavy with Cudlipptown* • Various
*The Book of Pimperne* • Jean Coull
*The Book of Plymtree* • Tony Eames
*The Book of Porlock* • Denis Corner
*Postbridge – The Heart of Dartmoor* • Reg Bellamy
*The Book of Priddy* • Various
*The Book of Rattery* • Various
*The Book of Silverton* • Various

*The Book of South Molton* • Various
*The Book of South Stoke* • Various
*South Tawton & South Zeal with Sticklepath* • Radfords
*The Book of Sparkwell with Hemerdon & Lee Mill* • Pam James
*The Book of Staverton* • Pete Lavis
*The Book of Stithians* • Various
*The Book of Studland* • Rodney Legg
*The Book of Swanage* • Rodney Legg
*The Book of Torbay* • Frank Pearce
*Uncle Tom Cobley & All: Widecombe-in-the-Moor* • Stephen Woods
*The Book of Watchet* • Compiled by David Banks
*The Book of West Huntspill* • Various
*Widecombe-in-the-Moor* • Stephen Woods
*The Book of Williton* • Michael Williams
*Woodbury: The Twentieth Century Revisited* • Roger Stokes
*The Book of Woolmer Green* • Various

## Forthcoming

*The Book of Bakewell* • Various
*The Book of Barnstaple, Vol. II* • Avril Stone
*The Book of Brampford* • Various
*The Book of Breage & Gurmoe* • Stephen Polglase
*The Book of the Bedwyns* • Various
*The Book of Bideford* • Peter Christie
*The Book of Bridport* • Rodney Legg
*The Book of Buckfastleigh* • Sandra Coleman
*The Book of Carharrack* • Various
*The Book of Castleton* • Geoff Hill
*The Book of Edale* • Gordon Miller
*The Book of Kingskerswell* • Various
*The Book of Lostwithiel* • Barbara Frasier
*The Book of Lydford* • Barbara Weeks
*The Book of Lyme Regis* • Rodney Legg
*The Book of Nether Stowey* • Various
*The Book of Nynehead* • Various
*The Book of Princetown* • Dr Gardner-Thorpe
*The Book of St Day* • Various
*The Book of Sampford Courtenay with Honeychurch* • Stephanie Pouya
*The Book of Sculthorpe* • Garry Windeler
*The Book of Sherborne* • Rodney Legg
*The Book of Southbourne* • Rodney Legg
*The Book of Tavistock* • Gerry Woodcock
*The Book of Thorley* • Various
*The Book of Tiverton* • Mike Sampson
*The Book of West Lavington* • Various
*The Book of Witheridge* • Various
*The Book of Withycombe* • Chris Boyles

For details of any of the above titles or if you are interested in writing your own history, please contact: Commissioning Editor Community Histories, Halsgrove House, Lower Moor Way, Tiverton Business Park, Tiverton, Devon EX16 6SS, England; email: naomic@halsgrove.com

In order to include as many historic photographs as possible in this volume, a printed index is not included. However, the Community History Series is indexed by Genuki. For further information and indexes to volumes in the series, please visit: http://www.cs.ncl.uk/genuki/DEV/indexingproject.html

*Rambler Cottage in Broad Lane, c.1905.*